CLARENDON LAW SERIES

Edited by
TONY HONORÉ AND JOSEPH RAZ

CLARENDON LAW SERIES

The Concept of Law
By H. L. A. HART

Introduction to Roman Law
By BARRY NICHOLAS

Legal Reasoning and Legal Theory
By NEIL MacCORMICK

Natural Law and Natural Rights
By JOHN G. FINNIS

The Foundations of European Community Law (2nd edition)
By T. C. HARTLEY

The Law of Property (2nd edition)
By F. H. LAWSON AND BERNARD RUDDEN

An Introduction to the Law of Torts (2nd edition)
By JOHN G. FLEMING

An Introduction to Administrative Law
By PETER CANE

Conflicts of Law and Morality
By KENT GREENAWALT

Bentham and the Common Law Tradition
By GERALD J. POSTEMA

An Introduction to the Law of Contract (4th edition)
By P. S. ATIYAH

The Principles of Criminal Evidence
By A. A. S. ZUCKERMAN

An Introduction to the Law of Trusts
By SIMON GARDNER

Public Law and Democracy in the United Kingdom and
the United States of America
By P. P. CRAIG

The Philosophical Origins of Modern Contract Doctrine
By JAMES GORDLEY

Principles of Criminal Law
By ANDREW ASHWORTH

Playing by the Rules
By FREDERICK SCHAUER

Precedent in English Law (4th edition)
By SIR RUPERT CROSS AND JIM HARRIS

INTERPRETATION
AND LEGAL THEORY

by
ANDREI MARMOR

CLARENDON PRESS · OXFORD
1992

Oxford University Press, Walton Street, Oxford OX2 6DP
Oxford New York Toronto
Delhi Bombay Calcutta Madras Karachi
Petaling Jaya Singapore Hong Kong Tokyo
Nairobi Dar es Salaam Cape Town
Melbourne Auckland
and associated companies in
Berlin Ibadan

Oxford is a trade mark of Oxford University Press

Published in the United States
by Oxford University Press, New York

British Library Cataloguing in Publication Data
Data available

Library of Congress Cataloging-in-Publication Data
Marmor, Andrei.
Interpretation and legal theory/by Andrei Marmor.
(Clarendon law series)
Based on the author's thesis (doctoral—University of Oxford).
Includes bibliographical references and index.
1. Law—Interpretation and construction. 2. Jurisprudence.
I. Title. II. Series.
K290.M37 1992 340—dc20 91–45001
ISBN 0–19–825691–4

Typeset by Pentacor PLC, *High Wycombe, Bucks*
Printed in Great Britain by
Bookcraft Ltd, Midsomer Norton, Avon

PREFACE

THIS book is based on a doctoral thesis submitted at the University of Oxford. Many people have helped me to accomplish it, but my greatest debt is to Joseph Raz, from whom I have learnt a great deal and could still learn much more. I am most grateful to him for his illuminating criticisms of drafts of this work, and for his continuous advice and encouragement throughout these years.

Ronald Dworkin was kind enough to comment on a substantial part of the book, and I am grateful for his invaluable criticisms. Peter Hacker's memorable seminars on Wittgenstein, and the conversations we have had, influenced my thought considerably. I am also indebted for his comments on the drafts of several chapters. I owe a special debt of gratitude to Chaim Gans of Tel Aviv University, who introduced me to legal philosophy several years ago, and who also provided me with valuable comments on parts of this work. Meir Dan-Cohen's comments on the drafts of several chapters were extremely helpful: he saw many issues which originally had eluded me, and saved me from some serious mistakes and obscurities.

Thanks are also due to G. A. Cohen, Carsten Hansen, Morton J. Horwitz, Marty Levine, Michael Moore, Gad Prudovski, and Ian Ramfit, all of whom read parts of this study and offered valuable comments.

My acknowledgments would be seriously wanting if I did not mention my gratitude to Adrian Zuckerman for his help and encouragement during my stay at Oxford; to Trevor Dickie, for the many hours he spent trying to improve my English; and to the members of Balliol College for the stimulating and enjoyable time I spent there.

My stay at Oxford was made possible by the Tel Aviv University Faculty of Law, Balliol College, and the University of Oxford, all of which provided generous funds. I am also indebted to the Cegla Institute for Comparative and Private International Law of Tel Aviv University Faculty of Law, which provided a generous research allowance enabling me to prepare the book.

A contracted version of Chapter 7 was published in the *Canadian Journal of Law and Jurisprudence*, and I am grateful to the editors for their permission to use the article here.

Finally, I would like to express my appreciation to Rela Mazali for her thorough revision of my English, editing, and style.

CONTENTS

1. INTRODUCTION   1

2. MEANING AND INTERPRETATION   13
   1. Radical Interpretation   14
   2. Pragmatics   24
   3. A Third Meaning of Meaning?   28

3. DWORKIN'S THEORY OF INTERPRETATION   35
   1. Constructive Interpretation   36
   2. Theory and Practice   40
   3. The Internal Point of View   44
   4. The Argumentative Character of Law   48
   5. Constructive Intepretation and the Hermeneutic Thesis   51
   6. Constructive Interpretation and the Principle of Charity   57

4. COHERENCE, HOLISM, AND INTERPRETATION:
THE EPISTEMIC FOUNDATIONS OF DWORKIN'S
LEGAL THEORY   61
   1. The Reflective Equilibrium   62
   2. Identity, Fit, and Soundness   69
   3. The Fish–Dworkin Debate   73
   4. The Concept of Fit   82

5. SEMANTICS, REALISM, AND NATURAL LAW   85
   1. The Meaning of 'Realism' and the Meaning of 'Law'   86
   2. Putnam's Theory of 'Natural Kinds' and the Concept of
     Law   93
   3. Critical Morality and Critical Law   97

6. CONSTRUCTIVE IDENTIFICATION AND RAZIAN
AUTHORITY   103
   1. Constructive Identification   104
   2. Constructive Identification and the Objects of Art   107
   3. Razian Authority and Constructive Identification in Law   113

7. NO EASY CASES?   124
   1. A Scarecrow called Formalism   124
   2. The Hart–Fuller Debate   129
   3. The Argument from Defeasibility   135
   4. Indexical Predicates and Empirical Defeasibility   138
   5. Wittgenstein on Following a Rule   146

8. LEGISLATIVE INTENT AND THE AUTHORITY OF
   LAW   155
   1. What is the Issue?   155
   2. Whose Intentions?   159
   3. What Kind of Intentions?   165
   4. Why Should Intentions Count?   172

REFERENCES   185

INDEX   191

1

INTRODUCTION

LAW is one of the most interesting and complex social phenomena of our culture. As such, it attracts scholarly attention from a wide range of different fields; historians, theologians, sociologists, economists, each equipped with his or her methods and theoretical objectives, find their own particular interests in this social enterprise. Philosophers in turn have their own perspective on law, but it is perhaps the most problematic one. Generally speaking, the interests of anglophone philosophers are divided, and often waver between two main philosophical objectives: the moral evaluation of law and legal institutions, and an account of its actual nature. But this latter, descriptive type of theorizing, the attempt to answer the question 'What is law?', is somewhat puzzling. What can philosophy contribute to our understanding of a social practice such as law? How would such an understanding differ from that of the sociologist or historian?

Historically, the *kind* of answer expected to the question 'What is law?' has typically varied with the dominating philosophical tradition. Thus when medieval essentialism lost its appeal, and it no longer seemed to make sense to speculate about the 'nature' or 'essence' of law, a different kind of answer was required. At times it was fashionable to seek a definition of 'law', thus manifesting, perhaps, the rising concern for logical and scientific accuracy. On the background of twentieth-century analytical philosophy, however, this definitional task was conceived of as rather naïve. The assumption was that law is too complex a phenomenon to be captured by any one definition. But if it is neither the essence of law nor its definition that legal theory should seek out, what then? Once again, legal philosophers could look to the dominating philosophical tradition of the time, in this case, to emerging analytical philosophy and its manifest interest in language and the concept of meaning. H. L. A. Hart is the founder and torch-bearer of the resulting tradition; the linguistic analysis undertaken in his monumental book, *The Concept of Law* (1961), has shown the methods and insights of recent analytical philosophy to be relevant to the classical questions of legal theory. Hart conceived the main task of legal philosophy as providing an analysis of the concept of law and related concepts essential to our understanding of law and legal systems. He believed a meticulous conceptual analysis of this type would lay the intellectual foundations for a rational and critical evaluation of law, free of romanticism or moralizing myths.

Needless to say, the analytical approach to jurisprudence raised methodological questions of its own. After all, it is far from self-evident what the analysis of concepts consists in. Is the analysis of the concept of law a matter of determining the ordinary uses of 'law'? And if so, how would this contribute to a better understanding of law as a social phenomenon? What makes it true that 'a sharpened awareness of words . . . sharpen[s] our perception of the phenomena', as Hart, citing J. L. Austin, proclaimed in his preface to *The Concept of Law*?

It seems remarkable that these methodological concerns have not come to the forefront of legal philosophy until quite recently, despite Hart's own awareness of them and some intriguing answers he suggested as early as his inaugural lecture of 1953, and later throughout his writings. Undoubtedly the reason for this lies at least partly in the substantive improvements Hart was able to offer on the existing (and exciting) models proposed by Austin and Kelsen. This may be indicative of the attention paid by philosophers to questions of method being inversely proportionate to the substantive progress being made in the given field. As long as the legal theories presented by Austin, Kelsen, and Hart could offer intriguing models for substantive philosophical discussions, observations about method tended to be rather casual and incidental to the main inquiry. But of course, the methodological puzzles were bound to surface sooner or later, as they have with the recent work of Professor R. M. Dworkin.

Since replacing Hart as Oxford Professor of Jurisprudence, Dworkin has turned out to be his predecessor's most extraordinary critic. Yet in the earlier stages of his criticism he followed in the methodological footsteps left by Hart and made his own contribution to the tradition of analytical jurisprudence. Recently, however, his critique has taken a sharp methodological turn: it consists in an outright rejection of the analytical approach to legal theorizing. This approach, which Dworkin identifies with what he calls 'semantic theories of law', is to be replaced by a theory of interpretation which, he argues, is the only kind of theory that can account for the interpretative nature of legal practice.

My main purpose in this book is to provide a critical assessment of this methodological turn, and of some of the substantive issues it gives rise to; but before the argument can begin it is important to place this methodological turn in the appropriate perspective.

Dworkin believes Hart, and many of his followers, to have presumed that an adequate account of the concept of law is, eventually, an account of the meaning of 'law'. It is with this, for the most part, that Dworkin now finds flaw in analytical jurisprudence in general, and legal positivism in particular. The semantic basis of these theories, he argues, is a serious impediment, since it provides them with no means of accounting for certain aspects of legal practice, those aspects which he finds most in need of explanation. Let us take a closer look at this argument.

It is a widely acknowledged fact that we can make propositions about the law in any given legal system which are either true or false. It is true, for example, that the law in England imposes a speed limit on driving, and it is false that the limit is 200 m.p.h. It is also widely acknowledged, although more so by lawyers, that there are numerous problematic cases; competent lawyers often have serious disagreements about the law. They can disagree, for instance, over the question of whether English law entitles a worker to compensation from a fellow worker. Nor are judicial decisions excluded from such controversies. Lawyers often argue that given judicial decisions were wrongly made, that is, from a legal point of view. All this is commonsensical for every law student. Yet Dworkin rightly points out that not all of these legal disagreements are of one and the same kind. Some are more profound than others, and in a rather special way: they concern the very basic question of legal theory, namely, the question 'What is law?' More precisely, these *theoretical* disagreements (as Dworkin calls them) are disagreements over the *conditions of legal validity*.[1]

A legal system is a system of norms. Validity is a logical property of norms in a way akin to that in which truth is a logical property

---

[1] Dworkin coins the expression 'grounds of law' here, which, if I understand him correctly, is meant to capture those propositions that are taken to constitute the conditions of legal validity in a particular legal system (1986:4).

of propositions. A statement about the law (in a given legal system) is true if and only if the norm it purports to describe is a valid legal norm. Thus the statement that 'the law in England imposes a speed limit on driving' is true because there exists a legally valid norm to that effect; and the statement that 'the speed limit in England is 200 m.p.h.' is false because no such norm is legally valid. It follows that there must be certain conditions which render certain norms, but not others, legally valid. Hence it also follows that there can be (at least) two types of disagreement over the truth of propositions about the law. People can disagree over the question 'What are the conditions of legal validity?', in which case their disagreement is a theoretical, that is, a jurisprudential one. But they can agree on the conditions of validity, and disagree as to whether or not those conditions are actually fulfilled in a given case.[2]

It is widely presumed, or so Dworkin contends, that it is only the latter kind of disagreement that one expects to find in courtrooms among lawyers and judges. They are expected to agree on the conditions of legal validity in their legal systems; arguments about the contents of the law on a given issue must be due to the fact that they cannot agree as to whether or not these conditions obtain. Lawyers would all agree, for instance, that precedent in England has legally binding force; disagreement on a particular issue supposedly settled by the common law must result either from failure to find the relevant precedents or from an inability to agree on the appropriate interpretation of the precedents that have been found. Theoretical disagreements about the conditions of legal validity are thought to be the business of legal philosophers and jurisprudence courses in universities.

Whether or not this view is a widely shared one is questionable. In any case, Dworkin is surely correct in characterizing it as naïve and unrealistic. Theoretical disagreements do form part of legal reasoning; lawyers sometimes support their cases, and judges their

[2] Dworkin (1986: 5) dubs this latter, 'empirical' disagreement, but this is not a very happy term. Even legal positivism must make allowance for the possibility that the conditions of validity for certain legal norms are such as to make their validity dependent upon various evaluative or moral considerations. In this case, lawyers and judges who agree on the conditions of validity could nevertheless disagree over the question of whether these (e.g.) moral conditions are actually fulfilled or not, which would hardly be an empirical disagreement. All the same, Dworkin's terminology is understandable as it is introduced while describing a very crude version of legal positivism, which he calls the 'plain fact view'.

opinions, with theoretical considerations, even with controversial ones, about the appropriate conditions of legal validity. Dworkin goes to some lengths to show this through a careful analysis of several concrete 'hard cases' from the United States and England (1986 : 15–30) Some of these, however, are more convincing than others. Not all would agree with him that, for example, disputes over the legal relevance of legislative intent and the legislative history of a statute are best characterized as disputes over the conditions of legal validity. Be this as it may, other examples may easily be provided. Thus, the dispute between various versions of the binding force of precedents in English law, to take another of Dworkin's examples, is indeed one which pertains to the question of legal validity; the difference between legal systems adhering to different rules on this matter amounts to a difference in the kind of norms recognized by each system as legally valid.

It is worth mentioning, however, that the kind of theoretical disagreement typically encountered in such legal cases is not very deep. The type of theoretical argument entertained by legal philosophers is one which concerns the concept of legal validity, and not the conditions of validity in a particular legal system. For a legal philosopher, the main question is not whether precedent in English law is binding in this or that manner; it is a more basic question, namely, 'How is the previous question to be decided: is it only a matter of conventions or is it also a matter of moral desirability?' and so forth. But, of course, there is no reason why judges should not engage in such deeper controversies, and I presume that examples, though perhaps rare, can be found.

All this seems quite straightforward. However, it should not be, at least not according to Dworkin's understanding of semantic theories of law, of which legal positivism is, allegedly, a prominent example. 'Our jurisprudence has no plausible theory of theoretical disagreements in law,' Dworkin (1986 : 6) contends. Why is this? What makes it a problem for legal positivism to account for theoretical disagreements in law? The argument, which Dworkin dubs the 'semantic sting', runs as follows: recent legal theories, particularly legal positivism, he claims, have been essentially semantic theories, aiming to determine the meaning of 'law'. They have presumed that we follow shared rules in using any word, rules determining the criteria for the given word's meaning. Legal positivism, then, is the thesis maintaining that 'our rules for using "law" tie law to plain historical fact' (1986 : 31). This semantic approach, however, leads to an embarrassing dilemma. If lawyers and judges share semantic rules which determine the meaning of law, any further theoretical argument over what the law is would not make much sense. It would boil down to two alternatives. One would be to admit to facing a semantically borderline example, in which case the argument would become rather silly (like one over whether a large pamphlet is a 'book' or not). The other would be to concede that, contrary to the rhetoric, the argument was not really about what the law is, but about whether to follow the law or change it. In other words, on this semantic approach, theoretical disagreements are either utterly silly, or a kind of pretence. As we would not wish to insult judges with the former option, we seem to be left with the pretence version; theoretical disagreements about the conditions of legal validity are in fact disguised arguments over what the law should be, how it is to be changed, supplemented, and the like. But this raises a series of difficult questions: after all, why not take legal rhetoric at face value? Why is such pretence necessary at all? And how can it have worked for such a long time—should judges keep their fingers crossed?

All these are difficult questions, which does not mean, of course, that they cannot be answered. I shall not attempt to discuss the pretence story at this stage, however, as no such explanation is required if the 'semantic sting' is shown to have stung no one. This, I am afraid, is just the case, or at least that is what I shall argue.

To begin with, there seem to be fewer semantic theories of law than Dworkin's account would suggest. In particular, as H. L. A. Hart forms one of the express targets of the 'semantic sting' argument, it would be fair to ask whether he actually adhered to the semantic approach attributed to him by Dworkin. Did he ever maintain that his account of the concept of law was in fact a semantic analysis of how people use the word 'law'? If *The Concept of Law* is taken as the basic statement of Hart's views, the answer will quite clearly be 'no'. In fact, Hart was very definite as to the word 'law' having more than one meaning, and determined that the dispute between rival legal theories over the appropriate concept of law is 'ill presented as a verbal one' (1961 : 204). The choice between rival concepts of law must be a reasoned one: 'it must be because one is superior to the other in the way in which it will assist our theoretical inquiries, or advance and clarify our moral deliberations, or both' (Hart 1961 : 204–5). This would seem to be the most explicit repudiation one could expect of the semantic approach. But of course, such statements do not necessarily settle the issue; after all, philosophers do not always hold to their programmatic proclamations.[3] Nevertheless, something of the incongruity this would imply seems to have bothered Dworkin, as at some point he feels that the fallacy he has revealed is so transparent as to require a diagnostic explanation of how the semantic approach could be maintained without anyone noticing its fallacy. He concludes that the semantic theorists suffer from a 'block': they must have presumed that if lawyers follow *different* rules in using the word 'law', then no genuine disagreement between them on the question 'What is law?' could be seen as an intelligent debate. Each lawyer would simply mean something different from the other when saying what the law is. Such an argument would be as pointless as an argument over 'banks', in which one person is referring to river-banks and the other to savings banks. Semantic theorists must thus have concluded that unless lawyers and judges follow the same rules in using the word 'law', there would be no genuine arguments over the question 'What is law?' to account for (1968 : 43–4).

Unfortunately, this diagnostic explanation is even more puzzling than what it aims to explain. To begin with, it is important to realize that the logic of the argument could be turned against almost any other philosophical question besides this one. Consider, for instance, the question, 'What is knowledge?' upon which epistemology turns. The semantic sting argument would seem to hold here as well: if it is presumed that people share a semantic understanding of the meaning of 'knowledge', then either analytical philosophers are quarreling over borderline examples, in which case they are acting foolishly, or else they are indulging in a kind of pretence (and acting what?).

But of course, this is a spurious dichotomy. There is a clear sense in which people can be said to know the meaning of a word or concept, without being able to articulate a correct theory about what it signifies. We use numerous concept-words according to the appropriate rules of language without being able to provide a complete explanation of the word's reference.[4] Sometimes this is simply a matter of

---

[3] Dworkin is not the only one who offers this semantic interpretation of Hart: see e.g. Coleman (1982) and Soper (1987 : 1171).

[4] It is quite remarkable that at some point Dworkin himself provides an example without realizing its full significance: 'We all use the word "cause", for example, in what seems to be roughly the same way . . . yet most of us have no idea of the criteria we use . . . it falls to philosophy to explicate these for us' (1986 : 31).

ignorance; most of us, I suspect, know very little about the chemical composition of plastic, yet we all know what 'plastic' means. Other cases are more complex in this respect. Philosophers' disagreements over the concept of knowledge, for instance, do not manifest anyone's ignorance; they are theoretical disagreements over the best way to understand that which the concept-word 'knowledge' signifies. Nor is it usually taken for granted that such concept-words have one meaning only. On the contrary, an analysis of the ordinary uses of such concept-words usually reveals a multiplicity of things meant by people in various uses of the word, and, as Hart aptly emphasized, it remains for us to propose a *reasoned* choice between the various uses we have revealed, a choice based on theoretical, rather than semantic considerations. In short, the fact that people have genuine disagreements about what a concept signifies does not entail that they do not know the meaning of the word, or that the disagreement is necessarily over borderline examples. But then why should this option be denied to lawyers and judges? Why should they not be able to have genuine arguments about the question 'What is law?' which neither concern borderline examples nor manifest semantic misunderstandings of any kind?

It seems that the only way of understanding these perplexities involves a recognition that what Dworkin is arguing against are not really semantic theories of law but conventionalism in general. In other words, the 'semantic sting' argument is, in fact, a new version of an old controversy argument against conventionalism. Dworkin has repeatedly argued for the existence of an unreconcilable tension between the conventionalism espoused by legal positivism and the controversial nature of legal reasoning. As the argument is stated in several ways in Dworkin's writings, it is not easy to provide a single definitive formulation of it. The essential point, however, seems to be the following. According to legal positivism, the conditions of legal validity are determined by the social rules and conventions prevalent in a given community. These conventions identify which actions or procedures create the law, or in other words, they identify the sources of law. An additional thesis of legal positivism is that all law is source based. This means that a norm cannot be legally valid unless it derives its validity from one of the sources identified by the pertinent conventional rules. (Hart has further maintained that in any given legal system these conventions can be formulated by one master rule, the Rule of Recognition.)

Now, according to Dworkin, this conventional account of law's validity cannot explain how the law is able to impose obligations in controversial cases. Conventions manifest a pattern of agreement, a convergence of beliefs; once their application turns out to be controversial there are no grounds for further argument on the basis of these conventions, as *ex hypothesi*, they have exhausted their binding force. Hence on this conventional theory of law, there is no binding law in controversial cases. But this latter conclusion, Dworkin argued, cannot be maintained. Lawyers and judges regard numerous norms as legally binding, despite their undeniably controversial nature. Hence his conclusion that as legal positivism is committed to the view that law is uncontroversial, it is patently false.

Now it is not difficult to see that the 'semantic sting' argument is a reformulation of this old controversy argument. Viewed from the vantage point of contemporary theories of language, legal positivism amounts to a conventionalist, that is, anti-realist, position on the meaning of 'law'. For those who claim that law is essentially a matter of social conventions, law is, *ipso facto*, what a community of lawyers and judges *thinks it is*. On a conventionalist account, there is nothing more to law than that which is perspicuous in the rules and practices which people actually follow. But then it seems that if Dworkin were right about the legal reasoning of lawyers and judges (at least in the United States and England), conventionalism would be self-defeating: if lawyers and judges recognize as legally binding not only those norms which are uncontroversially identifiable under the Rule of Recognition, that is, if what they recognize as binding is not only source-based law, then conventionalism turns out to be false on its own terms. In other words, either law is not what lawyers and judges think it is, in which case law is not a matter of conventions, or—if it is what lawyers and judges think— conventionalism is false, as they do not see the law as purely a matter of conventions.

It remains to be seen whether or not this allegation against conventionalism is sound, and I would like to believe that the rest of this book will show it is not. Nevertheless, once the 'semantic sting' argument is seen in the light suggested here, namely, as an overall objection to conventionalism, I think it becomes easier to understand and consequently recognize the importance of Dworkin's interpretative turn. The theory of interpretation he proposes is not a substitute for 'semantic theories of law' (a dubious concept in the first place), but a new conception of jurisprudence, aiming to present itself as a comprehensive rival to the conventionalism manifest in legal positivism. Furthermore, once the interpretative turn is regarded as an overall challenge to conventionalism, it is easier to see why it does not confine itself to a critique of method. Law as interpretation calls into question the main tenets of its positivist rival, in substance as well as method.

This book sets out to re-examine conventionalism in the light of this interpretative challenge. Following a preliminary analysis of the concept of interpretation, given in the next chapter, Chapters 3, 4, and 6 present a critical analysis of Dworkin's theory of interpretation. Chapter 3 examines some of Dworkin's main ideas on the concept of interpretation and its implications for the kind of legal theorizing he advocates. Two main tenets of Dworkin's theory are contested here: namely, the idea that the basic model of interpretation is what he calls 'constructive interpretation', and that the interpretation of a social practice, such as law, requires the endorsement of the 'internal', participants' point of view. These two interrelated points, I argue, are meant to substantiate Dworkin's thesis that legal theory is best seen as a theory of adjudication, a thesis which aims to challenge one of the basic presuppositions of analytical jurisprudence, according to which an account of the concept of law, and the justification of its particular requirements, are separate and basically independent issues.

The fourth chapter continues the analysis of Dworkin's theory of interpretation, focusing on its epistemological foundations. In particular, it includes a close examination of the relations between the various dimensions of interpretation proposed by Dworkin, that is, identity, fit, and soundness. I argue that an elaboration of these relations, in the light of a coherence theory of knowledge, constitutes a plausible reply to the kind of scepticism about interpretation raised by Stanley Fish. On the other hand, the application of this structure to Dworkin's jurisprudence raises grave doubts, since in this case coherence plays a substantive role as well, entailed by Dworkin's thesis of 'law as integrity'. I argue that coherence as a basic value of political morality is not easily reconcilable with the coherence theory of knowledge employed by Dworkin in his reply to Fish.

The argument points to certain difficulties, but it is not altogether conclusive. It is supplemented, however, in the sixth chapter, where

I argue that the kind of relation between the dimension of soundness and the identification of law advocated by Dworkin is conceptually implausible. The argument dwells on the distinct roles played by intentions in the identification, as opposed to the determination of the content, of a possible object of interpretation. I argue that intentions play a crucial role in identifying legal norms as such, since legal norms must be the expression of an authority's thoughts on how its alleged subjects ought to behave, or must at least be presented as such. The argument combines some of the points I make with respect to the concept of interpretation with Professor Raz's analysis of authority and the authoritative nature of law.

Chapter 5 aims to defend conventionalism against a different challenge, namely, the one associated with realism in semantics. Though this view differs from Dworkin's, the difference lies more in the reasoning offered to support it than in its final conclusions. Roughly speaking, it contends that a semantic analysis of 'law' would show that the term refers to a real or natural kind of entity, whose essence and constitution do not consist in social conventions. Hence the discovery of the 'real nature' of law renders anything like legal positivism false, and a version of natural law true. In this chapter I set out to criticize this view, which is, in substance though not in all the details, Professor Michael Moore's legal theory.

Finally, in Chapters 7 and 8 I turn to elaborate on some of the issues concerning interpretation in law as these are envisaged by legal positivism. The discussion in Chapter 7 focuses on the concept of 'easy cases'. Legal positivism is taken to be committed to the thesis that there is a distinction between (so-called) 'easy cases', where the law can be identified and applied straightforwardly, and 'hard cases', where the issue is not determined by the existing legal standards. Having explained and supported the view that legal positivism is indeed committed to this distinction, and outlined in what sense, I offer a defence of it on the basis of Wittgenstein's analysis of rule-following.

Chapter 8 concerns the age-old question of the role of legislative intent in statutory interpretation. In general, I suggest that the primary way to justify judges' deference to legislative intent involves the very same considerations which are taken to vindicate one's compliance with an authority's directives in the first place. Since the chapter advocates, if only in very limited cases, deference to legislative intent, it also takes up the task of answering two preliminary questions: 'Whose intentions count?', and 'What kind of intentions are potentially relevant for statutory interpretation?'

The discussion in these chapters is guided by the thesis, outlined in Chapter 2 and argued for throughout the book, that interpretation is an exception to the standard understanding of language and communication, as it pertains only to those aspects of understanding which are under-determined by rules or conventions.

In the course of this book I say very little, and assume a great deal, about the main themes in dispute among competing legal theories, particularly the so-called 'natural law' tradition, as opposed to legal positivism. I feel that a detailed account of these traditional disputes would be superfluous for those readers who are familiar with legal philosophy. On the other hand, certain parts of the book draw upon several traditional disputes in the philosophy of language. Readers whose primary interest is in jurisprudence might find it advisable to skip the second chapter and the last section 'of the third chapter, which concern issues in the philosophy of language that are, perhaps, more technical than those addressed by the rest of the book.

2

MEANING AND INTERPRETATION

BEFORE embarking on the main project of this book, which is to examine the concept of interpretation in law and legal theory, it might be useful to attempt an analysis of the concept of interpretation itself. But how should one go about such an analysis? The multifarious uses of 'interpretation' may prove quite confusing. This is not to say we should ignore the ordinary meanings of 'interpretation', but only that they should be treated with caution. First, because the concept of interpretation is a vague one, which means that there are bound to be disagreements about its applicability which are linguistically irresolvable. More importantly, interpretation, like numerous other concepts, has a variety of deviant and even dispensable uses. To say, for example, as is often said, that a scientific theory provides an interpretation of a given set of data, is no different from saying that the theory provides an explanation of those data. Here, and in many other cases, 'interpretation' and 'explanation' are used interchangeably. But this is not always the case: literary critics, theologians, and judges, to take a few familiar examples, typically engage in a kind of reasoning which we distinctively call interpretative. Or, to take another example, musicians debating the appropriate way to perform a Mozart sonata would not be described as arguing about the explanation of the sonata, or Mozart, or whatever; their argument is, again, a distinctly interpretative one. To be sure, I am not proposing that the distinction between interpretation and other forms of reasoning is a very clear one. All I wish to presume, at this stage, is that there are certain paradigmatic uses of the term with which we are all very familiar, and that these standard uses of 'interpretation' are considered to be the most appropriate ones. Furthermore, I will presume these paradigmatic uses to be intimately linked with the concept of meaning. Roughly speaking, interpretation can be defined as the imposition of meaning on a object. This, I will presume, is the sense in which the concept of interpretation is narrower than that of explanation. Hence also, only those objects which are capable of bearing some meaning qualify as potential objects of interpretation. These are typically, but not necessarily, acts or products of communication, such as utterances, texts, works of art, etc. Forms of behaviour, social practices, rites, and perhaps even dreams, also seem capable of bearing some meaning, due to which they too are cited and perhaps rightly so, as possible objects of interpretation.

This, however, would seem to advance us very little, as it still remains to be seen what the appropriate conception of 'meaning' is. Nevertheless, defining interpretation in terms of the attribution of meaning is a convenient move considering the extensive attention paid by contemporary philosophers to the analysis of meaning. I thus propose an analysis of the concept of interpretation by way of defining the appropriate notion, or notions, of meaning involved in this concept.

More specifically, I shall begin this discussion by questioning the possibility of perceiving the concept of interpretation from the viewpoint proposed by Donald Davidson's theory of radical interpretation. The choice seems to me to be justified, partly because some philosophers assume that this particular theory of meaning was meant to provide the basis for a general theory of interpretation, (or could be extended to encompass one).[1] Mainly though, it stems from my belief that its discussion will illuminate certain important differences between the concerns of interpretation and those of semantics. I shall then go on to examine the possibility of conceiving the concept of interpretation in terms of the notion of meaning as construed by pragmatics, arguing that although the interests of the two overlap, interpretation and pragmatics presuppose potentially different criteria of success.

It should be noted in advance that this chapter will not provide a comprehensive account of the concept of interpretation; it only prepares the ground for the subsequent discussion which will analyse in further detail some of the issues discussed here.

I. RADICAL INTERPRETATION

The general concern of semantics, since Frege and Wittgenstein, can be characterized as the analysis of meaning; or summed up in

---

[1] See e.g. J. Wallace, 'Translation Theories and the Decipherment of Linear B', in LePore (1986 : 211–34); Root (1986); McGinn (1986).

a somewhat different version (for instance Dummett's), in the question 'What is it to know what a linguistic expression means?' One of the dominating theories in this field is that of truth-conditional semantics. The basic idea here is that knowing the meaning of a sentence is knowing what has to be the case for it to be true or false. In other words, truth-conditional semantics maintains that one has grasped the meaning of a sentence if and only if one is able to specify the conditions which render it true or false. Since only a relatively small number of actual utterances can be said to have truth values, truth-conditional semantics introduced a rather special notion of meaning, employing Frege's distinction between the *sense* of a sentence and its *force*. (The latter has meanwhile come to be called 'illocutionary force'.) The notion of truth conditions is meant to be an explication of the sense of a sentence, which is taken to be the core of the theory. The assumption is that each well-formed sentence has a sense that is distinguishable from its illocutionary force. One can assert that such-and-such is the case, ask whether it is the case, wish that it were the case, and so on.[2] The assumption is that the component of sense remains basically intact regardless of the illocutionary force.

Now Davidson endorses this conception of 'meaning' and much of the theoretical burden attached to it. Yet his own theory of meaning is guided by a rather unique perspective on truth-conditional semantics, which—under the influence of Quine's (1960) 'radical translation' theory—he calls 'radical interpretation'.

A full presentation of Davidson's theory of radical interpretation would far exceed the scope of this chapter, and is in any case unnecessary. My interest lies in the range of this theory rather than its merits; what it is about, and how far, if at all, it can be conceived of as the basis of a theory of interpretation. In other words, granted that the theory is true, my main question is 'What is it that it states and provides?' More particularly, 'Does it provide the basis for a theory of interpretation?'

Unfortunately, Davidson himself is not sufficiently clear on what radical interpretation is about. He says, 'All understanding of the speech of another involves radical interpretation' (1984 : 125). This, it would seem, can only be taken as a stipulative definition of certain aspects of that which renders communication possible. The question remains, 'Which aspects?' No definitive answer to this is offered

---

[2] For a criticism of the distinction between sense and force, see Baker and Hacker (1984*a* : chs. 2–3).

when Davidson comes to state the aims of his theory. Consider the following remarks:

We interpret a bit of linguistic behaviour when we say what a speaker's words mean on an occasion of use.

The theory may be used to describe *an aspect* of the interpreter's competence at understanding what is said. (1984 : 141)

Having identified [his] utterance as intentional and linguistic, we are able to go on to interpret his words: we can say what his words, *on that occasion, meant.* What could we know that would enable us to do this? How could we come to know it? (1984 : 125, my emphasis.)

The problem is that the question of what words *mean* on an *occasion of use* is an equivocal one. Davidson claims to be interested in the question of what could constitute *sufficient* knowledge on the part of an interpreter which would enable him to interpret each one of the potentially infinite utterances made in his linguistic community. But this question can be understood in two distinct ways. On a very broad reading, it aims at an explication of linguistic communication. In a much more limited sense, it has to do with the explication of sentence meaning.

The gap between the two alternatives is fairly obvious. Consider the utterance, 'Do you know an honest politician?' In one clear sense, knowing what the *words mean* on an occasion of use would be insufficient for *understanding* what the speaker meant, or was trying to communicate. Such knowledge would fail to clarify whether it was a genuine question, a sarcastic remark, an exclamation of despair, and so on. On the other hand, some of Davidson's formulations seem to indicate that what he has in mind is a much wider question. For instance, his emphasis on notions such as 'linguistic behaviour' or his interest in the 'occasion of use', etc. All this would seem to imply that we should, perhaps, understand Davidson's project as much broader than an explication of sentence meaning. Radical interpretation would then be a theory aiming at the explication of that which renders possible the understanding of linguistic communication in general. Which concept of interpretation did Davidson have in mind? Which concept can his theory account for?

On the assumption that each competent member of a linguistic community is by and large capable of interpreting all the possible utterances of a speaker in that community, a theory of radical interpretation basically describes what people already know. As Davidson puts it, 'the theory is true if its empirical implications are true' (1984 : 142). In other words, the radical interpretation of a natural language can be looked at in terms of a meta-language, which we would want to see as entailing empirically correct interpretations of the object language. To account for this relation of entailment, Davidson employs Tarski's Convention-T, with appropriate modifications.[3] For each sentence s of the object language, a T-sentence is a theorem of the form:

> 's is true if and only if p', where 's' is replaced by a description of s, and 'p' is replaced by a sentence that is true if and only if s is. (1984 : 150)

But once this model is applied to the *interpretation* of an object language, correct interpretations would be entailed only if certain constraints were added. We want theorems of the form 'snow is white' if and only if snow is white, and not for instance, 'snow is white' if and only if grass is green: the T-sentences must give the correct meanings of the object-language sentences (1984 : 150). How is this to be achieved?

First it must be clear what is taken to be the data, and what constitutes the explanandum. Following Quine, Davidson contends that what one means by an utterance, and what one believes, are interconnected notions: one's beliefs cannot be inferred from an utterance without knowledge of what one means, and reciprocally, what one means without knowledge of what one believes (1984 : 195–6). Thus, the only thing which can be taken as given, Davidson argues, is one's propositional attitude of holding sentences true or false in each particular context. Hence, the challenge of radical interpretation is this: 'we suppose we know what sentences a speaker holds true, and when, and we want to know what he means and believes' (1984 : 145). The question is, of course, 'How should one proceed from here?' Davidson's (most important) answer is based on the *principle of charity*:

> The general policy . . . is to choose truth conditions that do as well as possible in making speakers hold sentences true when (according to the

---

[3] The most important modification introduced by Davidson is that he takes the notion of truth as given, or primitive, while Tarski was interested in a formal definition of truth for a formal language (1984 : 134; 1990 : 299). Note, however, that Davidson is anxious to retain the recursive aspect of the Tarskian model.

theory and the theory builder's view of the facts) those sentences are true. (1984 : 152)

The function of this principle should not be overstated, however. As Davidson warns, the task in question is not an absurd one of making disagreement or error impossible. The principle of charity is based on the assumption that mistake or disagreement is only comprehensible against some agreed background (1984 : 153). But this is an heuristic principle which serves to constrain a *theory* of meaning for a natural language, and not every potential disagreement one can think of.

Furthermore, Davidson does not presume that the theory will yield only one possible interpretation for each sentence of a natural language. Indeterminacies will occur, but this is hardly surprising, and should not be regarded as grounds for objecting to the theory (1984 : 154).

Be this as it may, we are now in a position to answer my initial question, namely 'What is the scope of this theory?' I wish to argue that radical interpretation can only (if at all) be an explication of sentence meaning, and cannot account for anything further than this. I shall argue further that this fact is instructive of an important aspect of the concept of interpretation.

Let me begin by considering Davidson's (1986*b*) recent critical reflections on his own theory.[4] Here he seems concerned with a question very similar to the one presented above. He claims that theories of meaning, including his theory of radical interpretation, only describe an interpreter's 'linguistic competence', that is, his or her ability to understand the meaning, or what he now calls 'first meaning', of sentences. The gist of Davidson's argument in this article is that linguistic competence (thus defined) is insufficient to account for numerous instances of successful interpretations where the speaker's use of language is in some way idiosyncratic. Davidson focuses attention on phenomena such as malapropisms, or more generally, the ability to interpret idiolects.[5]

---

[4] Although not the most recent; in the 1989 Dewey lectures (Davidson 1990) he provided an impressive overview of his semantics, reverting to most of his previous ideas. The critical reflections presented here are not restated in the lectures; in fact they are, by and large, ignored.

[5] It is puzzling why Davidson focuses on these unique phenomena; it seems clear that the need for, and ability to interpret, utterances whose interpretation must go beyond the literal meaning, so to speak, are far more trivial and pervasive than the example of malaproprism.

It is instructive to see how Davidson defines linguistic compet-ence. On his definition, it is that which enables interpreters to interpret 'first meanings', which in turn are characterized as having to be systematic, shared, and conventional (1986b : 436). Systematic relations must obtain between the utterances, otherwise there would be no way of accounting for the semantic relations between words and the structure of sentences. If a word is used to mean x in a given sentence, it must, by and large, mean x when used in other sentences in the same language. By the idea that first meanings must be shared, Davidson refers to what is often called the public aspect of meaning. Language could not be used for communication if the meanings of the words and sentences were not known to both the speaker and the interpreter. Lastly, the requirement that first meanings be conventional is of crucial importance: it points to the fact that the use of language is rule governed.[6]

Now we can return to Davidson's main argument. As shown clearly by these characterizations of first meaning, phenomena such as malapropisms introduce instances of interpretation which are inexplicable in terms of an interpreter's 'linguistic competence'. Accordingly, Davidson draws a distinction between 'prior' and 'passing' theories:

For the hearer, the prior theory expresses how he is prepared in advance to interpret an utterance of the speaker, while the passing theory is how he does interpret the utterance. For the speaker, the prior theory is what he *believes* the interpreter's prior theory to be, while his passing theory is the theory he *intends* the interpreter to use. (1986b : 442)

Unfortunately, it is not at all clear here whether Davidson is referring to the well-known distinction between what a speaker means and what his words mean. Dummett construes this distinc-tion somewhat differently. The line he draws falls between how the utterer 'wants the hearer usually to understand certain words that he has uttered, and how he wants him to understand that particular utterance of them' (Dummett 1986 : 461). Yet it is doubtful that this

---

[6] Davidson seems to have changed his mind on certain aspects of this point, as compared with his previous writings (1984 : 265–80). Notably, one of Hacker's main criticisms of Davidson's work consists in the claim that Davidson does not realize the full implication of this essential feature of language. See Hacker (1988), but cf. Davidson (1990 : 316).

is more successful in capturing what Davidson strives to account for, since Mrs Malaprop for instance, can hardly be said to have known the correct meaning of the words she uttered. In that case, Davidson would perhaps have done better to retain the traditional distinction between speaker's meaning and utterance meaning after all.

More importantly, the term 'theory' is utterly misleading here. Prior theory would better be described as the ability to use the language. This amounts to a cluster of capacities but not to a theory.[7] With regard to the passing 'theory', it is even clearer that whatever it is that enables one to interpret an idiolect does not amount to a theory one possesses. Does it make sense to say that Mrs Malaprop has a theory about the theory she intends her hearers to use? Or that the hearers have a theory about her theory?

Bearing these points in mind, I shall nevertheless go on using Davidson's terminology. Thus the gist of his argument in this article is that the passing theory cannot be explicated in terms of linguistic competence, because *'there are no rules for arriving at passing theories* (1986b : 446, emphasis mine). Hence the rather unusual conclusion of his paper, that 'there is no such thing as language, not if a language is anything like what many philosophers and linguists have supposed' (ibid.).

The soundness of this last conclusion is not our concern here.[8] We are interested in the possible scope of radical interpretation. It is clear enough that Davidson now sees his theory of radical interpretation as, at most, an account of *prior theories*. It is limited to an explication of the concept of first meaning and cannot, as a matter of principle, be extended to encompass passing theories. This is so, as the construction of what Davidson calls passing theories is *under-determined by rules* or conventions. On the other hand, radical interpretation initially proposes a recursive characterization of the concept of meaning, given by Convention-T. Under radical interpretation we assign to every sentence of the object language a T-sentence of the form. ' "s" is true if and only if p'. This definition makes no allowance for idiosyncracies. Indeterminacy is a different matter. It can be the case that even when the evidence is exhausted, we will end up with the conclusion that, for example,

---

[7] Cf. Dummett (1986 : 467); see also Hacker (1988).

[8] For criticisms of this conclusion, see Hacker (1988 : 169–71), and Dummett (1986).

' "s" is true and only if p', and/or ' "s" is true if and only if q'. But the problem we now face is not indeterminacy but idiosyncracy. What we need is an account of, for instance, how an interpreter can understand a speaker uttering 's' to mean that p, whereas the correct T-sentence of 's' is that it is true if and only if q (as in the case of malapropism).

To put it differently, though perhaps in a way that Davidson would not, what is needed is an account of the distinction between those aspects of communication which are determined by rules, and those which are not. To my mind, this is the key to the distinction, which Davidson's radical interpretation obscures, between the concepts of interpretation and semantic meaning. The latter, as opposed to the former, concerns those aspects of (linguistic) communication which are rule or convention governed. This is manifest in the kind of reasons one would typically provide for the explanation of the meaning of an expression as opposed to the interpretation of an expression. In explaining the meaning of a given expression, we typically refer to the rules of the pertinent language; but such rules are normally unavailable as reasons or justifications for an interpretation. On the contrary, interpretation is usually required *because* the issue is not determined by rules or conventions. To be sure, rules should not be confused with paradigms. Interpretation, like other intellectual activities, can be, and often is, guided by the paradigms of interpretation currently prevalent in a certain 'interpretative community'. These are typically examples of what count as good or acceptable interpretations in the given domain (see Fish 1980). But paradigms do not function like rules. They can be respected and emulated, but not followed as are, for instance, rules of the correct use of language. Deviating from an established paradigm—unlike failing to follow the rules of language—does not necessarily manifest a misunderstanding. Unconventional interpretations, idiosyncratic or crazy as they may be, are nevertheless possible interpretations; but Humpty Dumpty's private 'language' is not language at all.[9] Hence the conclusion that interpretation should not be equated with understanding the meaning of an expression, but seen as parasitic on the latter. Let me expand on this point in some further detail, since it is of crucial importance.

---

[9] On the distinction between paradigms and rules, see also Kuhn (1970), ch. 5.

Recall Davidson's contention that 'All understanding of the speech of another involves radical interpretation' (1984 : 125). As we have seen, Davidson must have meant this as a stipulation. But stipulative definitions are sometimes misleading. And in this case, I shall argue, Davidson's stipulation obscures the special role that the concept of interpretation plays in the understanding of an expression. Dummett rightly observed that:

when the hearer does not have to search for the speaker's meaning, but takes for granted that he is using words in just the way with which he is familiar, there is . . . no process of interpretation going on.

A crucial observation made by Wittgenstein in his discussion of following rules is that 'there is a way of grasping a rule which is not an interpretation' (*Investigations*, 201). Similarly, there is a way of understanding a sentence or an utterance that does not consist in putting an interpretation on it. (Dummett 1986 : 464)[10]

In short, one does not interpret that which is *determined* by rules or conventions. One can of course point to the rule or convention, and explain it to those who are unaware of the rule or its content. That, however, does not constitute an interpretation of anything.

Of course it is true that in ordinary cases, or most of the time, people do not reflect upon the meanings of the words they use, and I would assume that Davidson does not deny this. As Dummett puts it, 'in the normal case . . . the hearer simply understands. That is, knowing the language, he hears and thereby understands' (ibid. 471). Dummett does not indicate any disagreement with this observation on Davidson's part. It is equally clear that interpretation does consist in the reflection upon the meaning of, for instance, words and sentences. In other words, interpretation must consist, at the very least, in one's ability to specify (to oneself or others) how one understands a given utterance. But now, this observation, as Dummett rightly emphasizes, makes it clear that interpretation must be an *exception* to the standard instances of understanding expressions, as it requires the existence of a language in which, and about which, the interpretation is stated. One cannot reflect upon the meaning of words without knowing already what they mean in the ordinary, standard case. Even in the case of the supposedly

---

[10] Dummett is interested in the case of natural language, but the same point can be made with regard to other forms of communication, e.g. visual arts or music. Cf. Barnes (1988).

simple thought that an utterance means what it literally states, 'having that thought will not result in attaching the standard meaning to [her] utterance unless I know what that standard meaning is' (ibid. 464).[11]

Properly speaking, then, '*radical* interpretation' is not a coherent phrase, perhaps not even as a stipulative definition, that is, if what it suggests is that the explication of the meaning of expressions in natural language is basically a matter of interpretation, only more radically so. If *A* is an exception to *B*, and parasitic on it, then it makes no sense to suggest, or even to stipulate, that *A* is 'radical *B*' (unless, of course, '*B*' in the second phrase means something quite different). In any case, one should realize that Davidson's use of 'interpretation' utterly obscures the conceptual point made here by Dummett, that reflection on the meanings of words, sentences, etc., is parasitic upon the prior knowledge of the ordinary or literal meanings.[12]

This leads to the conclusion that understanding or explaining the meaning of an expression and interpreting it, are two conceptually separate enterprises. It also indicates that semantics can only be employed, if at all, to elucidate the concept of interpretation, by way of contrast: interpretation concerns those aspects of communication which are under-determined by rules or conventions.

Before proceeding, perhaps it should be asked whether it is possible to extend the scope of Davidson's theory, in one form or another, so as to encompass a broader sense of interpretation. The idea here would be application of the principle of charity, but with regard to a different set of assumptions, perhaps less 'radical' than those of Davidson's original project. In the next chapter I will consider some attempts to do this in the context of social explanation. Here, I shall confine myself to the following remark: whatever form an account of something like a passing theory might take, such an account could not employ the principle of charity, since this principle is not applicable to particular instances of interpretation. As Davidson himself emphasizes, the principle of charity makes

---

[11] See also Hacker (1988: 168). Notably, this also shows that unlike the concept of grasping the meaning of an expression, the concept of interpretation typically designates an activity; interpretation is something which must be carried out. In this respect, interpretation is closer to the concept of explanation than to that of understanding.

[12] This point is discussed in further detail on the basis of Wittgenstein's account of following a rule, in Ch. 7.

sense only upon a thoroughly *holistic*, 'across-the-board basis' (Davidson 1984:153). It would be perplexing to suggest that a particular utterance or text, or any subclass of language, should be interpreted with an underlying charitable aim, as it were. There is simply no inherent connection between the concepts of understanding and agreement; often the best explanation is that which brings a certain disagreement to light. In other words, the principle of charity amounts to the claim that one cannot have a theory of meaning for a natural language whereby the bulk of the speakers' beliefs would turn out to be false. But this applies to language and thought as a whole, not to bits and pieces of it.

2. PRAGMATICS

A different attitude, though largely motivated by the type of problem discussed in the previous section, is to be found in theories of pragmatics. Roughly speaking, pragmatists are generally concerned with the problems posed by discrepancies between 'utterer's meaning' and 'sentence meaning', that is, between what an utterer means and what his words or sentences mean. Thus it seems that theories of pragmatics are concerned with basically the same question as the one Davidson finds crucial, namely, that of an interpreter's ability to construct a passing theory, or, as I would prefer to put it, the question of an interpreter's ability to understand an expression (or an aspect of it) which is under-determined by semantic rules.

The origins of pragmatics are traditionally associated with the Griceian communication-intention theory of meaning (Grice 1957).[13] The basis on which Grice's theory may be understood is the distinction between two important senses of 'meaning': the *meaning of* an expression, which is what interests semantics, and someone *meaning that* such-and-such by a given expression, which was what interested Grice. He set out to provide an explication of the concept of someone meaning something by an utterance (non-naturally or non-standardly, as he called it) in terms of intentions to communicate. Sperber and Wilson point out that, according to

---

[13] Grice has since modified the details of his analysis in a series of articles and lectures. For a survey of Grice's views on the subject, see Grandy and Warner (1986).

Strawson's (1964) reformulation, for S to mean something by x he must intend

(a) S's utterance of x to produce a certain response r in a certain audience A;

(b) A to recognize S's intention (a);

(c) A's recognition of S's intention (a) to function as at least part of A's reason for A's response r.

(Sperber and Wilson 1986 : 21)

But now arises the question of what the connection is between this analysis of 'meaning that . . .' by an expression, and the meaning of the expression. Can the latter be analysed in terms of the former? In at least one important respect the answer seems to be negative. As Searle (1986) has rightly observed, an attempt to explicate the meaning of expressions in terms of intentions to communicate would leave at least one important aspect of meaning unexplained, that is, its public and *conventional* feature. Searle's argument cannot be explored in detail here. Suffice it to say that the Griceian analysis of meaning in terms of *intentions* to communicate seems somewhat too private, as it were; it would not capture that aspect of language which renders it public and learnable.[14] Whether or not this is a correct allegation against the Griceian model is not our immediate concern. What I want to claim is that this intuition, in one form or another, has led pragmatists (such as Searle himself) to employ the basic notions of sentence meaning derived from truth-conditional semantics. As we have seen, however, the most we can get through truth-conditional semantics is the concept of first or literal meaning explicated in terms of sense and illocutionary force. Quite often, though, literal meaning is not what is communicated. Hence the possibility of discrepancy between what words or sentences mean (that is, first meaning) and what an utterer means (that is, communication intention).

Thus, one way to view what pragmatics is about is to see it as an attempt to fill this gap between literal meaning and what is actually being communicated. In other words, it may be understood to attempt a 'reconciliation' between truth conditional and Griceian semantics. The key to this 'reconciliation' is usually described in

---

[14] The communication-intention theorists typically tend to provide an explanation of the public aspect of language in terms of its natural evolution. However, the point here is different; it regards the lack of a conceptual account of what it is for a sentence to have a meaning in this public-conventional sense. See Strawson (1969).

terms of the necessary and sufficient *contextual* knowledge which is
required to understand an utterance. Yet the concept of context
should be treated with caution here. The word 'context' is usually
associated with elements of locality and contingency; it is something
particular and immediate, as opposed to the more general and
lasting. However, as we shall see in a moment, many instances of
communication, though they require some knowledge which goes
beyond the literal meaning of words and sentences, are nevertheless
conventionally determined. In such cases, the context is a matter
of convention, as it were. Some familiar uses of indirect speech-acts
are good examples of this phenomenon. To mention one such
example; the question 'Do you have the time?' is not, in normal
circumstances, a question about possession, but a request to
provide a certain piece of information. Hence there is a certain
discrepancy here between the literal meaning (that is, the grammatical mood of the sentence) and the actual content of the communication. Nevertheless, this is an instance of communication which is
conventionally, though not semantically, determined. But, of
course, this is not always the case: the pertinent context, knowledge
of which is required to grasp the appropriate communication
intention of the speaker, is often of a kind not expressible in terms
of rules or conventions.

Let me mention two such general cases where the success
of communication is context-dependent in a non-conventional
manner. The first is the grammatical under-determinacy of literal
meaning. A rather familiar idea, though differently presented, is
the view that the understanding of literal meaning is always
preconditioned by some kind of background knowledge. This
position can be traced back to Wittgenstein's notion of 'form of life'
as a prerequisite for language use (1958, sects. 142, 241–2; see
also Dreyfus 1980), but I shall present Searle's more recent
formulation of this idea (1978). He argues that the literal meaning
of a sentence has application only relative to a set of contextual or
background assumptions. Consider the assertion 'The cat is on the
mat'. In normal circumstances we know what this sentence *means*
only because we share a whole set of assumptions about, for
instance, the gravitational force surrounding us, the cat, and the
mat. It is safe to say that on hearing this sentence no one would
assume that the cat was hanging on the edge of a vertically standing
mat. Yet were we to assume a very different environment in which

'the cat is on the mat' was uttered, that might be the precise meaning of such an utterance. Picture, for example, some bizarre experiment with cats and mats held in outer space by two astronauts.

Notably, the literal meaning of the sentence is variable; 'the cat is on the mat' has different truth conditions in each of the two situations and this variance is wholly context dependent. However, the crucial point, as far as Searle's argument is concerned, is not that background knowledge is required so as to determine literal meaning, but that this background knowledge is in principle semantically indeterminable. The contextual assumptions which are conventionally determined can be semantically represented and added to the sentence. Yet in the present case, Searle argues (1978:216), the contextual assumptions cannot be realized in the semantic structure of the sentence. First, that is because they are indefinite in number. The meaning of probably any sentence can be changed by an indefinite number of sets of contextual assumptions. Secondly, any literal statement of these contextual assumptions would itself be context dependent in the same way.[15]

For the second type of situation, in which the success of communication depends on context which is inexpressible in terms of rules or conventions, the term 'implicatures' was coined by Grice. Since then it has become the most widely discussed issue in the literature of pragmatics (Levinson 1983:97–166). The notion of implicature stands for the contextual assumptions which are required to account for a successful instance of communication where the context consists in a particular state of affairs, knowledge of which must be shared by the speaker and the hearer. Consider, for example, the following conversation:

A. Do you have the time?
B. The lecture begins in five minutes.

Assuming the success of this instance of communication between *A* and *B*, the implicature in this case is quite obviously the mutual knowledge that a particular lecture is supposed to begin at a particular time. Pragmatists find two main features of implicatures puzzling. First, that successful communication depends on the *mutual* knowledge of the relevant contextual background.[16] Second,

---

[15] See also Searle (1980:221–32).

[16] Pragmatists have found it difficult to specify the condition of mutual knowledge without falling into an infinite regress: the hearer and speaker must not only share the relevant contextual knowledge but also have a second-order knowledge of what

the inference of the communication content from the literal meaning and the contextual background assumptions is, as the example
shows, logically indeterminate (that is, it is a non-demonstrative
inference) (Levinson 1983 : 116). Why pragmatists find these features of implicatures so problematic is itself somewhat mysterious,
but we need not go into this here.[17] Suffice it to say that in such
cases communication is clearly under-determined by rules or conventions.

All this would seem to suggest that the interests of pragmatics
and interpretation converge at least on one point: both address that
aspect of communication which is not explicable in terms of
following rules or conventions. Interpretation, as we have seen, is
not a rule- or convention-governed activity. Hence, to the extent
that interpretation concerns communication, it apparently concerns
the very same problem tackled by pragmatics, namely, that of an
interpreter's ability to understand an expression, or an aspect of it,
which is not determined by rules or conventions. Perhaps there is
no substantial difference, then, between the interpretation that a
literary critic assigns to a phrase in a poem, for instance, and our
humdrum interpretations of expressions which go beyond the literal
meaning of the sentences we encounter. In both cases, it seems, the
interpreter must be engaged in the same kind of reasoning. Or is
there some difference? Arguably, there is at least one important
respect in which the concerns of pragmatics differ from those of
interpretation. This consists in the potentially different presuppositions held by each on what is considered to be the relevant criteria
of success. Let me explain this point.

3. A THIRD MEANING OF MEANING?

Pragmatics is basically interested in the question of how communication is being achieved. Consequently, the criteria of

is the knowledge they share; however, they also must assume that they share these
second-order assumptions, which makes it necessary to have third-order assumptions . . . and so on indefinitely. See Strawson (1964 : 157); Sperber and Wilson
(1986 : 16–17).

[17] One reason seems to be that pragmatics literature on implicatures often
oscillates between philosophical inquiry, e.g. of the kind practised by Searle, and
attempts to provide scientific or quasi-scientific explanations of the mental processes
involved in communication. This oscillation between philosophy and science, not to
speak of the problematic nature of the mental sciences, is the cause of a great deal
of obscurity in pragmatics.

success for a communicative act would be defined in terms of speaker's intentions. Recall the Griceian model of a speaker's communication intentions: for S to mean something by x, he must intend

(a) S's utterance of x to produce a certain response r in a certain audience A;

(b) A to recognize S's intention (a);

(c) A's recognition of S's intention (a) to function as at least part of A's reason for A's response r.

From the perspective of pragmatics, an act of communication succeeds if and only if the hearer recognizes S's intention (b) (Sperber and Wilson 1986 : 28). Suppose S tells H that 'Jim is a bad football player', intending (so we assume) H to believe this to be true. We judge the act of *communication* successful even if H fails to believe that Jim is a bad football player, so far as H recognizes that this belief was what S intended to convey to him, that is, realizing S's intention (b). Note that in normal circumstances, H's recognition of S's intention (b) is not only sufficient but also a necessary condition for the success of communication. Suppose H misunderstood S's utterance, hearing it as 'Jim is a good football player'. Suppose further, that for some reason he does not believe S (for instance, he thinks S has a good reason to lie), and hence he now believes the opposite, namely, that Jim is a bad football player. As it happens, S has succeeded in creating the appropriate response in H. Nevertheless, the act of communication has clearly failed, since H has not recognized S's intention to communicate *that* belief, that is, intention (b) has not been conveyed.[18]

But now, setting aside the interest in how communication is achieved, and taking up the perspective of interpretation, we must ask a different question; that is, 'What is it to understand, for example, an utterance or a text?' With regard to this question, the idea of successful communication is only one possible relevant consideration. In one clear sense it is of course true that one understands an expression if one recognizes the pertinent communication intentions of the speaker. Thus we can say that success-

---

[18] This is so, except in particular circumstances, when it is not part of the speaker's *intention* to secure a certain effect he strives to achieve by means of recognition of the intention to secure it, e.g. in cases of insinuating, manipulative speech-acts, etc. See Strawson (1964 : 162). See also Ch. 8, sect. 2.

ful communication is at least a sufficient criterion for understanding an expression. But is it also a necessary one? Not according to many philosophers and art critics, among whom it is a very familiar thesis that interpretation is not confined to an attempt to retrieve the communication intentions of the artist. They argue that successful communication is not the only criterion for the successful interpretation of a text or an utterance, etc.

Admittedly, if this thesis is correct, and I shall presume that at least contemporary interpretative practices render it undeniable, we still lack a conceptual account of what it is that enables one to make such interpretative statements. In order to pinpoint the issue, let me reiterate some of the conclusions reached so far. Interpretation, I have presumed, consists in the attribution of *meaning* to an object. We have encountered two senses of 'meaning' which are potentially relevant: the meaning *of* an expression, which is, at least in the linguistic context, basically determined by rules or conventions, and someone meaning *that* such-and-such by an expression, which is normally defined in terms of communication intentions. I have also argued that the concept of interpretation is not explicable in terms of following rules or conventions, and hence, that the semantic notion of meaning (that is, 'meaning of . . .') is not the appropriate one for the purpose of explicating the concept of interpretation. The pragmatic notion of 'meaning', understood in terms of communication intentions would seem more suitable, and we encounter its use in many interpretative contexts, but it is claimed that it fails to exhaust the full scope of interpretation. Hence the question 'Is there a third meaning of "meaning" which might do the job?'

It is sometimes suggested, particularly in the context of art criticism, that interpretative statements amount to formulations of the meaning of an object *for* the interpreter. Presumably, one refers here to expressions about the emotional impact of the work of art on the interpreter, the way it is experienced by him, and the like. Yet such emotional reactions to objects, even if they are reactions to works of art, are not normally presented as interpretations at all. Indeed, the term 'meaning' is used here in a very different sense, as it would be for instance, in saying that 'my wife means a lot to me'. This sense is rather remote from our present concerns. In using it, one is not offering an interpretation but rather expressing a certain emotion. On the other hand, when a literary critic claims that a certain novel is about such-and-such, despite the fact that the author may have had no such intention, the critic wishes to make a statement about the meaning of the novel, and not about his personal reaction to it. Hence we are back to the question of what the meaning can be of for example, 'the meaning of a work of art', if it is neither its literal meaning, nor the meaning intended by the author.

In general, I will suggest that the answer to this question consists in the fact that meaning is assigned through a counter-factual statement. Given that x is the meaning attributed to, for instance a text T, and x is not the literal meaning of T, nor is it the meaning of T intended by its author, then the attribution of meaning x to T can only be understood as the contention that on the basis of certain assumptions a certain fictitious speaker would have meant x by expressing T.[19] In other words, an interpretative statement is either a statement on the communication intentions of the actual speaker, or else it must be a counter-factual statement, characterizing the communication intentions of a fictitious speaker, whose identity and nature are either explicitly defined or, as is more often the case, presupposed by the particular interpretation offered.

It should be emphasized that the point here is actually twofold. First, that interpretation is essentially a matter of attributing intentions, that is, in the pragmatics sense of 'meaning', namely, meaning that such-and-such by an act or expression. At the same time, interpretations need not be based on the intentions of actual authors; the meaning of an act or expression is understandable in terms of counter-factual intentions, that is, in terms of the intentions one could attribute to a fictitious author characterized in certain ways. This characterization of 'the author' constitutes a certain framework of reference, as it were. It defines the parameters employed throughout the interpretation in question. The point is, however, that while these parameters are potentially variable, the logic of interpretative statements is such that they are typically reducible to the attribution of intentions.[20] Hence there is no need for a third meaning of 'meaning' to explicate the concept of

[19] Cf. Fish (1983a : 282–3). Note that generally, a counter-factual statement can be either contrary to the facts, or in a weaker version, regardless of the facts. Of course, the weaker version is more relevant here.

[20] Psychoanalytic interpretations may present one general exception to this thesis. As the status of psychoanalysis is itself subject to extensive controversy, I cannot hope to dwell on this matter in any satisfactory way. Generally speaking, though, it would seem that psychoanalysis presents an intermediary case, combining elements of interpretation and scientific explanation in a rather intricate manner.

interpretation. In other words, the difference between interpretations which confine themselves to attempts to reveal the intentions of the author, and those which do not, does not lie in the grammar of interpretation. The difference consists in variant characterizations of the 'author' whose intentions the interpreter strives to illuminate.

The characterization of a fictitious author can vary in various dimensions, and be presumed or presented at various levels of abstraction. The dimensions would vary, for instance, against different historical settings, or different generic affiliations, or whatever else might affect the meaning of the object in question. With respect to the level of abstraction, we could say that the most concrete characterization presupposed is the one which coincides with the actual, historic author. One could then move away, so to speak, from the concrete author, employing various degrees of abstraction. Say, for example, that the object of interpretation is a certain character in Shakespeare's *Hamlet*: interpretations at the most concrete level typically attempt to discover Shakespeare's intentions—that is, the ones he actually had—with respect to the character in question. At a somewhat more abstract level, one might also consider those intentions which one presumes that Shakespeare would have been willing to recognize as his own, despite his unawareness of them while writing. Progressing to a more abstract characterization, one might ask, for instance: what Shakespeare would have intended had he written *Hamlet* in the twentieth century, or had he been aware of Freud's conception of the Oedipus complex, and so on. Finally, one can abstract even further by departing from Shakespeare altogether, conceiving the author of *Hamlet* in terms of some ideal representative of a certain genre, for example.

I suppose that there are philosophers who would want to argue that the attribution of counter-factual intentions does not concern intentions at all. Or perhaps as others might put it: when an interpreter attributes intentions counter-factually, in the manner described, the intentions in play are those of the interpreter, not those of any author. There is, of course, more than a grain of truth in these contentions (or complaints, as one may wish), but they are beside the point. My thesis is confined to the explication of the grammar of interpretation, and was not meant to imply anything further. The thesis advocated here is not meant to deny (or to confirm, for that matter) that the concept of intention designates a mental event. Still, there is no conceptual flaw in the counter-factual attribution of intentions. There is, of course, a conspicuous logical difference between actual and counter-factual attribution of intentions, which resides in the nature of the truth conditions of each of these classes of statement. The truth conditions of the former would be given in terms of the mental events that those statements purport to describe. Hence also, statements of this kind would be verifiable in ways which are unavailable with respect to counter-factual statements. This is not meant to suggest that interpretative statements about actual intentions can be verified in ways which are somehow better or easier than the verification procedures which are available for other types of interpretative statements. It is often much more difficult to know what the author actually meant than what he would have meant had he been working on the basis of certain assumptions which we can attribute to him. The difference is only a logical one. But these logical differences do not affect the possibility of counter-factual attribution of intentions. Perhaps one can question the point of making such counter-factual statements, or doubt their objectivity, if I may have recourse to this problematic term, but these doubts pertain to a very different dimension of the matter than the one I have been concerned with. Generally speaking, these doubts pertain to the distinction, or better, to the problem of distinguishing, between interpretation and invention. Whether such a distinction can be substantiated in a satisfactory manner, is a question I would wish to discuss at a later stage.

There is one point, however, which can be made now: it is arguable that the more abstract the characterization of the fictitious author, the greater the interpretation's tendency to become invention. And vice versa, the more one commits oneself to retrieving the intentions of the actual author, the less creative freedom the interpreter allows himself, as it were. To be sure, this is not meant as more than a very general and rough observation. Much depends on the particular assumptions on the basis of which the given interpretation is conducted. It is important to realize, however, that those assumptions on the basis of which the speaker—whether actual or fictitious—is characterized, provide the basic criteria of success for the proposed interpretation. To the extent that one strives to retrieve the actual author's intentions, for instance, one commits oneself to certain criteria, in this case historic, that are taken to determine the success or failure of the particular interpretation offered. Likewise, if the author is characterized in terms of some ideal representative of a certain genre, for instance, the presumptions which are taken to determine this characterization would provide the criteria of success for the particular interpretation offered.

Consequently, one of the interesting questions about the concept of interpretation is whether there is any one criterion of success that is inherently suitable to all instances of interpretation in a particular field, or perhaps even in general. The possibility that there is, as suggested by Dworkin, will be discussed in the next chapter.

For the time being, let me summarize the conclusions that I see as justified at this point. Interpretation, I have argued, consists in the imposition of meaning on an object, whereas the appropriate notion of meaning is given in terms of communication intentions. This still leaves open the possibility of attributing intentions counterfactually to a fictitious speaker, whose supposed identity and characterization determine the criteria of success presumed by the kind of interpretation offered. This view of interpretation coincides with the thesis, advocated in the first section, that interpretation is an exception to, and parasitic on, the prior knowledge of literal meanings, as it normally concerns those aspects of communication which are under-determined by rules or conventions.

3

DWORKIN'S THEORY OF INTERPRETATION

THE basic presumption underlying the analytical approach to jurisprudence is that a distinction exists between the abstract concept of law and its realization in particular legal institutions. An attempt to characterize the concept of law is basically independent of attempts to answer questions on what the law requires in this or that situation. 'What is law?' and 'What is (or should be) the law on a given issue?' are, according to this traditional view, separate and basically independent questions.

Dworkin's theory of Law as Interpretation[1] challenges this conceptual division. On the thesis that 'law is interpretative throughout', Dworkin argues not only that accounting for the concept of law is a matter of interpretation, but also, and more interestingly, that such accounts are inevitably tied up with considerations of what the law is there to settle. In other words, as he sees it, jurisprudence is basically a theory of adjudication as both concern one and the same issue, namely, imposing the best available interpretation on a given practice. Notably this amounts to a frontal attack against analytical jurisprudence; Dworkin challenges its basic presupposition, that is, that the concept of law and the justification of its particular requirements are separate issues.

An analysis of this challenge forms the main topic of this chapter. Its first three sections are mainly explanatory; they outline Dworkin's concept of interpretation, and the role he assigns it in linking theory with practice. Sections 4 and 5 explore Dworkin's

---

[1] The ideas presented here and in Ch. 4 were published by Dworkin in two or three stages: in 1981 he published two articles on the interpretative nature of legal theory, first in 9 *Critical Inquiry* (Autumn, 1982), 179, and a similar version in 60 *Texas Law Review* (1981), 527 (the former is reprinted in Dworkin 1985 : 146). This was followed by a reply to Stanley Fish (Dworkin 1983), and, eventually, the most comprehensive elaboration of the theory in *Law's Empire* (Dworkin 1986). Where the arguments are essentially the same, I have allowed myself to refer rather randomly to the different texts, but I shall concentrate mainly on *Law's Empire*.

arguments in support of the main thesis in question, that is, the interdependence of jurisprudence and adjudication, and present the conclusion that none of them is convincing. Lastly, I shall attempt to draw a distinction between Dworkin's thesis and Davidson's principle of charity, arguing that the latter can provide no support for the former, even if it is considered acceptable of itself. The consequences of this failure to identify theory with practice are not spelled out fully in the present chapter. The subsequent chapters go on to complete the discussion.

I. CONSTRUCTIVE INTERPRETATION

Dworkin (1986:50) identifies two main categories of interpretation, 'conversational interpretation' and 'constructive interpretation'. The former is based on the communication-intention model described in the previous chapter. Dworkin acknowledges that in cases of ordinary conversation, interpretation typically amounts to an attempt to reveal the communication intentions of the speaker.

Not all forms of interpretation are based on this model, however. Other cases, Dworkin argues, notably social explanation and art criticism, have to be considered on the basis of a model which he calls the 'aesthetic hypothesis' (1985:149), or 'constructive' interpretation:

Interpretation of works of art and social practices, I shall argue, is indeed essentially concerned with purpose not cause. But the purposes in play are not (fundamentally) those of some author but of the interpreter. Roughly, *constructive interpretation is a matter of imposing purpose on an object or practice in order to make of it the best possible example of the form or genre to which it is taken to belong.* (1986:52, my emphasis.)

Two immediate and interrelated questions arise here, 'What are the logical relations between these two models of interpretation?' and, 'What is the scope within which the constructive model is applicable?' Dworkin seems to waver between two answers to the first of these questions. On the one hand he is aware that the conversational model may be derived from the constructive one. In other words, the constructive account . . . could perhaps provide a more general account of interpretation in all its forms' (1986:53). Consider an ordinary conversation: why should we care at all about the speakers intentions? One possible answer might be given in terms of the constructive model: an effort to ascertain the speaker's intentions presents the particular utterance situation in its best light. Acting upon any other presumption would amount to construing the utterance situation as a poor example of ordinary conversation.[2] On the other hand, in arguing against the precedence granted to the author's intention in literary criticism, Dworkin relies more than once on what he sees as the fact that a literary work is created, initially, with the intention of becoming a 'distinct entity' (1985 : 154–8; 1986 : 55–7). But if authors' particular intentions should be disregarded by attempts to interpret their works, only because they typically *intend* for these to become 'distinct entities', then it is the conversational model that holds here after all.[3]

Which model is the more basic one then? In which direction is the dual relation to be read? I believe that if Dworkin had been forced to choose (and he should have chosen) he would undoubtedly have preferred the former. When the conversational model is taken to be the basic one, the constructive model makes very little sense. We could turn to it, for instance, only when convinced that the creator of a given text had such an intention. But this might not happen very often. An author, not to speak of a legislator, might just as easily show his or her clear intention that the text be understood in a particular way, regardless of whether another interpretation might present it in a better light. Accordingly, the constructive model should be regarded as the basic model of interpretation in all its forms. Furthermore, we shall soon see that the logical priority of the constructive model is a thesis which Dworkin cannot easily dispense with.

Note that assigning logical precedence to the constructive model does not automatically amount to a rejection of the conversational model, either in art criticism or in any other realm. Dworkin rightly emphasizes this point: 'I am not arguing that author's intention theory of artistic interpretation is wrong (or right), but

[2] On the role of value-related considerations with respect to the presumption of sincerity and Grice's Co-operative Principle in this context, see Ulman-Margalit (1983 : 157–60).

[3] This may be even more apparent in Dworkin's account of constitutional interpretation, where he relies on the distinction between concept and conceptions. He argues for instance that one should take into account the concept of 'cruel and unusual punishment' the framers have 'chosen deliberately,' and not the more concrete conceptions such a concept can be taken to yield (see 1985 : 131). But Raz rightly notes that 'moral considerations are here assigned this role on the basis of a communication model of the Constitution, that is, on the basis of the intentions of the framers of the Constitution' (1986a : 1110).

whether it is wrong or right and what it means . . . must turn on the plausibility of some more fundamental assumption about why works of art have the value their presentation presupposes' (1986 : 61). In other words, the conversational model, or 'intentional-ism' as I shall often call it, makes sense only as a particular *instance* of the constructive model. To be sure, Dworkin acknowledges that a statement of the form '*A* interprets *T* as *x*' does not entail of itself that '*A believes* that *x* presents *T* in its best light.' This would often be false as a matter of fact. Nevertheless, he claims that in the 'usual critical circumstances we must be able to attribute some such view to him' (1986 : 61). Otherwise we 'are left with no sense of why he claims the reading he does' (1986 : 421).

Suppose we are presented with two interpretations, *A* and *B*, of a text, for example, a novel. Suppose further, that *A* presents the novel in a better light, whereas *B* is the interpretation which the author had in mind (whatever this may mean). What might support the plausibility of an argument to the effect that interpretation *B* was, nevertheless, to be preferred? Without going into any details, it seems quite clear that one would eventually have to draw upon the presupposed values believed to be embodied in literature. For instance, that literature is better viewed as realizing the value of personal ingenuity, of the author's ability to convey a particular message, etc., and not the values supporting interpretation *A*. In other words, in deferring to the author's intentions in literary interpretation, one displays, at least implicitly, a more general attitude towards literature. This is an attitude which consists in valuing the communicative aspect of literature, or of art in general.

The converse conclusion also holds. When the interpretation of a literary text takes no account of the author's intentions, this means that what is most highly valued by the interpreter is the work's significance, its impact on contemporary readers, and the like. In any case, then it is the presupposed value of literature which supports (or undermines) intentionalism. Hence intentionalism can only be grounded on the constructive model; it cannot compete with it.[4]

---

[4] Disputes over the role of intentions in historical studies are subject to similar considerations (cf. Tully 1988). There is one difference, however, consisting in the fact that in case of history, it is not the value of the subject (i.e. history) that comes into play, but rather the value attributed to the very study of history and our aim in learning it.

We have thus reached a unified concept of interpretation, underlying the interpretative endeavour in all its forms, that is, the constructive model. Hence, we can now supply an answer to the question of scope as well; the constructive model is applicable, in fact inevitably so, to all forms of interpretation (at least all standard ones).

The idea that interpretation is fundamentally constructive is of crucial importance to Dworkin's theory, since it clarifies how it is that all forms of interpretation are radically value dependent, or in other words, how it is that evaluative judgements profoundly determine our interpretations. On the constructive model, any interpretation attempts to present its object as the best possible example of the genre to which it is taken to belong. It follows that we must come to any interpretative task, already equipped with an idea of what is valuable in the pertinent genre (1986 : 52–72). This may be termed the primary evaluative judgement. It must then be supplemented by secondary evaluative judgements, which enable us to present a particular object as the best performance or manifestation of the supposed primary values (1986 : 66).

To see why the value dependence of interpretation is so central to Dworkin's jurisprudence, a few words must be said on his concept of law. Dworkin has always argued that the law in a particular community cannot be identified in value-neutral terms. Notably, he has been at odds with legal positivism. Consider the two claims of legal positivism mentioned in Chapter 1: first, that each legal system contains a rule (or rules) of recognition identifying the acts which are law creating acts, that is, the sources of law, and second, that all law is source based. Dworkin is at odds with both these tenets. To begin with the second, he claims that the source-based law fails to exhaust the entire body of the law in any given legal system. With respect to the first, he claims that the identification of source-based law itself cannot be defined in value-neutral terms. Both objections combine to form Dworkin's alternative concept of law as the *justified* use of collective force.[5] In keeping with the first objection this concept holds the law to consist of source-based law as well as all the norms derivable from the

---

[5] As a matter of fact, Dworkin's concept of law has two parts, or levels. The concept of law as the justified use of collective force (or past political decisions) is the general or more abstract part. 'Law as integrity' is Dworkin's more concrete suggestion for the justification of collective force.

soundest political theory justifying the source-based law. The second objection is manifest in the thesis that the precise identification of source-based law also depends partly on the soundest political theory justifying it.

Of course, these substantive points are not novel ones.[6] Now, however, they have emerged as anchored in methodological considerations, that is, the concept of interpretation. Nevertheless, Dworkin's move here is not straightforward. To claim that law is the *justified* use of collective force, he must first show why it is not just what it happens to be as a matter of social fact. It is not enough to show interpretation to be an intrinsically value-laden explanation. It must be shown that the interpretative methods characteristic of the theory are also indicative of the practice; that the practice itself is interpretative, as it were; and vice versa, it might be the case that the practice itself is essentially interpretative, while its proper description is not. Consider the practice of literary criticism, which is undoubtedly an interpretative enterprise. It is not clear from the outset that one who sets out to describe the basic concepts of this practice is necessarily engaged in anything like interpretation.

In other words, the relations between theory and practice must be elaborated in detail, before anything can be deduced from the concept of interpretation, as regards the concept of law.

2. THEORY AND PRACTICE

In some social practices, notably law and art, so Dworkin (1986: 47) claims, the participants develop 'a complex "interpretive" attitude' towards its rules and conventions, an attitude including two components:

The first is the assumption that the practice of courtesy[7] does not simply exist but has value, that it serves some interest or purpose or enforces some principle—in short, that is has some point—that can be stated independently of just describing the rules that make up the practice. The second is the further assumption that the requirements of courtesy . . . are not necessarily or exclusively what they have always been taken to be but are instead sensitive to its point.

---

[6] See Dworkin (1977: chs. 1–4).

[7] 'Courtesy' is an imaginary community Dworkin employs to elucidate his point. The fact that the discussion is conducted with reference to this imaginary example does not always help one to understand the scope of his arguments.

Unfortunately, Dworkin does not identify the kind of social practices which can be said to display this interpretative attitude. My suggestion is the following: the interpretative attitude characterizes social practices which are constituted by norms. Let me explain. Not all the social phenomena where people's behaviour conforms to rules are social practices, properly so called. The distinction here is between normative rules which constitute a social practice, and rules which merely reflect social regularities.[8]

I take it to be a defining feature of normative practices that the existence of the rules or conventions is of itself reason for action.[9] Thus, consider the following example. Suppose we observe a regularity in a certain society, for instance, that most people drink tea at five o'clock in the afternoon. Is this a social practice which can be said to have a value or purpose or some point? We would hardly say that eating meals is a social practice, and that as such it enhances a value, since people have reason to eat meals regardless of any considerations about what other members of their society do, or should do. In other words, eating meals is not an instance of following a rule. When the reasons for doing something are socially independent, it is inappropriate to call the regularity of actions a social practice, even if it occurs as a social regularity. This might be the case with regard to five-o'clock tea; but then again it might not. It is possible that people in our imaginary society adhere to this regularity for reasons which are not socially independent. On the contrary, it may be meaningful for the participants that the regularity is a practice rather than mere coincidence, and they may act as they do, at least in part, for this very reason. It is in such cases that the social rule is normative. (One need not conclude that socially independent reasons are necessarily excluded in these cases. Sometimes they are, for instance, when the rule functions as a co-ordinative factor such as the one determining on which side of the road cars are driven, but this is not always the case.)

Now, the point is that our story cannot be concluded here. It still lacks an explanation of why or in what sense the participants in a practice conceive of its rules as reason for action. This is where the

---

[8] By the term 'norms' I mean prescriptive, or rather what Raz calls 'mandatory' norms. See Raz (1975 : 49).

[9] See Hart (1961 : 78–83). Of course, a norm can also be a reason for condemning or praising behaviour, etc., but these are parasitic on the fact that the norm is primarily considered a reason for action. Norms can also determine beliefs, attitudes, etc., but we need not go into this here.

concept of the value or the point of this practice comes in. To make sense of the idea that a rule or convention is of itself a reason for action, we must assume that it is of some meaning or value for the participants. This then yields the answer to the question posed above. Constructive interpretation is the imposition of 'meaning' or 'point', or in general a value, on a normative-based practice in order to render intelligible the idea of norms or rules being a reason for action. In other words, social practices, that is, practices constituted by sets of norms, are only intelligible against the background assumption of a purpose or value that the practice is taken to enhance. In this sense it can be said that from the point of view of the participants, law, *qua* normative system, ought to be seen as justified.[10]

So much for the first component of the participants' interpretative attitude. What about the second one, namely, the view of the requirements of the practice as sensitive to its supposed value? Dworkin (1986 : 47) rightly acknowledges this as a distinct feature which is not logically entailed by the former. Again, he is not very clear in identifying the kinds of practice taken to be typically value sensitive. But the issue is both important and problematic. It is only natural to suppose that any activity performed (among other things) to advance a value or purpose, should display a sensitivity to the value or purpose it is taken to advance. But things become more complicated when we concentrate on social practices.

Most significantly, different social practices vary according to the different ways in which their requirements are institutionalized. By this I mean the various ways in which the requirements of the given practice are themselves determined, modified, etc., by a set of established rules and institutions. Thus, for instance, table manners and law probably fall at opposite poles of this continuum, the former representing one of the least, and the latter one of the most, institutionalized practices. (Art is an interesting intermediate case: viewed as a social enterprise, it certainly has many institutional features, manifest in the role of museums, galleries, art dealers,

---

[10] In this, Dworkin shares the views of Kelsen and Raz on the normativity of law, but not those of Hart (see nn. 11 and 12 below). One should realize, of course, that it is not necessary for all the participants in a social practice (constituted by normative rules) to regard the rules as normative. As we know very well from our legal systems, some of the participants can be anarchists, while many others comply with its rules for various prudential or personal reasons, or for no reason at all.

etc., in affecting the way art is viewed in a specific community. On the other hand, it is not clear that the concept of art is necessarily affected by such institutional elements.)

The institutional aspect of law is relevant here for the following reason: Dworkin's assumption that the requirements of law are sensitive to its point or value seems contradictory to the positivist doctrine of the separation of law from morality, that is, to the distinction of what the law is from what it should be. However, to be more precise, legal positivism need not deny that the requirements of law are sensitive to its point or value, as a matter of historical development. Over a certain period of time, people's actions are bound to be influenced by the way in which they understand or interpret the point or value of the practice, and this itself shapes the emergent forms in which the practice will be realized in detail. Such an account can hardly be denied. The dispute lies elsewhere. The question is, at what stage, and how, do evaluative judgements regarding the value of law actually become part of the law? Positivists argue that due to the institutionalized aspect of law, it is never *sufficient* for a rule or decision to be morally (or, according to Raz (1985), even logically) required to count as law, without an actual and authoritative decision to this effect. However, this being one of the main points of dispute between him and his positivist opponents, Dworkin cannot at this initial stage presume law to be sensitive to its value in the manner that courtesy is, without incurring the charge of having assumed the very point at issue. Avoiding this requires the restriction of his claim to the historical sense of this second feature of the interpretative approach, which indeed should not be denied by legal positivism.

To sum up, the discussion so far has shown that the normative aspect of legal systems requires its participants to adopt a 'complex interpretative attitude' towards its rules. Now it must clarify the relation between the legal theory and the practice, providing an answer to the question of why the theory should also be interpretative. The reply Dworkin proposes is rather surprising, namely, that there is no difference between theory and practice in this respect. Any attempt to explain a social practice such as law, must involve exactly the same kind of reasoning required for participation in the practice, that is, for accounting to oneself what it is that the practice requires. (For the sake of brevity, I shall henceforth refer to this thesis as the 'hermeneutic thesis', not because it epitomizes the main ideas of German hermeneutics, but because in this Dworkin claims to have been inspired by this school.) The following is the relevant passage:

A social scientist who offers to interpret the practice must make the same distinction. He can, if he wishes, undertake only to report the various opinions different individuals in the community have about what the practice demands. But that would not constitute an interpretation of the practice itself; if he undertakes that different project he must give up methodological individualism and use the methods his subjects use in forming their own opinions about what courtesy really requires. He must, that is, *join* the practice he proposes to understand; his conclusions are then not neutral reports about what the citizens of courtesy think but claims about courtesy *competitive* with theirs. (1986 : 64)

One can hardly overemphasize the importance of this thesis to Dworkin's jurisprudence, being, after all, the only account he offers of the interpretative nature of legal theory, and of the theory's identification with practice.

The hermeneutic thesis gains some of its plausibility from a potentially misleading example. Dworkin often compares legal theory to literary criticism (1985 : 158–9; 1986 : 50). The latter, as I readily conceded, is undoubtedly an interpretative enterprise. But is literary criticism analogous to legal theory? This is far from clear. More plausibly, it is analogous to adjudication. It is the role of judges, like the role of literary critics, to decide what certain texts mean. While jurisprudence might be construed as analogous to some form of literary theory, the same questions on the relations between theory and practice would hold here as well. In other words, is a theory *about* literary criticism an interpretation of literature? Dworkin seems well aware of this problem, claiming as he does at the very beginning of the book (1986 : 14) that he will make the 'judges' viewpoint' the paradigm of his theory. But this only pushes the question one step further: why should the judges' point of view determine the perspective of legal theory? In short, the analogy between jurisprudence and literary criticism does not hold independently; it can only follow from an argument which we have yet to explore, and cannot serve as a self-explanatory premiss of this argument.

3. THE INTERNAL POINT OF VIEW

We have seen why it is that the hermeneutic thesis is so important to Dworkin's jurisprudence and his concept of law. Two more things now remain to be seen. First, what precisely does this thesis amount to? Second, what are the arguments Dworkin offers to support it, and are they sound?

The appropriate account of the normativity of law has always been one of the most disputed topics among legal positivists. Bentham and Austin sought to provide a reductionist account of legal statements. Austin (1832: lecture 1), for instance, claimed that statements about legal duties are fully expressible in terms of the likelihood that one may come to harm of a certain kind.

Yet this reductionism formed one of the main targets in Hart's criticism of early positivism. Hart (1961: 78–83) distinguished between the external and the internal points of view of normative systems. The Austinian description is external in the sense that it is a description of legal practice, or better, its regularities, as viewed by an outsider attempting to understand the participants' behaviour with no knowledge of their reasons for behaving this way. Such an alien sociologist could, for instance, observe that most people stop their cars when the traffic-light is red, and that most (or some?) of them are liable to sanctions when they do not. He could thus only describe the 'normativity' of law in terms of predictions of liability to sanctions. But an analysis of law confined to the external point of view would, Hart argues, be a serious distortion. Legal theory must take account of the internal, participants' point of view. Most of these (particularly judges and other officials) regard the law as *reason* for actions, hence their statements about the law are normative statements.

Hart himself, however, seems to offer yet another type of reduction. He strives to explain the internal point of view in terms of what people *believe* to be reasons for action. He thinks it sufficient for legal theory to account for the normativity of law from this sociological perspective, as it were; that is, in terms of people's beliefs, attitudes, tendencies, and the like. Thus, according to this Hartian view, we encounter two types of normative statement:

1. Made by people who believe in the validity of the normative system (that is, full-blooded normative statements), and
2. Made as statements about (1) by someone who does not necessarily believe in the validity of the norms.

Raz (1975: 171) recognizes the same two varieties of explanation of norms (which he dubs 'normative based' and 'belief based', respectively) and acknowledges them as basic types. However, he also argues that a third category, which he calls 'normative statements from a point of view' (1975 : 170–7) or 'detached legal statements' (1979 : 153), cannot be reduced to either (1) or (2). These are statements of the form:

3. 'According to law A ought to do x.'

Nothing follows from statements like (3) as to what the speaker believes ought to be done (all thing considered), or as to what anyone else believes. They are statements 'from a point of view or on the basis of certain assumptions which are not necessarily shared by the speaker', or indeed by anyone in particular (Raz 1979 : 156).

Raz's identification of this third type of normative statement, irreducible to the other two, helps explain for instance, how normative concepts (such as 'ought' and 'duty') do not have different meanings when used in different normative contexts (for example, law, positive morality, critical morality), while preventing the confusion of this issue with the question of the necessary connections between law and morality (Raz 1979 : 158). But most important, it enables positivists like Raz (and Kelsen as construed by Raz) to reconcile positivism with the position mentioned earlier, that from the point of view of the participants, law ought to be conceived as justified. Raz can explain Kelsen's dictum that even 'an anarchist, if he were a professor of law, could describe positive law as a system of valid norms, without having to approve of this law' (Kelsen 1967 : 218 n.),[11] while preserving Kelsen's concept of legal validity in terms of justification.

This is a crucial point. Dworkin has previously argued (1977 : 48–58) against Hart's concept of normativity, that an adequate account of the internal point of view cannot be 'belief based', to use Raz's expression. This is so, as when the participants in a normative system make claims about what this system requires, they do not typically make claims about what other people believe ought to be done, but simply about what ought to be done. We can now gather that Kelsen and Raz could agree with Dworkin on this point without discarding legal positivism.[12] Legal positivism need not deny that the participants in a legal system (particularly judges) make full-

[11] See Raz (1979 : 156); see also his 'Kelsen's Theory of the Basic Norm' (ibid. : 123–45).

[12] I should mention that Hart himself objects to this account of the normativity of law, as depicted by Raz. He claims that 'when judges . . . make committed statements . . . it is not the case that they must necessarily believe or pretend to believe that they are referring to a species of moral obligation' (1982 : 161). Hart's argument seems to dwell on the fact that people, judges included, can have various

blooded normative statements which are irreducible to belief-based explanations; but it is also, on the other hand, under no obligation to admit that an account of such statements must adopt the internal point of view, in a full-blooded, normative manner.

In other words, in-so-far as the issue is an account of normative statements, there does not seem to be any real difference between Dworkin and Raz. Both would agree that when a theorist or a participant seeks to account for what the law requires in a given case, he or she is bound to make some normative statements which are (at least in some cases) irreducible to belief-based explanations. Yet neither of them is logically obliged to contend that such an account must adopt the committed, rather than the detached point of view.

But now it is vitally important to see where the disagreement does in fact lie. It indeed has to do with the relevant point of view, not with regard to the explication of normative *statements*, but regarding the explication of the *concept* of law. Dworkin seems to be claiming that the concept of law is also a normative concept, that is, a concept which may only be accounted for from a normative point of view. This is why, or rather this is the sense in which, Dworkin's jurisprudence is a theory of adjudication. Dworkin declines to distinguish between the interpretation of the law, that is, its particular requirements, and the interpretation of law, that is, the general concept. For him, both endeavours amount to one and the same thing: imposing a purpose or value on the practice so as to present it in its best possible light (Dworkin 1986 : 90).

To sum up so far: the hermeneutic thesis should not be understood to deny the possibility of normative statements from a point of view. What it amounts to is a contention that jurisprudence—viewed as a theory of the concept of law—and a theory of adjudication, must adopt the *same* point of view, that is, the point of view of a committed participant.

In the following sections I shall try to present what seem to me to be Dworkin's arguments in favour of the hermeneutic thesis, arguing that none of them in fact turns out to be successful. Later, I shall say something more about the consequences of this failure.

reasons for accepting the normativity of law, reasons which are not necessarily moral or political. I think Raz would not deny this, yet he would claim that these are somehow parasitic cases, i.e. parasitic upon the standard, moral conception. However, a full account of the dispute between the two would exceed the scope of this chapter, and in any case, even Hart does not deny that Raz's account of the normativity of law is compatible with legal positivism (1982 : 158).

4. THE ARGUMENTATIVE CHARACTER OF LAW

Dworkin first refers to the internal perspective on law in a reply to the possible claim that a proper understanding of law requires a scientific or historical approach. As the same argument is also mentioned later, however, in the context of the hermeneutic thesis, it deserves close examination. Consider the following passage:

Legal practice, unlike many other social phenomena, is argumentative. Every actor in the practice understands that what it permits or requires depends on the truth of certain propositions that are *given sense only by and within the practice*; the practice consists in large part in deploying and arguing about these propositions.

... the historian cannot understand law as an argumentative social practice ... until he has the *participants' understanding*, until he has his own sense of what counts as a good or bad argument within that practice. (1986: 13–14 my emphasis.)

The main point here seems to turn on the question of what one must know or experience so as to be able to understand a social practice such as law. Yet the distinction drawn here by Dworkin between a sociological or historical approach to law and a 'jurisprudential' one (1986: 14) indicates that he is dealing with two separate questions in one breath. The question of whether a causal explanation of social practices is possible, and if so, whether and to what extent it is preconditioned by an interpretative explanation, is a rather familiar issue, extensively debated in the philosophy of social science.[13] But the question we are facing now is entirely different: it pertains to the role of the participants' point of view in an interpretative explanation. The two should be kept distinct, since answering the latter requires no reference whatsoever to the former (although, the opposite may not be the case).

Dworkin's answer to the second question would seem to run as follows: in the practices he has classified as 'argumentative', the intelligibility of certain requirements of the practice depends on understanding concepts or propositions 'that are given sense only by and within the practice'. But the term 'argumentative' may be misleading here. Consider games, for instance: terms such as 'checkmate', 'goal', etc. are clearly 'given sense only by and within' a certain game. Let us call these 'institutional concepts', concepts

[13] See e.g. Taylor (1971) and (1985). See also Winch (1958), and cf. MacIntyre (1973).

which gain their very meanings from the existence of a practice or institution. Certainly, one needs to know the pertinent practice in order to understand these terms. Someone with no idea of what chess is, for instance, would have to be taught the rules of the game (and perhaps, in some cases, the point of playing games at all) in order to understand what a 'checkmate' is.

The same point, however, can be taken a step further: background knowledge is not confined to institutional concepts. Clearly, for instance, a knowledge of the pertinent natural language is also required to render the requirements of law intelligible. Furthermore, recall Searle's argument that the literal meaning of sentences is only applicable relative to a set of background assumptions.[14] What emerges then is a multi-layered picture of the necessary background knowledge which makes the propositions of a social practice intelligible. Needed at the most basic level is a knowledge of the natural language, which in fact amounts to knowing a great deal about the world as conceived of by the pertinent community. Yet the closer the attention paid to institutional concepts, the more necessary it becomes to know about the particular background of these concepts. The nature of the background information required here may also vary according to the nature of the concept. In some cases the institutional background is very specific, a particular game for instance (as in the case of understanding 'checkmate'), or a particular theory (required to understand 'quantum', for example). In other cases it is much more holistic, absorbed in large portions of our knowledge (for instance, the concept of 'contract').

These considerations thus establish that social practices are intelligible only relative to a body of background information, knowledge of which any interpreter either shares already, or must acquire. Does this prove the hermeneutic thesis? Clearly not. It only shows that in a familiar sense, all statements or propositions, especially those employing institutional concepts, are only intelligible against a complex background. But as we have seen, the hermeneutic thesis presents a stronger claim than this. It contends that participants' and theorists' interpretations must adopt one and the same *normative* point of view. Nothing in the necessity of background information can be taken to establish this.

Dworkin, I believe, would reply that I have missed a point here. It is not the necessity of background knowledge on which he relies,

---

[14] Ch. 2, sect. 2.

but the fact that it is controversial, and that these controversies form an essential part of the practice itself. (Perhaps this is why he calls such practices 'argumentative'.) Note, however, that the possibility of normative statements from a point of view does not depend on the assumption that the pertinent point of view is uncontroversial, either in its concrete judgements, or in the background assumptions that make the statements intelligible. Nor do I think that Dworkin would wish to deny this. As we have seen, the debate concerns the relevant point of view with regard to the concept of law, not its particular requirements. Nevertheless, Dworkin sees the problem of controversy as pertinent here.

Consider the following improvisation on a rather familiar example: while not a vegetarian myself, I could still tell my friend, whom I know to be a devout vegetarian, not to eat a certain dish, since it contains fish. According to Raz, I thus make a normative statement from a point of view. Now, suppose that it is controversial among vegetarians whether fish should or should not be eaten. Suppose further, that this controversy is due to different conceptions vegetarians hold on the requirements of their practice, and even different conceptions of nature. Should this make any difference with regard to my ability to make a detached normative statement?

To begin with, we must distinguish between two possible cases. First, perhaps there is a problem of identity here pertaining to the concept of vegetarianism: is vegetarianism a single normative practice or are there, for example, two such practices, one prohibiting the consumption of fish and the other allowing it? Thus, in saying 'according to vegetarianism, *A* should not eat fish', I might be making the mistake of over-generalization. I should have said, 'according to one school of vegetarianism, *A* should not eat fish', or something to this effect.

Alternatively, if it is not a question of identity, the issue of controversy boils down to the problem of applying rules to novel cases. It will not do just to repeat how the rule has been applied, since the case in question is a new and, so far, unsettled one. Here (and this has nothing to do with the nature of the background information required to understand a social practice), Dworkin would argue that both the participants and the theorists would have to decide what vegetarianism 'really requires' (1986 : 64), that is, in such a way as to present it in its best light. This, I take it, is the main argument offered by Dworkin in support of the hermeneutic thesis, and it is to this argument that I now turn.

5. CONSTRUCTIVE INTERPRETATION AND THE HERMENEUTIC THESIS

As we have seen, the normativity of law requires the participants to develop a 'complex interpretative attitude' towards the requirements of their practice. Now suppose we accept Dworkin's contention that any interpretation strives to present its object in the best light, as the best possible manifestation of its genre. Seemingly, there should be no difference between the way participants understand their practice and the way a theorist would account for it: both would have to account for full-blooded normative statements, and both would have to present the practice in its best moral light. In other words, it seems that establishing the hermeneutic thesis involves the substantiation of two points: first, that for both participants and theorists an account of the concept of law is a matter of interpretation; second, that the constructive model underlies all forms of interpretation.

It is this second contention upon which I wish to concentrate. (Partly because I think there is little to gain in arguing about the first, but mainly because rejection of the second would make the entire argument inadequate anyway.) In other words, we must return to the question of the scope appropriate to the constructive model; does the model underlie all forms of interpretation? More particularly, should we concede that the interpretation practised by theorists and participants is of one and the same kind, that is, constructive?

Dworkin's reply clearly relies on the rejection of the communication-intention model (1986 : 62–4), assuming it to be the only plausible alternative to the constructive one. Its main ideas, already presented above, may be briefly recounted as follows:

1. Any interpretation presupposes certain criteria of success.
2. The criteria of success can be either (*a*) mentalistic, based on the communication intention model, or (*b*) value dependent, based on the constructive model.
3. On any plausible account, the mentalistic answer (*a*) is only an instantiation of the constructive model (*b*). Hence
4. The constructive model is the only plausible candidate for (1), that is, the criteria of success in all forms of interpretation.

In the previous chapter I argued that (1) should be accepted. I will also presume that the arguments supporting (3) are sound. Now I would like to argue, however, that the dichotomy in (2) is not exhaustive and hence that the conclusion (4) should be rejected as well. Furthermore, I will argue that even if the argument (1)–(4) is accepted, it cannot establish the hermeneutic thesis since even on the constructive model, theoretical and practical interpretations presume different (evaluative) criteria of success.

As the mentalistic conception is the only one Dworkin considers as a possible rival to his constructive account, the impression is that once this option is dismissed, constructive interpretation remains the only plausible option. As a matter of fact, though, there is a much wider range of options.

Consider the following example. Some critics argue that early cubism (particularly the works of Picasso and Braque from 1906 to 1912) should be seen as 'realistic' painting, which embraces a particular notion of 'representation of reality'.[15] Hintikka goes even further, comparing the concept of realistic representation embodied in cubism to Husserl's phenomenology and his own semantics of possible worlds.[16] Now, can Dworkin's constructive model account for such interpretations? Is the interpretation of cubism as realistic painting an imposition of purpose on cubism 'in order to make of it the best possible example of the form or genre to which it is taken to belong'? Not necessarily: it is not at all clear that such an interpretation should fail if it falls short of presenting cubism in the best light, as compared to rival interpretations. Basically this is due to the fact that interpretation is often a matter of presenting an object in a certain light, or in a different light, rather than in the best light, as Dworkin insists.

As a matter of fact the objection here is twofold: first, that often interpretations are not presented by the interpreter himself in the way described by Dworkin. Second, that sometimes interpretations cannot be presented according to the constructive model. Let us take up these two points in detail.

Evaluative judgements are generally of two kinds. One can either intend the judgement to be universally accepted or not. Moral judgements are typical examples of the former, and judgements

---

[15] See e.g. Cooper (1971).

[16] I refer to a lecture given by Hintikka in Israel in 1974, which was translated into Hebrew from MS by David Heyd, and published in 25 *Eayun* (1974), 139–57.

of taste, such as one's preference for violin rather than piano concertos, are prominent examples of the latter. Clearly then, Dworkin cannot concede that interpretative statements may be of the latter kind, since in such cases it would make no sense to speak of 'the best' interpretation. Yet counter-examples are easily supplied. Many interpretations are not presented with the pretensions Dworkin attributes to them. To take another example, consider for instance a modern adaptation of a Shakespearian play, say *The Merchant of Venice*, set in the City of London, with Shylock as an ambitious Yuppie merchant banker. Would the interpreter claim that this presents *The Merchant of Venice* in its best light? That this interpretation ought to be accepted as *the* right way to see the play? Not necessarily. Instead, one would probably say, 'I'm inviting you to see *The Merchant of Venice* in this possible light—better than some, worse than others—but interesting, nevertheless'.

Admittedly, the fact that interpretative claims are, in practice, being made contrary to Dworkin's analysis is inconclusive either way. It still remains to be seen whether such interpretative contentions make any sense. People often present their moral statements, for instance, as if they expressed only judgements of taste which, arguably, makes no sense. Philosophers have repeatedly contended that the meaning of morality and moral concepts render such 'subjective' statements nonsensical or incoherent.[17] Can Dworkin argue that the same holds with respect to the concept of interpretation? Would it be nonsensical or incoherent to propose an interpretation which one does not intend to be universally accepted?

Dworkin faces two difficulties here. From a methodological point of view, he might find it difficult to answer the above questions in the affirmative, without falling prey to his own 'semantic sting' argument (see Chapter 1). If it does not make sense to propose an interpretation which is not intended to be universally accepted, this must be due to the *meaning* of 'interpretation'. But of course, this might be true, and the 'semantic sting' false.

Be this as it may, the difficulty is also substantive. Consider what Dworkin's rejoinder would be: he would argue that when someone proposes an interpretation of X, and at the same time admits that X could be presented in a better light, 'we are left with no sense of why he claims the reading he does' (1986: 421). But although this

---

[17] See e.g. Hare (1964).

might sometimes be the case, it often is not. We have a very good sense of why one would want to present *The Merchant of Venice* set in the City of London, although it is probably not the best reading of Shakespeare's play. If it is good, the performance may contribute to a better understanding of the complexity and richness of Shakespeare. But this is not on a par with the thesis that an interpretation ought to present its object in its best possible light.[18]

Furthermore, and this takes us to the second part of my objection, it is arguable that often one *cannot* present an object of interpretation in its *best* possible light. Finnis (1987 : 371) rightly observes that Dworkin ignores the fact that interpretations are very often incommensurable. Both the realist and the traditional interpretations of cubism, for instance, may be better than others, but this does not mean that one of them must, or indeed could, be the 'best' interpretation. On Dworkin's own account, interpretations reflect certain values that the interpreter finds embodied in the pertinent genre. But different primary evaluative judgements may be incommensurable. The same holds with regard to secondary evaluative judgements. A work of art can be presented in different and incommensurable ways, each of which presents the object in a different light, though based on the same presumptions about the value the genre is taken to manifest. In short, very often it is pointless to insist on the best answer to an interpretative question. Note, however, that this argument does not imply scepticism (Finnis 1987 : 372). It does not present the claim that all interpretations, as such, are incommensurable, that 'anything goes' in interpretation. It only holds that some interpretations are. A, B, and C can be incommensurably good interpretations of X, while another interpretation, D, can still be worse (or better) than A (or B or C).[19]

---

[18] Needless to say, Dworkin could not account for satire or parody as forms of interpretation, since they aim at mocking given works of art or political events, presenting them in a ridiculous, rather than the best, light. But then, Dworkin could claim that satire and parody are original works, not interpretations.

[19] The argument from incommensurability is not necessarily confined to aesthetic or moral values. Consider the philosophy of action: according to a certain conception of practical reasons, e.g. Anscombe's, standard belief/desire-based explanations do not exhaust the possible ways of accounting for actions. After drawing a distinction between mental causes, intentions, and motives, Anscombe says, 'To give a motive . . . is to say something like, "See the action in this light"' (1956 : 150). Motives, though they partly explain actions, do not determine actions in the sense of causing them (1956 : 148). Thus, it might often be pointless to ask which motive is the *right* one.

In short, Dworkin's concept of interpretation seems too narrow, in the sense of resting on unnecessary and unwarranted assumptions as to the commensurability of all interpretations of the same object. I think this suffices to cast serious doubts on Dworkin's assumption about the unified purpose (and hence criteria of success) of all forms of interpretation.

However, could Dworkin respond that the 'best' light does not necessarily mean 'the only one which is the best'? In other words, could he claim that the constructive model is compatible with a group of incommensurably best interpretations, each of which is the best according to certain assumptions?[20]

Although this seems a much more plausible and realistic picture of interpretation, it would not do for Dworkin's purposes. Most importantly, recognizing the multiplicity and incommensurability of interpretations would undermine the hermeneutic thesis. Recall that this thesis gains its plausibility only from the unified conception; even if both participants and theorists were indeed to strive to present law in its best light, the thesis could not be established unless the 'best' reflects the *same kind* of evaluation from both perspectives. But I will try to show that this is not the case, and that different notions of evaluation are involved here. In other words, I shall try to show that regardless of the argument from incommensurability, and even on the constructive model, this unified concept of interpretation cannot be maintained.

The concept of evaluation indicates that one has to make judgements of preference between certain competing options. A criterion is evaluative if it is based on such judgements. But not all evaluative judgements are of one and the same kind. The point is that Dworkin seems to have failed to distinguish between evaluative judgements as opposed to descriptions or observations, and evaluative judgements as opposed to neutrality. If neutrality means total abstention from judgements of preference, then in a familiar sense no theory can be neutral. Any descriptive theory is evaluative throughout, and not only in the social realm, as it is part of its aim, *qua* theory, to evaluate the data it purports to cover (as opposed to

---

[20] Notably, the text of Dworkin's discussion can hardly be taken to indicate this option. He refers to what the practice 'really requires' (1986 : 64), to the 'formal structure' of interpretation 'as if this were the product of a decision to pursue one set of themes' (1986 : 58), and uses additional, similar formulations, all of which indicate that in referring to 'the best light' Dworkin means precisely what he says.

for instance, sporadic assertions or observations). Any theory, for example, relies on certain evaluative presuppositions as to what is more important for it to achieve or explain.[21] Suppose a widely accepted physical theory yields inaccurate predictions in a certain section of its field of application, while it is very attractive in (*inter alia*) the extreme simplicity of the formulations on which it is based. This might offer scientists two options: either to prefer the simplicity and elegance of the theory, and to attempt its accommodation to the relatively narrower scope of application, or to strive to replace it with a totally different and perhaps more complex theory. Clearly, the option selected, whatever it is, reflects judgements about the relative importance of simplicity versus accurate predictions in physical theories. These judgements are evaluative in the relevant sense: they reflect certain preferences for specific criteria of success in physics. (Of course, the fact that these are preferences and not, for instance, observations of data, does not entail that they cannot be accounted for, argued and justified.)[22] In other words, if evaluation is taken to mean the opposite of neutrality, then any theory or explanation is profoundly determined by such evaluative judgements.

However, nothing in this sense of evaluation entails that the evaluation in question is necessarily moral or aesthetic. It is only when the competing options are initially moral ones, that is, when they emerge from a moral dilemma or have specifically moral consequences, that the evaluative preference must also be a moral one. The same holds for aesthetic values and the like.[23]

To sum up, Dworkin would be correct in claiming that neutrality or impartiality in theoretical explanation is impossible, and that, in this sense, evaluations are inevitable. However, this is not a feature peculiar to interpretation or social explanation, and it does not entail that the evaluation involved is necessarily moral (or aesthetic).

It should be clear by now why the hermeneutic thesis is not entailed by the constructive model. Suppose we concede Dworkin's thesis that interpretation should strive to present its object in its best light. Now it is true that for the participants in a practice like

---

[21] One might object immediately here, that it is the discovery of the truth which theories aim at. Of course, I do not wish to deny this, but evaluative judgements concern questions about how one gets there.

[22] On the role of evaluative judgements in science, see Kuhn (1970).

[23] Cf. Raz (1986a : 1114).

law this would naturally mean 'best' in its moral sense. But this is due only to the fact that the participants must regard law as *reason for their actions*. Still, for a theorist, the 'best possible example of its kind' does not necessarily mean morally best. What it does mean depends upon the purpose of legal theory. Once we realize that the 'best' is not necessarily 'morally best', we can acknowledge that interpretations might have various purposes, and hence various criteria of success. If legal theory had been confined to answering the question 'Is there an obligation to obey the law?' then it might have been the case that law ought to be presented in its morally best light. If, however, the project is taken to be a different or broader one, then the evaluations underlying it must vary accordingly.

For instance, it is thought to be one of the main purposes of jurisprudence to reveal those features of law which are common to all legal systems; to try to distinguish the features which are conceptually common from those which are only contingently so, and the like. Or to return to Hintikka's interpretation of cubism, it is an interpretation not only of cubism, but also of 'realism', of 'representation', and of the complex relations between these three concepts. Both these examples clearly display the underlying evaluative judgement that this comparative and conceptual aim of interpretation is important in providing for a better (or the 'best'?) understanding of our concepts, and of the conceptual scheme which constitutes our intellectual world. Yet none of these judgements, evaluative though they indeed are, necessarily involves moral or aesthetic preferences.

To conclude, Dworkin obscures the possibility that interpretations may have various purposes and hence various criteria of success, as he presupposes evaluative judgements to be of one kind only. His failure to make this distinction seriously undermines the hermeneutic thesis, whose sole source of support lies in a unified concept of the purpose of interpretation (and hence its criteria of success).

6. CONSTRUCTIVE INTERPRETATION AND THE PRINCIPLE OF CHARITY

In the previous section, I have tried to show that the hermeneutic thesis can only be grounded upon a unified concept of interpretation, and that such a concept cannot be maintained, since it is based on three unwarranted assumptions: (1) that all interpretations are intended to be universally accepted; (2) that all interpretations are commensurable; and (3) that all interpretations are based on the same kind of evaluative judgements.

I would like to conclude this chapter with an examination of an alternative line of reasoning which might be thought to support Dworkin's theory, that is, the principle of charity. Although Dworkin himself refers to this option only briefly (1986 : 53), there is a striking similarity between his account and some of the existing attempts to apply Davidson's principle of charity to the realm of social explanation. Recall that according to the principle of charity, 'the general policy . . . is to choose truth conditions that do as well as possible in making speakers hold sentences true when (according to the theory and the theory builder's view of the facts) those sentences are true' (Davidson 1984 : 152). As I have already mentioned in the previous chapter, this principle makes sense, on Davidson's own account, only within a holistic conception of language and thought. One thing should thus be clear from the outset: the constructive model is not entailed in any straightforward sense by the principle of charity. Nor do Davidson's further conclusions, denying the possibility of conceptual schemes (Davidson 1984 : 193–8), have any direct bearing on our present concern. The hermeneutic thesis is not a denial of conceptual schemes or of radically different minds. My question then is this: is there any other form, perhaps less direct, in which Davidson's principle of charity could support Dworkin's constructive model?

Consider the following account. Root, exploring the application of Davidson's theory to social explanation, argues that the principle of charity 'tells against the idea that there may be a great difference between the perspective of the insider and the perspective of the outsider. Charity counsels the outsider to attribute a perspective to the insider that is very close to her own' (1986 : 291). I take it that what Root has in mind is not the hermeneutic thesis, but a somewhat weaker principle. Nevertheless, his arguments are instructive. He identifies three main features in Davidson's concept of interpretation that have a bearing on social explanations: (1) that interpretation is holistic; (2) that it is critical and normative; and (3) that the norms of interpretation are the norms of rationality. Most interesting is Root's characterization of the second and third features, in terms of the 'reflexivity' of interpretation. Since the norms that guide interpretation are the norms of rationality, 'the norms of interpretation are the norms that guide the interpreter . . . and the interpreted as well' (1986 : 279), and '[a]s a result, the critical principles that guide interpretation will limit the differences between the participant's account . . . and the interpreter's account' (1986 : 291). Root, however, is careful to avoid an obvious mistake. He acknowledges that the 'principle of charity does not preclude disagreement; what it precludes is inexplicable disagreement' (1986 : 287). Nevertheless, he claims that '[A]ccording to Davidson, a weighted majority of the beliefs that the interpreter attributes to her subject must be beliefs that, on the interpreters own view, are true' (1986 : 285). But the point is that even this seemingly modest formulation should have been further qualified. First, recall the problem of incommensurability; 'rationality' is not a magic word capable of dismissing it. I do not intend to argue that there *are* radically different minds (or cultures), so different from our own as to make them inscrutable. The problem of incommensurability is a domestic one, as arguments in the previous section have pointed out. The idea that there is *one* principle of rationality guiding our behaviour, that is, even within our own culture, is far from obvious. But unless such a unified concept of rationality is presumed, it cannot be concluded that interpretation is necessarily guided by the same norms as the interpreted. Furthermore, the more general (and hence perhaps more plausible) the principles of rationality are taken to be, the less bearing they will have on the interpreter–subject relation.

Secondly, and more importantly, Root seems to be content to apply the principle of charity as a heuristic principle of interpretation of particular actions or practices. This takes the principle of charity closer to Dworkin's constructive model, but much further away from the truth. Root's mistake is due to the following unwarranted inference: suppose we concede Davidson's general assumption that disagreement of any kind is intelligible only against a background of agreement (Davidson 1984 : 153). It clearly does not follow that each particular interpretation must attribute beliefs to a subject in such a way as to make most of *his* beliefs true. Davidson himself (and Quine for that matter), cannot be accused of this *non sequitur*. When Davidson refers to 'a speaker', or a subject, it is a speaker of a natural language, *qua* speaker of such language. (Recall Davidson's own proviso on the applicability of radical interpretation to a 'passing theory'.) As far as the principle of charity is concerned, people who believe in voodoo can be interpreted as being utterly mistaken. The fact that one cannot understand voodoo unless one understands a great deal about these people does not entail that the interpreter has to attribute any true beliefs *about* voodoo, let alone presenting voodoo in its best light.

The inevitable conclusion, therefore, is that despite apparent similarities between the principle of charity and constructive interpretation, the two are essentially different, and the former can lend the latter no support.

I believe we are now in a position to draw conclusions. As we have seen, according to the traditional view of analytical jurisprudence, legal theory comprises *inter alia* a theory of adjudication which concerns the unique features of judicial reasoning. The hermeneutic thesis challenges this division. It contends that jurisprudence *is* basically a theory of adjudication, as both amount to one and the same form of interpretation, namely, imposing a point, purpose, or value on a practice in order to present it in its best possible light.

In this chapter, I have argued for the rejection of the hermeneutic thesis. This suggests a need to shift from an interpretative account of jurisprudence to the broader (and traditional) conception of jurisprudence as comprising a theory of interpretation. Furthermore, as we have seen, there are no grounds for assuming that a theory *of* interpretation is itself a matter of interpretation. Interpretation is part and parcel of the legal *practice*. Jurisprudence should comprise a theory to account for this, a theory which is not itself an interpretation of the law, but a philosophical account of what it is to interpret the law.

4

COHERENCE, HOLISM, AND INTERPRETATION: THE EPISTEMIC FOUNDATION OF DWORKIN'S LEGAL THEORY

THE concept of coherence has always been of fundamental importance to Dworkin's legal theory. A legal system, he has repeatedly argued, comprises not only the settled or conventionally identifiable law, but also those norms which can be shown to fit or cohere better with the best theory of the settled law. It has recently become clearer, however, that the concept of coherence also plays a crucial role in the epistemic foundations of his legal theory. Thus, we can discern two distinct levels to which the concept of coherence is pertinent: the level of content, to which it applies as a basic value of political morality, and the level of method, recently articulated in the form of a theory of interpretation. This chapter will propound the view that the roles assigned by Dworkin to coherence on the two levels of his theory of interpretation, are ones which are not easily reconcilable.

I shall begin my discussion with a few observations about the concept of coherence in general and about Rawls's 'reflective equilibrium' in particular—a thesis which has influenced Dworkin's thought considerably. I shall then turn to a closer examination of the epistemic foundations of Dworkin's theory of interpretation, focusing on the relations between the various dimensions of interpretation he proposes, that is, identity, fit, and soundness. I shall argue that a construal of these dimensions in the light of a coherence theory of knowledge, constitutes an interesting reply to the brand of scepticism regarding interpretation which is raised by Stanley Fish. Finally, in the last section, I shall outline the difficulties which arise when this interpretative structure is applied to Dworkin's jurisprudence, where coherence also plays a substantive role, as entailed by his thesis of 'law as integrity'.

I. THE REFLECTIVE EQUILIBRIUM

Coherence and holistic theories of knowledge have received increasing philosophical attention since the publication of W. V. O. Quine's 'Two Dogmas of Empiricism' (1953). This pair now seems to dominate the main trends in epistemology, on the ruins of traditional empiricist foundationalism. Kuhn's contribution to our understanding of scientific knowledge (1962), and Rawls's elaboration of the reflective equilibrium as the epistemic foundation of his *A Theory of Justice* (1971), would seem to have completed this philosophical revolution. Yet as Kuhn himself has taught us, a shift in the paradigms of a discipline does not solve its problems but rather engenders new puzzles. Substituting coherence for foundationalism does not seem to be an exception.

Any theory of knowledge based on the concept of coherence faces two immediate difficulties. First, coherence is typically meant to designate something more than mere logical consistency. But it is not perspicuous (and it is rarely made explicit) just what this additional feature is taken to be.[1] Consider the pair of propositions: 'One should always obey the law' and 'All swans are white.' The two are quite obviously consistent but there is hardly any sense in which they can be said to be coherent. One is tempted to say that coherence is the requirement of consistency as applied to *theories*. This would make the example irrelevant since the two propositions cannot be conceived of as belonging, together, to any theory whatsoever. This answer, though perhaps basically correct, is insufficient. In fact, it begs the question, for in what sense is a theory more than a set of consistent propositions? In other words, it only pushes the question one step further.

The second and more interesting difficulty encountered by a coherence-based epistemology concerns the relation between coherence and truth. There is a rather trivial sense in which we all seem to agree that these two notions are intimately linked. We tend to presume, at least intuitively, that a set of incoherent beliefs cannot, ultimately, be true. Ethics, however, may be a rather unique case in which coherence may be denied even this seemingly innocuous role. This could be termed the 'no-theory' view, although it does not necessarily amount to a radical scepticism. Roughly, it embodies the idea that moral principles, even if we hold them to be objective and true, cannot be comprised of a set of coherent

[1] Cf. MacCormick (1984).

principles, as the contradictions between them reflect genuine contradictions inherent in our moral lives, or entailed by the very nature of our social lives, etc.[2] Be this as it may, what the coherence theories confront is more than just this 'no-theory' stance. To begin with, some philosophers have sought to explicate the notion of 'truth' itself in terms of coherence alone, that is to say, as a repudiation of the correspondence conception of 'truth'. Coherence, in this sense, is employed to explicate what 'truth' *means* or consists in: when saying that a proposition, p, 'is true', the only thing we can mean is that p is consistent with other propositions which we also hold to be true.

A coherence theory of truth, however, is not a very popular philosophical position. There is no need to repeat the well-known difficulties involved in such an explication of the meaning of truth.[3] Opponents of the correspondence conception of truth usually prefer to abandon the notion of truth altogether,[4] or—taking a less sceptical attitude—to construe it as a 'primitive' notion which resists further analysis or reduction of any kind.

A coherence theory of *knowledge*, on the other hand, is best seen as a rejection of foundationalism. Foundationalism (both in its traditional empiricist and rationalist manifestations) amounts to the claim that some of our beliefs, within a given realm of knowledge, do not require justification; they constitute the foundations of knowledge. Hence the foundational propositions cannot be refuted by the rest of the theory, but only vice versa. At the opposite pole, coherence conceptions can take two possible forms. According to a strong coherence theory, none of our beliefs should be taken to constitute the foundation of a realm of knowledge, all the propositions in a given realm requiring equal justification. Thus the only pertinent epistemic criterion for the correctness of theories is logical consistency. Patently, this is a highly implausible view, if for no other reason than the fact that there are infinite possibilities of constructing sets of consistent propositions. (And indeed, it is questionable whether anyone has ever held such a view.)

---

[2] Cf. Nagel (1979). If I have understood him correctly, Bernard Williams (1981) also seems to hold such a view.

[3] See e.g. Russell (1959: 119–23). See also Davidson (1986a).

[4] In fact, there are two versions of this redundancy conception of 'truth'. According to the kind of pragmatism advocated by Rorty (1982), the notion of truth is *epistemically* redundant. According to others, 'truth' is *semantically* redundant. The proposition 'it is true that p' is, on this view, semantically equivalent to the proposition that 'p'. See Strawson (1969).

The second and much more plausible version of a coherence theory of knowledge runs more or less as follows: some beliefs have a quasi-foundational status, in the sense of not initially requiring any justification. However, even these quasi-foundational beliefs are not exempt from possible refutation at some later stage, when the theory has been fully articulated. This could be put, roughly, as a matter of priority. As opposed to foundationalism, such a theory assigns to consistency among the total relevant set of beliefs, precedence over the force of those beliefs that constitute the foundations.

Once the notion of coherence as an explication of the meaning of truth is abandoned, however, coherence theories of knowledge run into serious difficulties in justifying this precedence. I shall exemplify these difficulties through the case of the application of a coherence theory of knowledge to moral theory (that is, through meta-ethics).[5]

There is presumably an indefinite number of possibilities of constructing sets of logically consistent moral principles. Hence, the first question facing advocates of a coherence theory of morality is how to choose among the possible sets of moral principles. Rawls's proposal of reflective equilibrium (1971 : 34–53) seems to provide the most attractive and comprehensive answer to this question. The values or principles must be consistent not only among themselves but also with an additional set of judgements, namely, our firmly held intuitions. As Rawls himself admits, this does not provide a logical solution to the problem of indefiniteness, but it at least imposes a practical constraint. It is quite implausible to assume that several theories could be constructed so as to be coherent with *all* our actual moral intuitions. On the contrary, it even seems highly unlikely that a single set of coherent principles might account for all our actual moral intuitions. Hence the notion of a *reflective* equilibrium. Our intuitions and the moral principles must be mutually adjusted in a special manner. First, the intuitions taken into account are only those which are held firmly and meet certain conditions.[6] Second, in the process of constructing the moral

---

[5] On an attempt to solve the problem in a manner different from the below, see Davidson (1986a). An examination of Davidson's suggestions, however, would exceed the scope of this chapter.

[6] Which is why Rawls does not use the term 'intuitions' in this context but 'considered judgements' (1971 : 47).

theory, some of our intuitions must be amended or even jettisoned in the interests of consistency with the principles. Third, Rawls assumes that the relation between principles and intuitions may, in certain cases, be self-reflective; once the principles are fully articulated, we may want to change our initial intuitions or view them in a different light.

Now Rawls's model of the construction of moral theories, attractive as it may seem, raises two difficult, interrelated questions. First, it is not at all clear why the fact that we can reach an equilibrium between our firm moral intuitions and principles serves to justify the epistemic precedence of coherence over the force of firmly held intuitions. Suppose we have discerned that we have a set of n firm moral intuitions, yet the most coherent set of moral principles, say P, can account for only $n-1$ of these. If we assume that intuitions reflect correct moral judgements, which apparently we must as it would otherwise be pointless to refer to them, it is not clear why we should prefer P to continued adherence to our original set of n judgements. Suppose another coherent set of principles, Q, accounts for only $n-5$ intuitions. If we have reason to prefer P to Q, it is that more truth, so to speak, is covered by the former. But then, holding the initial position would be even more truthful.

This leads us directly to the second problem pertaining to Rawls's model, namely, the highly problematic status it assigns to intuitions. On the one hand, they must be held to be true in order to function as constraints on the available moral principles. On the other hand, we must be prepared to disregard or jettison some of them for the sake of the moral theory's coherence. What clearer instance, then, of 'having one's cake and eating it'?

The alternative conclusion seems to be that only (a set of) coherent moral intuitions can be true. This is a very troublesome idea, though, as we know that different sets of coherent moral principles would account for different sets of intuitions. Suppose theory P is coherent with $n-a$ intuitions, and theory Q with $n-b$ intuitions (where n stands for all our firmly held moral intuitions). This would compel us to say that a is true and false; it is true in Q but false in P. Needless to say, this result is very uncomfortable unless, of course, one subscribes to a coherence theory of truth as well. To sum up, the presupposition that intuitions are independently true and the converse one, that their truth depends on fitting a coherent scheme, both seem to yield paradoxical results. Needless to say, a sceptical attitude towards the correctness of intuitions would naturally render Rawls' coherence approach equally dubious.

In one of his earlier articles, titled 'The Original Position', Dworkin (1975) presented his own interpretation of the reflective equilibrium, one which might be thought to have averted some of the difficulties of Rawls's position.[7]

Dworkin considers two possible construals of the reflective equilibrium as an account of the construction of moral theories. The 'natural' model presupposes that moral principles are discovered rather than created. That is, our moral intuitions, and accordingly the principles which emerge from them, are clues to the existence of some moral reality. The other, 'constructive' model, 'does not assume, as the natural model does, that principles of justice have some fixed, objective existence, so that descriptions of these principles must be true or false in some standard way', but rather that 'men and women have a responsibility to fit the particular judgements on which they act into a coherent program of action' (1975 : 28). In other words, the natural model presupposes *ethical realism*, while the constructive model does not. One important difficulty arising from an attempt to apply the natural model to Rawls, is that under the natural model, any theory which does not account for an intuition, at least for one which is held firmly, cannot be wholly satisfactory, just as a scientific theory which does not account for certain observational data it is supposed to cover, would not be satisfactory in a familiar way. Hence Rawls, Dworkin claims, cannot be taken to be an ethical realist. Imposing the natural model on Rawls would be inconsistent with one of the main features of the reflective equilibrium, namely, the claim that we are justified in neglecting or discarding some of our intuitions for the sake of coherence. Such concessions from the perspective of the natural model 'would be nothing short of cooking the evidence' (1975 : 32). We are thus left with the constructive construal of the reflective equilibrium; but what, exactly, is this model? Dworkin says, '[i]t demands that we act on principle rather than on faith. Its engine is a doctrine of responsibility that requires men to integrate their

[7] A word of caution: in this article Dworkin presents an interpretation of Rawls which he never explicitly endorses. Nevertheless, as he neither denies nor criticizes this interpretation, I shall assume that Dworkin is presenting his own views in this article.

intuitions and subordinate some of these, when necessary, to that responsibility' (1975 : 30). Consider the two difficulties raised by the model of reflective equilibrium described above. Dworkin's answer to the question of why coherence justifies the moral theory is based on considerations of political morality, that is, a doctrine of responsibility:

It is *unfair* for officials to act except on the basis of a general public theory that will constrain them to consistency, provide a public standard for testing or debating or predicting what they do, and not allow appeals to unique intuitions that might mask prejudice or self-interest in particular cases. (Ibid. my emphasis.)

The main thing to notice here is the fact that Dworkin regards coherence as an *instrumental value* of political morality. It is a constraint to be imposed upon officials for the sake of *fairness*.

His answer to the question of the status of intuitions is somewhat more obscure. Intuitions are not to be considered as true 'in some standard way'. But we are not enlightened as to what this is, or told in what other sense they can be considered true. I believe that by 'standard way' Dworkin has in mind a correspondence conception of truth, according to which moral judgements are true when they correspond to some reality, just as the proposition 'there is a chair in this room' is true if and only if there is a chair in this room. Dworkin is quite unclear about any (other) sense in which moral convictions might be true, apart from determining the fact of their existence, that is, that people have these convictions and that they are indeed convictions. The constructive model 'takes convictions held with the requisite sincerity as *given*, and seeks to impose conditions on the acts that these intuitions might be said to warrant' (1975 : 31, emphasis mine).

In short, Dworkin is saying that people have moral convictions which they typically take to be true. However, he is not interested in an account of how it is that such intuitions *can* be true or of what their truth consists in. Instead, he turns to a different question, of what is the fair and just scheme within which such convictions ought to be taken into account and constitute reasons for actions, especially political actions. Officials, he submits, should be allowed to *act* upon their moral convictions only to the extent that these convictions can be invoked within a coherent scheme of principles. These two points, taken together, constitute an interesting and rather unique version of a coherence theory of political morality.[8]

On the other hand, regarding the constructive model as a basis for a moral theory's construction, that is, as a methodological alternative to the natural model, will raise the following difficulty: it simply *cannot* serve as an alternative in the relevant sense. To reiterate: the main problem with the natural model is that if the truth of one's moral convictions is presupposed, a coherence conception which requires neglecting the truth in some cases cannot be justified. Hence, coherence should be ignored or at least assigned second priority (as, for example, an ideal which one might some day hope to achieve). The constructive model propounded by Dworkin as an alternative averts both the question of whether our moral convictions are really true, and that of what their truth consists in; it introduces coherence as a *moral* constraint on the practical reliability of these convictions. However, if coherence is justified, as it is here, with reference to certain moral values, that is, a specific conception of fairness, then we face the following problem: the presupposed values of fairness must themselves be based upon intuitive convictions, in which case the question of *their* truth cannot be ignored. If they are taken to be true (in 'some standard way'?) we are driven back to the perplexities of the natural model. (Recall that one cannot adopt a sceptical attitude here since this scepticism would affect the value of coherence as well.)

It would seem that the only way of escaping this circularity is to presuppose that the basic values of fairness Dworkin relies upon have some pre-eminent status as compared with other moral convictions. This, however, will not do. Firstly, it is false—simply as a matter of fact. One's conviction that it is morally wrong to torture people just for fun might well be much more firmly held than any convictions about political fairness. Secondly, and more importantly, such a view would amount to a *foundationalist*, rather than a coherence theory of morality. If some values are taken to be pre-eminently true, then it is these values that vindicate the theory, not a concept of coherence.

All this indicates that Dworkin's interpretation of the reflective equilibrium actually constitutes a shift from a coherence theory of

[8] A similar, though not identical, strategy is adopted by Rawls himself in his later writings. See Rawls (1980) and (1985). However, my critical remarks in the following pages are not meant to have any direct bearing on Rawls's recent formulation of his theory. For a similar line of thought with respect to Rawls, see Raz (1990).

morality (that is in the epistemological sense) to a moral theory which endorses coherence as one of its basic values. In this case, much of the text remains largely unclear (for example, why the whole model is discussed as an alternative to the natural model, that is, ethical realism; why it is presented as an interpretation of Rawls who undoubtedly takes coherence to be an issue of method) though logical perplexities are at least avoided. Nonetheless, it must be clear that such a move can offer no alternative to ethical realism or, for that matter, to any other meta-ethical stance. Its brand of coherence can offer no *method* of choosing between rival theories since it is itself a substantive moral principle which rests upon substantive moral convictions.

2. IDENTITY, FIT, AND SOUNDNESS

At a later stage in his thought, when Dworkin comes to elaborate on the epistemic foundations of his interpretative theory, his conception of coherence becomes much more meticulous. In his interpretative theory of law, Dworkin clearly distinguishes between the role played by coherence at the methodological level, namely, in the form of a coherence theory of knowledge, and at the level of soundness, namely, as a particular value of political morality. In other words, Dworkin's concept of interpretation presupposes a coherence theory of knowledge which, however, once it is applied to law, must leave room for coherence as a distinct value, as entailed by his concept of 'integrity'. As such a value, coherence is rendered a guiding principle for one particular interpretative strategy which may be chosen from among various others. Law as integrity urges judges to grasp their adjudicative assignment as guided primarily by concern with the moral value of coherence. Judges ought to interpret past political decisions (for example, statutes, precedents) only in a way and to the extent that would render (or reveal?) these past political decisions consistent in principle.

Thus from the outset Dworkin has taken up a rather difficult task on the methodological level. He has to explain how, on the one hand, interpretation is guided by judgements of value, for instance, moral, aesthetic, etc., while on the other hand providing it with a firm basis of some kind and refuting the view that 'anything goes', as it were, under interpretation. As we have seen in the previous chapter, according to his *constructive model* of interpretation, every interpretation attempts to present its object as the best possible example of the genre to which it is taken to belong. Hence, evaluative judgements play a decisive role in all interpretations, in two complementary ways. First, it follows from Dworkin's constructive model that one must come to an interpretative activity already equipped with an idea of what is valuable in the pertinent genre. This is what I have called the primary evaluative judgement. Then one must supplement this with secondary evaluative judgements, allowing for the presentation of the given text, practice, etc., as the best performance or manifestation of the supposed primary values.

Now consider law as integrity. Judges have certain type of texts to interpret, that is, past political decisions. Dworkin argues that any interpretative attitude they adopt is always guided by basic evaluative judgements. His preferred option is integrity. At the same time, however, the value of integrity would be rendered absolutely pointless in the absence of an assumption that texts themselves somehow *constrain* the meanings available for extraction. This gives rise to the crucial question, can we distinguish between interpretation and invention? Are people justified in holding a 'right—wrong' picture of interpretation, and assuming that it makes sense to speak about 'the correct interpretation' of a given text? In other words, what is Dworkin's answer to the charge that 'anything goes' in interpretation?

Note that under the constructive model, this charge becomes a very serious one. Once we realize, as Dworkin urges us to do, that the purposes and intentions at play are those of the interpreter, and that the entire enterprise is wholly dependent upon evaluative judgements, it is tempting to say that even if people do entertain a 'right—wrong' picture of it, they are simply mistaken. This is not (primarily) because values are not objectively true (whatever that means) but because it is the interpreter who has to single out or designate the relevant values in each given case. I take this to be the meaning of Dworkin's contention that the 'purposes in play . . . are those of the interpreter' (1986 : 52). Thus, even if the values' *content* is uncontroversial, their designation, if it turns out to be wholly subjective, will still render interpretations basically incommensurable. Some notion of the constraints that will prove essential arises from this last problem.

To put it differently, the very idea of a constructive model of interpretation presupposes the availability of constraints. The requirement of presenting an object in its best light makes sense, only if rival interpretations are indeed interpretations of *the same object*. But are there any such constraints? Dworkin believes so. His answer is very subtle, though, and needs careful explication.

Considered as a process, interpretation comprises the pre-interpretative, the interpretative and the post-interpretative stages. Considered structurally, it contains three elements: identity, fit, and soundness (1986 : 65–72). Let us consider the structural dimension first. When approaching an interpretative activity, one must first have an idea of what it is that is to be interpreted. In other words, one must identify the relevant 'text'.[9] The second feature, fit, renders the element of identity essential. As the soundness of a particular interpretation depends, at least roughly speaking, on how it fits the bulk of the 'text', it is crucial to know just what this 'text' is.

Dworkin's concept of identity[10] defines conditions which are rather weak in some respects, and rather strong in others. They are weak in their emphatic renunciation of the need for a precise identification of the boundaries of the 'text', so to speak. This, at least, is the case when the 'text' is a social practice, such as law. One of the initial conditions enabling interpretation to flourish within the practice, in the case of law, is precisely the assumption that the extension of the practice is sensitive to its point or value (the other initial assumption being that it has a point or value). Furthermore, although we must typically be capable of pointing to paradigm cases as part of our identification of the 'text', in the sense that they are taken to be parts of it if anything is, such a paradigm case is nonetheless never 'secure from challenge by a new interpretation that accounts for other paradigms better and leaves that one isolated as a mistake' (1986 : 72).

---

[9] For the sake of convenience, I shall use the word 'text' in quotation marks to indicate all that which constitutes a possible object of interpretation. The question of whether almost anything can be an object of interpretation raises difficult issues which I cannot explore here.

[10] To be precise, Dworkin should have distinguished between questions of identity and questions of identification or individuation. The former is basically a matter of sameness. The typical form of an identity question is 'Is *A* the same *f* as *B*?' where *f* stands for the pertinent sortal concept. On the other hand, questions of identification are typically of the form 'Is *A* an *f*?' In this case we seek to single out something *as* an *f*. Thus when Dworkin speaks about 'identity' it is really identification that he has in mind. See Ch. 6.

However, the conditions outlined by Dworkin as defining the 'text's' identity emerge as rather strong ones upon noting that the constructive model is radically genre dependent. Interpretation aims at presenting an object as the best of its kind. An initial identification of the kind or genre is hence a precondition for any interpretation. But, as Dworkin himself readily admits (1986 : 66), kinds and genres do not carry identifying labels. More naturally, one would tend to regard the designation of genres as products, rather than preconditions, of interpretation. We shall return to this point later on. At the moment, suffice it to say that identity imposes fairly loose conditions with regard to the 'text's' extension and rather rigorous ones with regard to the classification of its kinds or genres.

The concept of fit seems to play a double role in the scheme of interpretation.[11] To explain, a few words must now be said on the *process* of interpretation. In the pre-interpretative stage we identify the 'text', at least tentatively. Dworkin emphasizes two highly important features of this stage. First, that 'some kind of interpretation is necessary even at this stage' (1986: 66) (for example, consider the issue of identifying genres, mentioned earlier). Second, for an interpretative enterprise to exist, that is, as a social practice such as literary criticism or adjudication, 'a very great degree of consensus is needed' among interpreters with regard to the identification of what counts as the 'text' (ibid.).

In the second, interpretative phase of the process of interpretation, the constructive model comes into play; an interpretation is actually offered. This tentative offer is then refined and rechecked in the course of the last, post-interpretative stage.

Now, returning to fit, it seems (though Dworkin is not explicit on this point) that the main difference between the interpretative and the post-interpretative stages is as follows: in the former, fit is basically a threshold requirement. The proposed interpretation 'must fit *enough* for the interpreter to be able to see himself as interpreting that practice, not inventing a new one' (1986: 66, emphasis mine). But this may not be enough, as several and conflicting interpretations may fit the 'text' in this sense. The post-interpretative stage introduces another, more evaluative notion of fit. It involves the choice of that interpretation which is attributed the better, or actually, the best fit. In other words, when fit operates as

[11] Cf. Alexander (1987).

a threshold requirement, it is more like a quasi-logical condition; the interpretation must account for enough parts of the 'text' and must consider paradigm cases as such (with the proviso mentioned earlier). An interpretation of a novel requiring us to disregard every second line in the book, or a legal theory claiming that statutes are not part of the law of England are easy examples of unfitness in this sense. Fit in the post-interpretative stage is more substantially evaluative. It is roughly tantamount to what I have called the secondary evaluative judgements. At this stage, the interpreter 'adjusts his sense of what the practice "really" requires so as better to serve the justification he accepts at the interpretative stage' (ibid.).

As Dworkin affirms explicitly, the echo of the reflective equilibrium sounds very strong here. Once past the threshold requirement of fit, we must seek an equilibrium between the soundest value a 'text' can be taken to manifest, and its features as identified in the pre-interpretative stage. As he puts it in the case of law, the purpose of legal theory is 'to achieve equilibrium between legal practice as [we] find it and the best justification of that practice' (1986 : 90) see also (ibid. 424). Note that it is a *reflective* equilibrium since it involves a process of mutual adjustments (between identity, fit, and soundness) in the Rawlsian sense explained in the previous section.

It would seem that all this leads to a coherence theory of interpretation. I shall postpone the analysis of the theory's coherence basis, however, as I believe that an examination of Stanley Fish's criticism will help reveal Dworkin's deeper presuppositions.

3. THE FISH–DWORKIN DEBATE[12]

The pretext for Fish's criticism is Dworkin's celebrated metaphor of the chain novelists. Dworkin asks us to imagine a group of novelists who accept the following assignment: each is to write a single chapter of a novel. The first author writes the opening chapter, and all the rest will then add their consecutive chapters. Yet every novelist entering into this endeavour accepts the special responsibility of creating the best and most unified novel that he or she can. Hence, 'every novelist but the first has the dual responsibilities of interpreting and creating because each must read all that

---

[12] Dworkin's first articles on interpretation were criticized by Fish (1983*a*); Dworkin's (1983) rejoinder was followed by Fish (1983*b*). In *Law's Empire* Dworkin referred to most of those issues again (e.g. pp. 78–86, 424). Finally, see Fish (1987).

has gone before in order to establish, in the interpretivist sense, what the novel so far created is' (1985 : 158). Dworkin intends this metaphor to explain the role of judges in his conception of law as integrity: 'Deciding hard cases at law is rather like this strange literary exercise. . . . Each judge is then like a novelist in the chain. He or she must read through what other judges in the past have written . . . to reach an opinion about what these judges have collectively *done*' (1985 : 159). Fish has two main objections to the metaphor and its implications. First, he argues against Dworkin's assumption that there is, or could be, any difference between the assignment given to first novelist in the chain and those given to the rest. Dworkin assumes, so Fish claims, that the first novelist has a purely creative role, while the others must both create and interpret.

But in fact, the first author has surrendered his freedom . . . as soon as he commits himself to writing a novel . . . the very notion of 'beginning a novel' exists only in the context of a set of practices that at once enables and limits the act of beginning.

　　Moreover, those who follow him are free and constrained in exactly the same way. . . . That is, the later novelists do not read directly from the words to a decision about the point or theme of the novel but from a prior understanding . . . of the points or themes novels can possibly have to a novelistic construction of the words. (1983*a* : 273)

Admittedly, this passage seems somewhat obscure but the main idea is clear enough and it is anchored in the concept of *prior understanding*.[13] Upon approaching a text, be it a novel or a legal precedent, we must already possess a whole set of convictions enabling us to grasp and refer to it as belonging to a certain kind of text, that is, to assign it a specific location within our intellectual environment. These interpretative convictions do not usually rise to the surface, since they are strongly embodied in our cultural and professional ambience; they are latently shared by groups of people who therefore constitute an 'interpretative community'.[14] But still, Fish argues, one must realize that these convictions amount to nothing more than the fact that they are convictions which happen

[13] See Fish (1980 : 268–92).

[14] Needless to say, the notion of an 'interpretative community' is drawn from Kuhn's account of 'scientific communities' and their role in scientific inquiry. See his *Scientific Revolution* (1962, 1970). In general, Kuhn is a major hero of Fish's intellectual background, as is Derrida.

to be shared by a group of people at a given time and place; they manifest a certain convergence of beliefs and attitudes which may easily change across time and space.

One may well wonder whether Dworkin denies any of this? And why is it so important? The answer to the first question is that he certainly does not. The task of the first novelist in the chain is not totally creative; surely, to begin a novel he must have some idea about what novels are, and such an idea is partly a matter of interpretation. Dworkin does not deny this.[15] In fact, it is compatible with his view that interpretation is generally involved even in the pre-interpretative stage. Furthermore, Dworkin explicitly concedes that a rather substantive amount of *agreement* between interpreters on points such as identifying features of genres and 'texts' is necessary in order for an interpretative enterprise to flourish . As he later came to admit, this kind of consensus is what constitutes an interpretative community (1986 : 66). But the point is that all this may fail to answer the question, which is not what Dworkin says but whether what he says is consistent with his theory. Fish, I think, is advancing the claim that it is not.

As far as I can see, the following argument, his main objection to the chain novelists' example, is an argument to that effect. The significance of this 'chain enterprise', says Fish (that is, of law as integrity) depends on the presupposition that there is a discernible and defensible distinction between interpreting a 'text' and changing it or inventing a new one. But this distinction is unsustainable, he argues, since *any* reading or interpretation changes the 'text'. The only way in which the 'text' 'is there' to be read or interpreted is determined by the convictions constituting the prior understandings of a given interpretative community.[16] Furthermore, this body of shared convictions reflects nothing more than a convergence of beliefs, attitudes, etc., which can change in time or from one community to an other. There is nothing in the 'texts' themselves, Fish contends, to warrant the conclusion that the prior understandings of one interpretative community are more correct than those of another; there are no *textual facts*, that is, facts which

---

[15] Although one must admit that Fish's complaint is not textually groundless: at some point (i.e. Dworkin (1985 : 158), cited above) Dworkin does seem to draw a distinction between the first novelist, whose task is creative, and the rest, who must both create and interpret. Under the best interpretation of Dworkin, however, this should be regarded as a slip of the pen (or the keyboard, as the case may be).

[16] See Fish (1983a : 281). See also Feyerabend (1972).

can be identified independently of particular interpretative strategies.

Fish then goes on to draw two conclusions. First, that all interpretations are 'enterprise specific'. Neither a chain novelist nor a judge is able to 'strike out in a new direction'. This is not a conceptual possibility, since any such move is either conceived of as an institutional possibility (that is, in accordance with the prior understandings shared by the interpretative community) in which case it would not count as a new direction; or judged to belong to or constitute a separate enterprise, should it be so 'new' as to go beyond the boundaries of the prior understandings (for example, a judge deciding a court case according to the colour of the plaintiff's hair).

Second, Fish claims, across the various enterprise-options, no particular interpretation can be identified as better (or worse), being measured only with reference to the prior understandings of the given enterprise and, *ex hypothesi*, being necessarily compatible with it. In other words, if there are no textual facts independent of interpretative strategies, then there is no sense in speaking about 'the best' interpretation. An interpretation can, of course, be more or less persuasive within a given interpretative community, but this is a sociological criterion, not an epistemic one.[17]

Now the question that emerges here is whether Dworkin can maintain his acceptance of the argument's premises (that is, of the interpretative and evaluative nature of the pre-interpretative stage) while rejecting these sceptical conclusions.

Before continuing to Dworkin's reply, it would be useful to see just why he feels committed to subscribe to the premises of Fish's argument. This is basically because Dworkin wishes to avert the claim that interpretation is somehow *conceptually* or *conventionally* constrained. Consider the possible alternatives. The object of interpretation might be thought to be given from the outset, that is, independently of whatever might present it in its best light. This would not do, however, as it could undermine one of Dworkin's major objections to legal positivism, that is, his claim that the extension of the object of interpretation, in this case the identification of law, is sensitive to its supposed values. A second alternative to the premises in question would be a position according to which

---

[17] Ibid. 276–85. Basically, the same argument reappears throughout the debate with Dworkin.

the supposed purpose, point, or value of the object of interpretation is somehow determined conventionally, independently of the particular interpretations offered. One could claim that some purposes or values are *conceptually* connected to specific objects or practices and that thus presupposing any other value or purpose would amount to changing the concept. For instance, consider someone whose conception of cars has nothing to do with the purpose of transportation: what he has in mind is simply a different concept.

Dworkin cannot endorse the latter view as it is one which he denies explicitly. He emphasizes that social practices, such as law, have no conceptually defining features, whether evaluative or factual (1986 : 69). Furthermore, such a view might prove inconsistent with the constructive model; regardless of the purpose or value taken to be conceptually embodied in the given practice, law for example, the possibility that another value might present it in a better light could not be eliminated. A commitment to the constructive model, however, would always require the precedence of this latter value.

The above is a crucial point. It is a hallmark of Dworkin's theory that interpretation (or knowledge in general?) is not conceptually constrained. Consider Dworkin's distinction between the *concept* and its *conceptions*.[18] The concept constitutes the most abstract level of 'agreement [which] collects around discrete ideas that are un-controversially employed in all interpretations'. As opposed to this, the particular conceptions are the interpretations which manifest the 'controversy latent in this abstraction' (1986 : 71).

Notably, Dworkin's concept of 'concept' is very much like Fish's notion of the prior understandings which constitute an interpretative community. Concepts do not reflect 'linguistic ground rules everyone must follow to make sense', but only a convergence of beliefs which happens to prevail within a certain community, a pattern of agreement 'that might . . . disappear tomorrow' (ibid.). No wonder then, that Dworkin must maintain that concepts are too abstract and precarious to yield any significant constraints on the available conceptions (that is, interpretations) to be extracted from them.

---

[18] Dworkin has adopted this distinction from Rawls, assigning to it an important role in his writings. See e.g. Dworkin (1977 : 134).

Having said as much, we can return to Dworkin's rejoinder to Fish. His refutation of Fish's criticism comprises two arguments, both of which seem to provide Kuhnian answers to Fish's Kuhnian puzzles. The first is based more explicitly on the concept of coherence: 'There is no paradox in the proposition that facts both depend on and constrain the theories that explain them. On the contrary, that proposition is an essential part of the picture of knowledge as a complex and interrelated set of beliefs confronting experience as a coherent whole' (1983 : 293). The idea is as follows: we have already noticed that, in keeping with its very concept, the constructive model requires some form of constraint. However, accepting (as Dworkin does) the view propounded by Fish, that the 'text's' identification, which might be regarded as a constraint, is itself a matter of interpretation, might mean the inability of this element to operate as a constraint in any meaningful sense. In other words, Fish's argument boils down to the claim that Dworkin's theory of interpretation postulates a circular relation between the notions of identity, fit, and soundness, which is incompatible with any notion of a *better* or *best* interpretation. Now, Dworkin admits to the circle inherent in his argument, but denies that it is a vicious one. It would only be vicious under a very crude version of realism, according to which propositions are expected to match some kind of 'brute facts'. In fact, though, even with regard to scientific theories, it is already a commonplace that facts can be theory laden, with no paradox attached. 'It is now a familiar thesis among philosophers of science and epistemology, after all, that people's beliefs even about the facts that make up the physical world are the consequence of their more general scientific theories' (1983 : 293). There thus seems to be no reason why interpretation should not be constrained by prior understandings, even if such understandings reflect only one possible convergence of interpretative convictions.

One might still wonder what the answer really is. Have we not just admitted to the charge of vicious circularity? We would have, Dworkin says, in one specific case: were the relations between facts and theory not sufficiently complex. Again, consider scientific knowledge:

[T]he constraints of scientific investigation are imposed . . . by the internal tensions, checks, and balances of the complex structure of what we recognize as scientific knowledge. Of course the constraint would be illusory if that system were not *sufficiently complex and structured*, if there

were no functional distinctions, within that system, among the various
kinds and levels of belief. But there are, and that is why scientists can
abandon theories on the ground that they are inconsistent with the facts
deployed by the remaining structure of the body of knowledge. (1983:
293, emphasis mine.)

This passage is of crucial importance, since it contains the core of
Dworkin's answer to the question of constraints. It provides an idea
of what Dworkin presupposes in the notion of coherence, and of
how this agent may operate as an internal constraint. But we should
proceed with caution. Although Dworkin moves back and forth
from holistic to coherence formulations of his theoretical assumptions, seeming to endorse both concomitantly, the two concepts are
quite distinct. Both amount to a rejection of foundationalism, but
each gives this rejection a different form.

Holism urges the realization that the totality of our knowledge is
a network of logically interrelated beliefs. As a consequence, it
amounts to a rejection of the assumption that singular propositions
can have empirical content in isolation.[19] Holism, however, does
not necessarily lead to a coherence theory. It is a negative view in
the sense that it provides no answer to the question of a substitute
for foundationalism, for which status a coherence theory of knowledge is only one candidate.[20] Apparently, Dworkin endorses this
option. In fact, he endorses a specific concept of coherence,
namely, one which rests on the idea of complexity. As our system
of knowledge is 'sufficiently complex and structured', coherence
amounts to achieving consistency between the various kinds and
levels of beliefs, and it is this fact which renders the achievement
of consistency non-trivial.

On the other hand, it is important to realize that a coherence
conception of knowledge—as opposed to a coherence theory of
truth—makes much more sense when it concurs with holism. If
coherence is not offered as an explication of what truth consists
in, but is viewed as an indication of the truth, then the more
encompassing the coherence, the better the indication it is likely to
provide. Hence the fact that Dworkin subscribes to holism as well
should not be regarded as an accidental feature of his epistemological presuppositions.

[19] According to Quine (1953), holism also amounts to a repudiation of the
analytic–synthetic distinction. This is a highly controversial issue. See e.g. Dummett
(1978: 375 ff.).
[20] Quine himself seems to have endorsed the pragmatist solution (1953: 46).

In the following section I shall pursue this issue more directly. First, let us examine Dworkin's second reply to Fish. It takes up the challenge of scepticism implied by Fish's argument. Dworkin begins by drawing a distinction between internal and external scepticism. The former is a sceptical attitude adopted from within the enterprise, whereas the latter is a scepticism directed at the whole enterprise. 'External scepticism is a metaphysical theory, not an interpretative or moral position. [His] theory is rather a second-level theory about the philosophical standing or classification of these [e.g. moral] claims' (1986 : 79). Internal scepticism, though grantedly a plausible attitude, *ex hypothesi* adopts the internal (for example, moral or aesthetic) point of view. Hence it must rest on moral or aesthetic arguments. It follows that internal scepticism presupposes the general 'right–wrong' picture and argues only against some (or most) of our moral or aesthetic *conclusions*. Surely Fish's argument cannot be grounded on this type of scepticism.[21]

But external scepticism, Dworkin claims, is harmless since it is irrelevant. The external sceptic typically makes the following claim: the only way to give any sense to propositions of the form; 'A moral judgement, *p*, is true', is by assuming that moral judgements are meant to reflect some reality. Scepticism arises from the denial that any plausible sense can be made of such a reality.[22] Hence external scepticism only makes sense if it is true that we regard our evaluative claims as claims about some 'external reality'. However, and here we reach the crux of the matter, the point is that we do not. Moral judgements can be justified or argued for, only by other moral judgements; aesthetic judgements can be justified only by other aesthetic judgements, and so forth. In other words, external scepticism denies a claim which we need not make, namely, that by affirming the objectivity of our evaluative judgements we refer to something external to the domain of those judgements:

> The only kind of evidence I could have for my view that slavery is wrong, the only kind of justification I could have for acting on that view, is some substantive moral argument.

---

[21] It is somewhat difficult to see why the so-called 'internal' sceptic is a sceptic at all. But of course, it is a possible position. Perhaps in referring to internal sceptics, Dworkin had in mind those legal theorists who deny the possibility of understanding the whole body of legal material on the basis of a coherent scheme of principles. Whether this is a genuine sceptical stance or just sceptical rhetoric is a difficult question I need not resolve here.

[22] For an interesting exposition of this argument, see Mackie (1977 : 38–42).

the 'objective' beliefs most of us have are moral, not metaphysical, beliefs
. . . they only repeat and qualify other moral beliefs. (1986 : 81, 82)

Unfortunately, this answer is too crude even on Dworkin's own
account. It gives the impression that moral judgements constitute
a closed system, as it were, which can be organized coherently only
within its own boundaries. But this is inconsistent with the holism
which is required of, and indeed is manifest in, Dworkin's theory
of interpretation.

To see this point more clearly, let me contrast my construal of
Dworkin with that of Simmonds (1987 : 472). He argues that the
constructive model leads to infinite regress. Take, for instance, the
interpretation of legal practice. It must, according to the model, be
based on the best conception of justice capable of accounting for
the practice. But justice, according to Dworkin, is itself an interpretative notion, and the interpretation of justice must also appeal
in turn to some, more basic level of reflection, on 'nonpolitical
ideas, like human nature or the theory of the self' (Dworkin
1986 : 424). But, Simmonds argues, we have no reason to stop at
this level. Surely any theory of the self must also be an interpretation. Hence, according to the constructive model, an even more
fundamental level of evaluation must be appealed to so as to satisfy
the requirement of soundness, and so on, *ad infinitum*.

I believe it should be clear by now what Dworkin's answer would
be, given that my reading of him is correct: Simmonds wrongly
attributes a linear structure to Dworkin's theory, as if each realm
of reflection were justified by another, more basic one, until we
must either admit to infinite regress or decide to stop arbitrarily at
one of these levels. But in fact, the theory is circular; the relation
it postulates between different realms of knowledge (for instance,
law, justice, self) is not a reductive one but rather a reflective
equilibrium, that is, a relation of coherence. Thus, for instance, we
can 'stop' non-arbitrarily at the level of a theory of self, since
soundness of interpretation can be provided at this level by fitness
to other aspects of our knowledge, including for example, justice.
But again, it is important to realize that this circularity is vindicated
by the complexity thesis and the holism presumed by Dworkin.

Finally, before turning to some of these issues in greater detail,
it should be remarked that when the role of coherence is extended
in this manner, some of the forms of scepticism which Dworkin
would classify as external might be 'internalized' and become very

relevant. This is so, as they may now be translated from attempts to repudiate ethical (or aesthetic) realism into rejections of the very possibility of coherence. Although such scepticism can take various forms, it is most likely to be propounded by adherers to the belief that certain realms of reflection are in fact incommensurable. Surely, if it can be shown that different realms of reflection are incommensurable, the possibility of coherence is undermined from the outset. Furthermore, the more encompassing the role assigned to coherence, the more plausible it becomes to deny the possibility of its realization. Even those who wish to avoid the 'no-theory' view in ethics may be tempted to find such a view more cogent in the light of a holistic framework. It would seem, in other words, that within such a holistic context, the distinction between external and internal scepticism may be less helpful than Dworkin would like to assume.

4. THE CONCEPT OF FIT

To sum up so far, we have been looking for available constraints on interpretation. Fish's argument boils down to the claim that there are none, since the identity of the object of interpretation is totally dependent upon the particular interpretations offered, that is, upon the dimension of soundness. Dworkin's reply did not deny this dependence, but shifted the theoretical burden of constraints from the dimension of identity to that of fit. Now we must face the consequent question, can Dworkin's concept of fit really do the job?

Let me begin by presenting an argument, proposed by Simmonds (1987 : 478–80) in an attempt to reply in the negative:

1. Our convictions about fit, at least when it operates as a threshold requirement, must be *independent* of the substantive value judgements constituting the element of soundness, otherwise there would be no way of distinguishing interpretation from invention.

2. How do we know how much fit would suffice in each particular field? The most plausible answer seems to be that this is determined by the extent to which we think it matters to distinguish interpretation from invention in that particular realm. For instance, consider the difference in this respect between a judge and a legal historian referring to the relevant legal history, each for his particular institutional purposes.

3. Now consider a theory of adjudication. Why does it matter that a judge is interpreting rather than inventing the legal history of his country? Dworkin's only answer rests on the concept of integrity. Law as integrity explains just this; why it is a judge's role and duty to interpret rather than invent.

'There is just one small problem,' Simmonds says, 'law as integrity is also the substantive interpretation of legal practices that is being offered. Dworkin therefore violates his own injunction that the criteria of fit must be independent of the substantive criteria' (1987 : 479).

Apparently, either something is wrong with the argument, or something is deeply wrong with Dworkin's theory of interpretation. Let us take a closer look at the first premiss. Can Dworkin defend his theory by denying it? Can he claim that no damage results from allowing our convictions about fit to depend on the evaluative judgements constituting the dimension of soundness? We have already seen Dworkin endorse a similar strategy in his reply to Fish. Now, however, we face a difficulty. The plausibility of the reply to Fish was grounded on the complexity thesis; but this thesis will be placed under serious doubt if the first premiss of Simmonds's argument is denied. To reiterate, the charge of circularity in the mutual dependence of identity and soundness was evaded through the assumption that the dimension of fit is sufficiently complex. But in admitting that fit too depends on soundness, that is, on the self-same values meant to vindicate the given interpretation, we leave very little room for complexity. And as we have already seen, Dworkin himself concedes that the coherence attitude is rendered dubious without the presumption of complexity.

One must take caution at this point; value dependence *per se* does not necessarily lead to simplicity. Consider science for instance: suppose it is agreed that scientific inquiry is basically motivated by the idea of prediction. Now apply Simmonds's argument to this model, on the assumption that scientific inquiry is similar to interpretation in the relevant respects. We would soon end up with the same conclusion about fit. When asked, 'Why does it matter that a scientist interpret rather than invent?' we would have to reply that it matters as long as, and to the extent that, prediction is taken to be the scientist's aim. The general justifying value determines the level of fit in this case too. However, this does not undermine the concept of fit in scientific theories; fit can be a significant constraint in the case of science because the complexity thesis holds, not because fit is independent of justifying values.

This will not rescue Dworkin's theory of interpretation though. To see why, consider the possible criteria of complexity in further detail. My suggestion is as follows: first, as I have already indicated, the idea of complexity must embrace a quantitative criterion. A theory which accounts for very few of our beliefs and shows them to be coherent would hardly ever rise above triviality. But the concept of complexity must also embrace a qualitative criterion. A theory is warranted in relying on the complexity thesis if it accounts for beliefs which (at least prima facie) are different in *kind* or *source*. This is a crucial point; consider what the concept of fit involves in a physical theory. It embraces notions such as sense datum, prediction, logic, mathematics, laws or regularities, probabilities, and so forth. At least some of the beliefs embodied in these concepts differ in kind or origin, and even belong to very different realms of knowledge. This is why the idea of complexity can play a significant role in such a theory.

Does Dworkin's interpretative theory of law meet these criteria? Hardly, since our convictions with regard to both identity and fit so clearly depend on the substantive justification. The whole idea of 'checks and balances' becomes suspect when it turns out that everything emerges from the same evaluative judgement, that is, coherence. In other words, it is not value dependence, *per se*, which undermines the idea of complexity in Dworkin's legal theory, but the fact that all the elements of interpretation seem to depend on the proposed value.

Is the upshot of all this that Fish's sceptical conclusions are inescapable? As Dworkin's theory stands at the moment, it does seem to entail this type of scepticism, notwithstanding Dworkin's rhetoric which avoids admitting this. If I am right, one might be drawn in two opposite directions: towards endorsing the project and accepting its sceptical conclusions, or regarding the sceptical implications as a good reason (though not the only one) for revising the theory altogether. Elaborating upon my reasons for preferring the latter, and upon the alternative I have in mind, is the topic of other chapters in this book. My purpose here was a more limited one: to show that those wishing to subscribe to Dworkin's interpretative theory of law must first clarify a few points regarding its epistemic foundations.

5

SEMANTICS, REALISM, AND NATURAL LAW

THE view this chapter will scrutinize is opposed to Dworkin's, but more so in the reasoning offered to support it than in its final conclusions. First, unlike Dworkin (or myself, for that matter), adherents to this legal theory advocate a semantic approach to jurisprudence. They explicitly affirm just what Dworkin's inter-pretative approach strives to deny, that is, that legal theory is in essence a theory about the meaning of the term 'law'. Second, this theory espouses semantic *realism*, thus linking an account of the meaning of 'law' with a natural law doctrine. The following three theses should provide a rough summary of the theory I have in mind:

1. The appropriate account of the concept of law is a semantic analysis of what the word 'law' means (and, perhaps, of the meanings of other, related, concepts characteristic of legal language).
2. Such a semantic analysis of 'law' would show that the term refers to a real or natural kind of entity whose essence and constitution do not consist of social conventions.
3. Hence, discovery of the real essence of law renders anything like legal positivism false, and a version of natural law true.

The present chapter sets out to criticize this view, which is, in substance, tantamount to Michael Moore's legal theory, though probably divergent from it in certain details.[1] I shall refer to it as 'Semantic Natural Law', because my primary concern is with a certain type of reasoning which has attracted several legal philosophers, rather than with the details of any particular theory.

---

[1] See particularly his 'Semantics of Judging' (Moore 1981), 'A Natural Law Theory of Interpretation' (1985), and 'The Interpretive Turn in Modern Theory: A Turn for the Worse?' (1989*a*). See also Hurd's 'Sovereignty in Silence' (1990), and Kress's critique of Dworkin (1987).

I shall begin by explaining what realism in semantics means, and how a realist account of the meaning of 'law' can support a doctrine of natural law. But the main portion of this chapter will strive to show that the attempt to analyse the concept of law on the basis of semantic realism is one which is bound to fail. Later on, in Chapter 7, I shall be saying something about a possibly more modest version of semantic natural law, which employs semantic realism in statutory interpretation.

I. THE MEANING OF 'REALISM' AND THE MEANING OF 'LAW'

Realism is seen as a position on a metaphysical issue, a view on the way our thoughts and language relate to the world. Dummett captures this intuition in the following formulation:

The primary tenet of realism, as applied to some given class of statements, is that each statement in the class is determined as true or not true, independently of our knowledge, by some objective reality whose existence and constitution is, again, independent of our knowledge. (1981 : 434)

The gist of this formulation is a non-epistemic notion of truth: a realist, above all else, must maintain a clear distinction between the truth of a statement and the recognition of its truth. A realist must maintain, with respect to a certain class of statements, that there is a determinant reality rendering the statements in that class either true or not true, independently of whether we can recognize or confirm this.[2] In other words, realism regarding a given realm of knowledge entails the possibility of verification-transcendent truths within that realm. But, as Dummett emphasizes, this formulation also bears upon the theory of meaning appropriate to the relevant class of statements, because 'of the intimate connection between the notions of truth and meaning' (1981 : 434).

Most importantly, realism entails the principle of bivalence, which states that every statement is determinately either true or

---

[2] Note that one need not hold a realist (or anti-realist) position *tout court*; it makes perfect sense to hold different positions with respect to different realms or classes of statement. For instance, one can maintain realism with respect to statements about the physical world, and deny realism in mathematics or morality, etc. On the other hand, it is questionable whether this formulation of realism is capable of capturing the nominalist–realist debates concerning universals (see Dummett (1981 : 437), and cf. (1978 : preface)). In any case the ontological status of universals is quite irrelevant to our concerns.

false (where 'false' is the classical negation operator, equivalent to 'not true'). This requires several clarifications, however. To begin with, there is the question of truth-value gaps. Consider Strawson's analysis of statements, given utterances of which contain a singular term with no reference, as in Russell's classical example, 'The king of France is bald.' Contrary to Russell, Strawson (1971: 1–28) argues that specific utterances of such statements (an utterance of the above in 1990, for example) are devoid of truth-value. Thus, admitting truth value gaps may not seem inconsistent with realism. According to Dummett, however, 'even the belief in truth-value gaps due to failure of reference for singular terms represents a repudiation of realism in the relevant aspect: it is opposed to realism concerning non-existent objects, as maintained explicitly by Meinong' (1981: 438). An alternative strategy for coping with this type of truth-value gap would be to maintain the following: for a realist to deny that the principle of bivalence holds with respect to a subclass of statement within the class he is a realist about, he would have to maintain that certain conditions for a statement to be *correctly asserted* must have failed to obtain in that subclass (ibid.). The complex notion of correct assertability cannot be articulated within the bounds of the present discussion. Suffice it to say that examples of failure to satisfy the conditions of correct assertability would typically involve vagueness, equivocal statements, and failure of reference for singular terms. In such cases the realist adhering to this strategy would hold that the linguistic expressions in question were not genuine statements, from a logical point of view.

Morality might be thought to be a case in which realists need not subscribe to the principle of bivalence. According to Moore:

John Finnis, for example, is a realist about moral entities and qualities yet believes that we can 'run out' of moral reality. Finnis accordingly rejects the principles of bivalence and stability for moral assertions, for to 'run out' of moral reality is to admit that there are sentences about morality that are neither true nor false. (1989*a* : 879)

This is a mistake, however, since the moral gaps to which Moore is referring are not truth-value gaps. For a realist with respect to moral statements, gaps consist in the fact that certain competing moral claims may turn out to be incommensurable, in the sense that one might not have any further moral grounds on which to adjudicate between them. But this is still consistent with the

principle of bivalence. Suppose that in a particular situation both
'A ought to do x' and 'A ought to do y' are true statements.
Suppose, further, that it is impossible for A to do both x and y, and
that no further moral grounds are available for deciding between
the two options; the moral principles underlying each carry equal
weight. Now, one might be inclined to say that in such cases the
statement 'A ought to prefer x over y' is neither true nor false. This
would be a mistake, though, since the statement is simply false,
and its negation true: 'It is false that [A ought to prefer x over y]'.
In short, moral realism which admits of gaps is consistent with the
principle of bivalence, as the latter demands that every statement
expressing a moral prescription be determinately either true or
false, not that every possible practical choice, all things considered, be either morally right or wrong.

Two further clarifications regarding realism are in place here.
First, it is important to realize that the relation between realism
and the principle of bivalence is not a symmetrical one. While the
former entails the latter, the opposite is not the case. One could
easily construct an artificial language game, for instance, in which
the principle of bivalence would hold, while one would hardly
need to be a realist about such a game. The fact that each
statement in a certain class is determinately either true or false,
does not entail that it is necessarily rendered true or false by an
objective reality whose essence and constitution are independent
of our knowledge.

The second point, which bears more relevance to our topic,
concerns the relation between realism and reductionism. It is
usually thought that a full reductionist thesis between two classes
of statement entails an anti-realist position with respect to the
reduced class. Intuitively, the idea is clear enough: when one,
given class of statement is fully reducible to another, this reductive
relation would seem to mean that statements apparently about
things of one kind are really about things of some other kind.
Hence, the reduced class does not really exist, as it were. Now,
suppose that such a reductive relation obtains between two
statement classes, A and B, and, suppose further, that one can
hold a realist position about B. If each and every statement in A is
fully translatable to a statement in B, and if one is a realist about
B, then one would seem, *mutatis mutandis*, to be a realist about A.
In other words, maintaining a realist position about A, only

requires a translation of each and every statement in *A* to a statement in *B*, which requirement is met by the reductive relation. Dummett believes this precisely to be the case with central-state materialism, for example, which maintains that each and every statement about the mental is fully reducible to a statement about the central nervous system. According to Dummett, 'far from calling realism concerning psychological statements in question, [such a reductive thesis] tends to reinforce it, because of the plausibility of the principle of bivalence for statements about the central nervous system' (1981 : 448).

Things are not quite this simple, however. Central-state materialism does call into question realism concerning psychological statements in at least one, rather obvious, sense; it is opposed to what might be termed full-blooded realism concerning psychological statements, a realist position on the realm of the mental that includes a denial of any possibility of reduction. Such a full-blooded realism asserts of the mental what central-state materialism denies, namely, that there is a *mental* reality which renders either true or false each and every psychological statement. It would hence be much more accurate to draw a distinction between two kinds of realism, as Dummett suggests. He has called these naïve and sophisticated realism. Central-state materialism is only an anti-realist position on the naïve version of realism; according to 'sophisticated realism' it can count as a realist position about psychological statements, subject to being a realist position about the central-nervous system (ibid.).[3]

It is important to realize, however, that in most familiar contexts it is the naïve version of realism which is debated, as the example of central-state materialism itself shows. This is not merely a matter of philosophical tradition. It is a prerequisite of sophisticated realism that reduction be complete, yet such full reductionist doctrines are not easily come by. Nevertheless the distinction itself is important, as will shortly become evident.

---

[3] I am not quite happy with Dummett's terminology. Naïve realism is not a new term; it is traditionally associated with the eighteenth-century distinction between primary and secondary qualities, naïve realism being the thesis that secondary qualities, such as colour for example, do really exist in the world, as we see them. Although this version of naïve realism fits Dummett's distinction quite well, it should be clear that contemporary debates over realism are not confined to this eighteenth-century (indeed naïve) controversy. Bearing this clarification in mind, I shall continue to use Dummett's terminology.

Having said as much on the minimal implications of realism, let us pause here to see what bearing such an account might have upon the nature of law. To begin with, we need an interpretation of the meaning of 'law' which would enable us to speak of the truth values of statements. This should not be too difficult. We can stipulate a class of statements, let us call it LP, which consists of all the statements about what the law requires (or permits, authorizes, etc.) in a given legal system. Thus, LP in a given legal system, S_i, would be comprised of all the statements of the form: 'According to the law in S_i, A ought to do x', or of any similar form.[4]

Note that there is no need to claim that LP is semantically equivalent to the meaning of 'law' in any standard use of the latter. A realist would merely have to show that there exists a possible interpretation of 'law' enabling one to speak of the extension (or reference) of 'law' in terms of a determinable class of statements. This is what LP is meant to signify. Thus realism as applied to law would entail that each and every statement in LP is rendered true or false by some objective reality whose existence and constitution are independent of our knowledge. Hence also, each and every statement in LP must be presumed to be determinately either true or false.

Now it is fairly obvious that such a realist account of the meaning of 'law' is incompatible with the main tenets of legal positivism, at least as maintained by Hart, Kelsen, and Raz. As I have already mentioned in Chapter 1, contemporary legal positivism entails an anti-realist doctrine on the meaning of 'law'. The reason for this is as follows: one of the main tenets shared by legal positivists is the thesis that law is essentially a matter of social conventions. Whether one prefers Hart's formulation of the Rule of Recognition, or (as I do) Raz's formulation of the sources thesis, the result remains the same; the truths of legal propositions cannot be conceived of independently of the conditions for the recognition of their truths. The conventionalism espoused by legal positivism, and realism about the meaning of 'law' are directly opposed.

It is also quite easy to see how realism concerning the meaning of 'law' would, if true, support a natural-law doctrine. If there

---

[4] The formulations would vary according to the kind of legal rule in question: if the rule does not impose an obligation, but, for instance, confers power, the formulation would vary accordingly.

were an objective reality rendering legal propositions determinately either true or false, then it would make sense to claim that the truth of statements in *LP* could be *discovered* or *revealed*, as one discovers a law of nature. I am by no means claiming that semantic realism must be maintained by anyone wishing to subscribe to a natural-law doctrine. In fact, we have already seen in detail, that Dworkin, for one, rejects realism in favour of a coherence conception of knowledge and morality. But again, it would surely be easier to maintain a natural-law doctrine if the plausibility of realism about *LP* could be substantiated.

Hence, I shall now turn to the question of whether or not it makes sense to hold a realist position with respect to the meaning of 'law'. Let me begin by asking whether it makes sense to claim that each and every statement in *LP* is determinately either true or false, that is, whether the principle of bivalence is applicable to law. In the first place, we should note that for a realist with respect to legal propositions, and especially one like Moore who wishes to maintain a natural-law theory, the first step would be to advocate a realist position with respect to the class of moral statements as well. This, due to the fact that legal propositions refer to moral considerations, often doing so explicitly and, perhaps even more often, implicitly. We should thus be willing to admit, at least for the sake of the argument, the plausibility of realism in morality.[5]

However, even from the perspective of natural-law theories, we cannot accept that a realist view of the class of moral statements would settle the issue over realism in law. The reason is quite straightforward: numerous legal issues are morally neutral (at least within a certain range), or morally insignificant. A prominent example is the case where the law operates as a co-ordinating factor. In such cases it may be of importance (morally or otherwise) to have an established decision, while it is absolutely (morally or otherwise) insignificant what decision is eventually taken (that is, within a certain range of options). Hence, to establish realism with respect to law, a realist would have to show that the principle of bivalence holds with respect to statements about the law, even when the case is not determinable on moral grounds.

At the same time the realist would have to disallow any contradiction between law and morality. Suppose it is held to be

---

[5] Moore (1982) has argued at length for a realist position in morality.

true that according to morality, 'A ought to do x (in a given set of circumstances)'. Can a realist about law then admit to the truth of the statement 'according to the law A ought to do not-x (in the same set of circumstances)'? Surely not! Maintaining the existence of a determinate *reality* which renders either true or false every statement in *LP*, as within the realm of morality, means the disallowance of any possibility of contradiction between these two realms; reality does not admit of logical contradictions.

Both of these theses, however, though necessarily required of the realist, involve serious, not to say devastating, difficulties. The latter makes it obvious that the type of natural-law theory entailed by the 'semantic natural law' doctrine is such a strong one as to make it doubtful whether anyone actually subscribes to it. It would mean taking Aquinas's *lex iniusta non est lex* much more seriously than proponents of modern versions of natural-law doctrine could wish. Furthermore, even if this difficulty were ignored, a similar, equally serious one would still emerge. If the principle of bivalence is held to apply to law, it follows that, at the very least, the law cannot impose a set of inconsistent demands. But this is simply false. Legal systems often comprise morally, and even logically, inconsistent prescriptions.

But suppose I am wrong here, and that one does want to take a full-blooded natural-law doctrine seriously. How would one cope with the first difficulty, namely, those legal issues which are not determinable on moral grounds? How is the principle of bivalence to be applied to such cases? Suppose, for example, that the possible applications of a legal rule are compatible with several conflicting interpretations, none of which is morally (or rationally) significant. Can we say that each of the options is determinately either true or false? What would enable us to do so? One natural suggestion might be a reductionist thesis about the meaning of legal propositions. As explained above, a full reductionist thesis with respect to a given class of statements is indeed compatible with a sophisticated version of realism. Thus, suppose one holds the view that a legal proposition is meaningful if and only if it can be fully reduced to a set of propositions about past events. In other words, any proposition of the form 'x is the law in S_i at time t', would *mean* that 'at some time prior to t, it has been actually *decided* in S_i, that x'—which is, plausibly, determinately either true or false. For someone like Moore, though, there is just one problem in conceding this proposal. It is, embarrassingly, a legal positivist thesis.

Now I am by no means claiming that contemporary legal positivism is a realist doctrine, even on a sophisticated version of realism.[6] On the contrary, as shown in Chapter 3, the possibility of full reductionism has been criticized and consequently jettisoned by positivists such as Hart, Kelsen, and Raz. The only conclusion I am indicating is that unless such a full-blooded reduction is presumed, it is hard to see how all statements about the law could be subject to the principle of bivalence, and hence, how a realistic thesis could be held with regard to them.

2. PUTNAM'S THEORY OF 'NATURAL KINDS' AND THE CONCEPT OF LAW

Despite its centrality to contemporary philosophy of language, Dummett's formulation of realism, which concentrates on the notion of 'truth' (and sentence meaning), is not popular with those legal philosophers who find semantic natural law appealing. If my arguments in the previous section are correct, then the reasons for this should be clear enough. Instead, those who subscribe to semantic natural law tend to draw their conclusions from Putnam's theory of reference, which concentrates on word meaning. Their reasons will become apparent once we take a look at Putnam's theory of natural-kind predicates.

A brief summary of Putnam's main theses will have to suffice here, though it falls far short of doing justice to the richness and subtlety of his theory.[7]

Putnam's central attempt aims at establishing externalism with

---

[6] Perhaps Austin is the only legal positivist one can think of whose views entail something like a sophisticated realism. According to a possible (though not necessarily accurate) interpretation of Austin, he maintained that all statements about the law are fully reducible to statements about past events, namely, about the commands of the sovereign. To the extent that one can be a realist about past events (of the pertinent kind), Austin's reductionist account would turn out to be sophisticated—though not naïve—realism about the law. But of course, this is not the kind of realism about law that semantic natural lawyers have in mind. It is the naïve version of realism which is presently being debated; semantic natural lawyers wish to assert that which Austin strove to deny, that there is an objective *legal* reality which renders determinately either true or false each and every statement about the law.

[7] The main source of the following presentation is 'The Meaning of "Meaning" ', Putnam (1975 : 215–71).

respect to the individuation of linguistic contents. That is, an 'internalist' would hold the following assumptions which, Putnam claims, cannot be satisfied jointly:

1. To know the meaning of a term is to be in a certain psychological state.
2. No psychological state presupposes the existence of any individual other than the subject to whom that state is ascribed.
3. The meaning of a term determines its extension (or reference).

To show that meaning (that is, as characterized above) does not determine reference, Putnam employs the now famous example of Twin Earth. Suppose that Earth and an imaginary Twin Earth differ only in the chemical composition of the substance called 'water' in both worlds. On Twin Earth it is composed of XYZ instead of H_2O, although it is perceptually indistinguishable from H_2O. Prior to the 1750 discovery of the chemical composition of water on Earth, people on both Earth and on Twin Earth could have shared the exact same psychological state when referring to water, despite the fact of referring to different substances. Identical mental states, then, need not indicate identical extensions. Furthermore, once such a discrepancy in the extension is revealed, we would say that XYZ on Twin Earth was *mistakenly* called 'water', not that the meaning of 'water' had changed. The example is thus taken to demonstrate how two speakers can be in exactly the same psychological state, while the extensions of the term associated with this state nonetheless differ in their respective idiolects.

Putnam's explanation for this possibility is that we use natural-kind words (and many other nouns) of a type which he calls indexical, to designate, 'rigidly',[8] specific kinds of entities, whatever their real nature may eventually turn out to be. This position is often called externalism, since it admits that reality— the actual nature of things—forms a part of meaning.

Now, to account for the fact that people can use indexical words despite their frequent inability to specify the precise extension of these words, Putnam incorporates a doctrine which he terms the division of linguistic labour: people are able to use words like 'gold' and 'elm' despite their inability to identify gold or elm with certainty, since they can rely on a subclass of speakers, that is,

---

[8] The term is of course Kripke's (1972), the idea being that indexical predicates are rigid designators.

experts, to reach such identifications. The meaning of an indexical word should not, however, be equated with any particular account of its reference given by experts in a specific field. The latter should always be regarded as only the best approximation of the real reference at any given time (Putnam 1975 : 227–9).

Finally, Putnam acknowledges that many predicates are not indexicals. Certain words (which Putnam calls 'one-criterion words') are synonymous with a description in terms of necessary and sufficient conditions. Over the last few years, Putnam has shifted the position of the line between the two. In the 'Meaning of "Meaning"', for instance, he holds than an artifact, such as a 'pencil' is 'an indexical as "water" or "gold"' (1975 : 243). Later, though, he seems to have conceded to the contrary (1983 : 74–5).

Be this as it may, we are now in a position to see why the Putnamian account of indexical predicates proves so appealing to legal philosophers.[9] Showing that 'law' is an indexical concept, such as 'water' or 'gold', would entail conclusions which are highly favourable to the semantic natural law doctrine. To see this, let us concentrate on the point at which Putnam's account of indexical predicates converges with realism.

One of the most important implications of Putnam's theory is the following: for any indexical word, it should be possible for a *whole community* of speakers to *misidentify its extension*. As the extension of a term is just what the term is true of, the possibility of misidentification rules out an anti-realist position which, as we have already seen, denies that truth and its recognition are completely separate notions.

Consider one of Putman's examples. Suppose that in Archimedes' time, certain pieces of metal, X, were indistinguishable from gold, while today with the aid of modern techniques, we could easily distinguish between the two. Now, assuming the indexicality of 'gold', Putnam is bound to say that although the Greeks of Archimedes' time could not distinguish gold from X, X did not lie within the extension of 'gold' *even then* (Putnam 1975 : 235–8). Or, consider again the Twin Earth example. For Putnam to be able to say that XYZ on Twin Earth is not water (although

---

[9] See Moore (1981 : 204). See also Kress (1987 : 854–60), who advances a Putnamian account of the meaning of 'law' as a rejoinder to Dworkin's 'semantic sting' argument. But unlike Moore, Kress seems to have failed to notice that such an account is incompatible with legal positivism (ibid. 854).

Twin Earthians may mistakenly have called it 'water'), he must presume that the extension of 'water' can be misidentified by Earthians as well (as indeed it could easily have been prior to 1750). The alternative view would be an anti-realist one, namely, that the ability to recognize the extension of words like 'water' and 'gold' is a constituent of their very meaning, ruling out the possibility of *extensive* misidentification, that is, on the part of a whole community of speakers.[10]

Thus, showing the concept of 'law' to be indexical would constitute a repudiation of the brand of anti-realism entailed by legal positivism. Surely, no conventional understanding of law could allow for the possibility of an extensive misidentification of the law. Furthermore, establishing the indexicality of 'law' would give meaning to the idea that there is more to discover about the 'real nature' of law, as it were, than that which is perspicuous in the rules or conventions themselves, and the practices of applying them. In other words, the indexicality of 'law' would support the age-old natural-law doctrine, that the law can be *discovered* even where there are no rules or conventions which settle the issue.

We are thus faced with the question of whether or not it makes any sense at all to see 'law' as an indexical word. Recall that for 'law' to be an indexical predicate, it must be possible for a whole community of speakers—including experts!—to misidentify its extension. Is it indeed possible? Is it possible for a whole community of lawyers to make a mistake about the identification of their laws?

Let us construct an example analogous to Putnam's story of the misidentification of 'gold'. Take a certain legal system, say Roman law in the first century AD; let us presume that a certain norm, P, was recognized by the Roman lawyers of the time as part and parcel of their legal system. Does it make sense to say that this community of lawyers has made a mistake, since according to the 'real nature' of law, P did not lie within the extension of their legal system even then, despite their inability to recognize this?

I presume that the negative answer to this question is almost self-evident; such an extensive misidentification in law would seem

---

[10] I am not claiming that an anti-realist view rules out the possibility of any misidentification. Clearly, even an anti-realist must admit that certain types of misidentification are possible, e.g. when a word is used incorrectly. But what the anti-realist cannot admit is the possibility of *extensive* misidentification, namely, when a *whole community* of speakers is concerned.

profoundly mysterious. But the fact that a philosophical doctrine yields mysterious results has never yet deterred all the philosophers, so perhaps something more should still be said about this issue.

3. CRITICAL MORALITY AND CRITICAL LAW

A comparison of law with other normative practices may be instructive here. Take morality, for instance: an extensive misidentification in morality would seem to make perfect sense. It surely seems to be possible for a whole community of speakers to display wrong moral attitudes and beliefs, or in other words, to misidentify (all? some of?) the true moral statements. But it is essential to draw upon two distinct notions of normativity which are being used here. Following Hart (1963:17), we should distinguish between *positive* and *critical* morality. The former consists in the moral beliefs, attitudes, etc., actually being held by a certain community, whereas the latter consists in the class of true moral statements. Thus, from the realist's point of view, extensive misidentification in morality is rendered possible due to the potential discrepancy between its critical and positive aspects.

The distinction between these two senses of normativity— critical and positive—is not confined to the realm of morality. The realm of aesthetics is, perhaps, another example where such a distinction is applicable. But it is important to realize that this is not always the case. There are normative domains which do not admit of any sensible *autonomous* critical aspect. To be sure, the lack of critical normativity with respect to a certain field of norm-guided conduct, does not entail the impossibility of critical evaluations in the field. What it entails is that critical evaluations be imposed from the perspective of a different normative domain.

Consider, for example, the contention that 'Game *A* is better than game *B*.' It surely poses the question. 'In what sense?' Is it intellectually more intriguing? Or healthier? Is it more enjoyable? More competitive? etc. Each of these questions represents a different normative perspective according to which games can be evaluated. But, and this is the crucial point, there is no general 'game perspective' as it were. Games are guided by rules, but these rules have no *autonomous* critical aspect. Hence also, people who play a game cannot misidentify its rules: the game consists in the rules people actually follow (or lay down).

I believe that the same is true of the normativity of language, but this is a point I cannot pursue here.[11] Instead, let us return to law. We can see that the crucial question with respect to the possibility of extensive misidentification in law is whether or not the concept of an autonomous or inherent critical normativity is applicable to this field. The realist, in other words, must substantiate a concept of critical law enabling him to distinguish between law's critical and positive aspects. He would have to maintain that even if a norm is legally valid, that is, from the perspective of positive normativity, it can turn out to be legally false, as it were, from the perspective of the critical normativity. Note, once again, that the notion of legal truth (and falsehood) must be distinct from moral right (and wrong). As we have seen, moral realism applied to law does not entail legal realism (as this notion is understood here).

At the most abstract level, there are two possible ways of construing the idea of critical law: the critical perspective of law may be conceived in either instrumental or non-instrumental terms. Moore's functional conception of law is a good example of the former. On his account law's critical normativity consists in its 'functional essence'. This functional essence can be discerned by asking: 'What are the distinct goals that law and legal systems serve?' (Moore 1989a: 887). Not surprisingly, Moore concedes that law's purposes are basically moral and political: 'that law serves the goals of liberty . . . of equality . . . of substantive fairness . . . of procedural fairness . . . of utility . . . etc.' (ibid.) Thus, critical law, according to Moore, is that which will 'maximally satisfy the rightly ordered set of some such values' (ibid., emphasis mine).

The problem with this instrumental conception of law's critical normativity is that instead of providing a concept of critical law, it simply provides an application of critical morality to law. If the criteria of legal truth are seen as given in terms of law's moral and political ends (or function, if one prefers), then there is no distinction between the critical evaluation of law from a moral as opposed to a legal point of view; law's 'functional essence' turns out to be critical morality in disguise.

Nor would it help to presume (counter-factually, I would add, as the presumption is simply false) that there are certain moral and

[11] Cf. Ch. 7 below.

political ends which are somehow *unique* to law. Suppose there are certain moral ends unique to the practice of promising. Surely that does not render the critical evaluation of promising autonomous, or independent of morality in general.

Thus, a non-instrumental construction of critical law would seem a more promising attitude. According to this view, recently articulated by Weinrib (1988), the truth of a legal norm—as opposed to its validity—is independent of the alleged ends it is taken to enhance. Law's critical aspect, or rather its 'form', as Weinrib prefers to call it, consists in what he calls the 'immanent rationality' of law (1988:955). By this latter he means, if I have understood him correctly, that law's critical evaluation is independent of any of its moral or political dimensions.

As Weinrib himself realizes, however, this non-instrumentalist understanding of critical law makes sense only if confined to the structure of legal reasoning.[12] This, in turn, leads the non-instrumentalist conception of critical law to a coherence theory of truth in law. As Weinrib explains:

The formalist's concern is not with whether a given exercise of state power is desirable, either in its own terms or in the terms of the larger ends it serves, but with whether it is intelligible as part of a coherent structure of justification.

The reason coherence functions as the criterion of truth is that legal form is concerned with immanent intelligibility. Such an intelligibility cannot be validated by anything outside itself, for then it would no longer be immanent.

Hence, he concludes:

Coherence is the criterion of truth for the formalist understanding of juridical relationship. (1988:973, 972)

But this is not quite clear. To begin with, the term 'criterion of truth' is ambiguous. Either it means that the truth of legal statements *consists in* coherence, or else that coherence is the only (or primary) *indication of* truth in law. The former option will not

---

[12] That is, unless one adopts a Platonist construal of legal form, but I have no idea how to understand the contention that legal form should be construed on such a Platonist ontology. Even Plato himself, to the best of my knowledge, did not advance such an extraordinary claim (but perhaps only because he was contemptuous of lawyers). In any case, it is clear enough that Weinrib does not espouse such an interpretation of legal form.

do for purposes of establishing the possibility of realism in law. Patently, a coherence conception *of truth* with respect to a certain class of statements, is directly at odds with a realist conception about that class. Hence, even if some notion of critical law can be construed on the basis of a coherence conception of truth, such a notion of critical law does not admit of realism.

Hence, we must presume that Weinrib means coherence to be an indication of truth. That is, we must shift from a coherence theory of truth to a coherence theory of knowledge. This, however, will still not do, not even if we presume the latter to be compatible with a correspondence conception of truth, and hence with realism. As shown in Chapter 4, a coherence theory of knowledge only makes sense within the context of a holistic conception of knowledge. But on such holistic grounds, the critical aspect of law can hardly be characterized as autonomous or immanent rationality; holism and the autonomy of law are not easily reconcilable.[13] Note that Weinrib must confine his construal of the criterion of coherence to the epistemological dimension. Maintaining that coherence was a justificatory *value*, along the lines suggested by Dworkin's concept of law as integrity, for example, would violate his injunction that formalism is not concerned with the moral or political desirability of legal arrangements or institutions. Nor would such a claim be compatible with the notion of critical law which the realist seeks to substantiate. This, for the very reason due to which Moore's functionalism fails: if the criteria of legal truth are given in terms of moral values, critical law cannot be distinguished from critical morality applied to law.

It might be objected at this point that we still have not reached the root of the matter: why is it the case that certain normative domains, such as morality, can be conceived of as having immanent or autonomous critical aspects, while others, such as law, can only be critically evaluated from the perspective of other normative domains? One is inclined to see the reason in the fact that law, unlike morality, is a matter of human creation, a product of culture. But this is not wholly satisfactory. It is not clear that a

---

[13] It is not clear that Weinrib himself wants to adopt a realist position with respect to the meaning of 'law', hence this is not necessarily a criticism of his article. But the fact that he seems unaware of the distinction between a coherence theory of truth and a coherence theory of knowledge unfortunately obscures his position.

realist, with respect to moral statements, for instance, must deny the possibility that critical morality be at all culturally dependent. We have already seen that realism with respect to moral statements is compatible with a view admitting of a certain amount of incommensurability among competing moral choices. Hence, realism may also allow for a certain degree of cultural divergence stemming from incommensurable cultural choices.

On the other hand, there seems to be a rather obvious connection between anti-realism and cultural relativity. It is difficult to see how the reference of concepts which are purely cultural products could ever be misidentified by the entire population of that culture. In fact, one can make a stronger claim: to the extent that something is a purely cultural product, its reference consists in what people think it to be, which renders the possibility of extensive misidentification a logical impossibility. This suggests a pertinent distinction between concepts which are the *products* of a culture, and concepts which are cultural-relative only in a partial or derivative sense. Realism, and consequently the Putnamian account of indexicals, makes sense with reference to the latter but not the former.[14]

The above distinction may be illustrated as follows: imagine yet another Twin Earth whose inhabitants differ from us in two respects, first, that Twin Earthians have no concept of morality or of moral evaluation of behaviour; second, that Twin Earthians have no form of legal system whatsoever. In my opinion, the moral realist could understandably claim that at least some kind of moral evaluations were applicable to the behaviour of Twin Earthians despite their inability to recognize this. It might, for instance, be morally wrong for a Twin Earthian to kill his fellow Twin Earthian without due cause. However, it would not be illegal. Moreover we can offer no idea of what would count as illegal behaviour on the part of a Twin Earthian. There is no way of evaluating the behaviour of Twin Earthians by any legal, as opposed to moral, standards.

Arguably, similar relations obtain between the concepts of art and aesthetics. From the vantage point of the distinction under

[14] Putnam sometimes gives the impression that for a concept to be a product of culture, and hence not accountable on the basis of indexical predicates, it must be possible to provide a definition of that concept in terms of necessary and sufficient conditions. See Putnam (1975:243), and Wiggins (1980:90–101). This is an utterly puzzling contention and I can only hope that my impression is mistaken.

consideration here, the relation between law and morality seems analogous to that between art and aesthetics. I have already mentioned that the concept of autonomous critical normativity, and hence realism, is perhaps also applicable to the realm of aesthetics. But the realist about aesthetic statements would have to maintain that aesthetic evaluations were not the products of culture (though perhaps partially sensitive to cultural divergence). On the other hand, realism about the meaning of 'art' seems to be no less implausible than realism about the meaning of 'law'. In the next chapter I shall argue, although from a different perspective, that artistic genres, like legal institutions, are *products* of culture, and hence cannot be misidentified extensively.

Be this as it may, I do not wish to assert realism about morality, aesthetics, or anything to be an acceptable view. I do want to suggest, however, that realism about morality is an understandable position only in so far as it is also maintained that morality is not altogether a product of culture (though perhaps partially sensitive to cultural divergence). The fact that law is a cultural product *par excellence* renders a realist position, and hence a Putnamian account about the meaning of 'law', incomprehensible.

6

CONSTRUCTIVE IDENTIFICATION AND RAZIAN AUTHORITY

DWORKIN's legal philosophy went through several stages between the 'Model of Rules' and *Law's Empire*. One central theme, however, remained mostly untouched: the *coherence thesis*, as it is usually referred to. A legal system, Dworkin argued repeatedly, comprises not only source-based law but also those norms which can be shown to be consistent in principle with the bulk of source-based law. His recent interpretative turn is basically an attempt to re-establish this thesis on novel grounds, namely, on the idea that law is interpretative throughout. From the outset, however, Dworkin has realized that an interpretative account of law might turn out to be inimical to the coherence thesis, that is, if interpretation is explicable only on grounds of the communication-intention model. This worry is expressed in the following passage:

The idea of interpretation cannot serve as a general account of the nature or truth value of propositions of law, unless it is cut loose from these associations with speaker's meaning or intention. Otherwise it becomes simply one version of the positivist thesis that propositions of law describe decisions taken by people or institutions in the past. (1985 : 148)

This formulation may be a bit too crude, even on Dworkin's own account, but it serves well to introduce the problem. According to the popular view, whenever a judge cannot apply the law straightforwardly, he is faced with two options. He can either interpret the law at hand—if there is one—or turn to extra-legal sources and thus, in the case of higher courts, create a new law. As we have seen, Dworkin's theory aims to challenge this dichotomy, offering the thesis that law is interpretative throughout. But suppose interpretation is only a matter of retrieving the communication intentions of the speaker or the author of the text. Then one could speak about the interpretation of law only in those cases where the alleged law was in fact the expression of someone's intention. In any other case, one would have to admit to the law's invention or creation. Patently then, Dworkin must deny that law is interpreted on the basis of the communication-intention model. Recall that according to the coherence thesis, a norm can be a *legal* norm even when it has never been created, or in fact previously contemplated as such. Thus, the communication model of interpretation and the coherence thesis are directly opposed.

It is not the purpose of this chapter to argue for the endorsement of the communication model of interpretation in law. I shall try to argue, however, that intentions do play a crucial role in the *identification* of legal norms as such and, moreover, that they do so in a way which is incompatible with Dworkin's coherence thesis. The argument focuses on the distinct roles that intentions play in determining the identification, as opposed to the content, of that which is interpreted.

I. CONSTRUCTIVE IDENTIFICATION

Legal practice, like art, according to Dworkin, is an interpretative enterprise. The participants in these practices presume that the practice has a value, a point, or some purpose it is meant to enhance, and the requirements of the practice are taken to be sensitive to these supposed values. A theoretical account of such a practice is basically a matter of achieving an equilibrium between the practice as we find it (roughly!) and its best possible justification (Dworkin 1986:90). We have already seen in detail (Chapter 3), how the interpretative nature of both practice and theory yield their value dependence. Yet there are two aspects of the value dependence of interpretation which ought to be kept separate here. One is the thesis that the interpretation of works of art, legal norms, or whatever, is made possible and intelligible only against the background of a conceptual scheme constituted by, *inter alia*, evaluative judgements. In the previous chapters I have tried to show that, important as this insight may be, it cuts no ice with the dispute between Dworkin and his positivist opponents.

However, the kind of value dependence which might serve to support the coherence thesis is a different matter altogether. Here, one must maintain that evaluative considerations are *sufficient* to determine (at least sometimes) whether something *is* a legal norm or a work of art, etc. In other words, what must be demonstrated is the value dependence of the identification of law (or art) as such, not of its content or meaning. I shall henceforth refer to this thesis as the *constructive identification* thesis.

One immediate objection might be raised here, namely, that this formulation of the constructive identification thesis ignores the dimension of fit. This is not the case, however, first, because fit itself, as Dworkin admits, is partly value dependent; but mainly because once the threshold of fit is passed, moral considerations can, according to Dworkin, provide sufficient grounds for identifying a given norm as a legal one. And this is the very essence of the idea of constructive identification. In other words, it is definitely not the case that whatever is 'the best' is law (or art). Dworkin's position is, rather, that considerations of what is the best can sometimes determine what law is.

What he seems to have overlooked though, is the fact that constructive identification is diametrically opposed to two distinct versions of the communication model, not one. Patently, as we have seen, the thesis is irreconcilable with the idea that interpretation amounts to a retrieval of the author's intentions. But, for the very same reasons, it is also irreconcilable with the idea that something can be identified as a legal norm (or a work of art) only if it is presumed to have been created as such. According to the latter option, the author's intentions are not referred to for purposes of determining what, for instance, a text means, what its content is, so to speak. Yet its identification as a text—under a covering concept of a given kind, that is, a type of texts—requires that one at least presume the intention to create a text of this kind. These are two separate versions of intentionalism. One could subscribe to the latter without endorsing the former. A particular text's identification *as a novel*, for instance, on the basis of the assumption that it has been created as such, does not mean or entail that its content ought to be determined by considerations about what its author had in mind.

The main part of this chapter will argue that presumptions about intentions play a crucial role in the identification of law, and hence that the coherence thesis should be rejected. However, it will be convenient to begin with a discussion of the possibility of applying the thesis of constructive identification to the realm of art. To justify this move I can only appeal to Dworkin's own work, which often relies on the analogy between the interpretative nature of these two enterprises. I should make it clear from the outset, however, that it is not the nature of art that interests me here, so much as the kind of considerations capable of supporting or undermining the possibility of constructive identification; art is just an example. But two clarifications are required before we proceed.

In saying that something has been created as such-and-such, it is typically assumed that the agent had actually formed an intention with respect to what he has produced. The relation between action and intention, however, is not always so strong; most of the time people act intentionally without forming any particular intention with respect to the act performed.[1] Now perhaps it is sometimes possible to see something as being created as a result of an intentional action in this weaker sense. In any case, nothing in the present context depends on an answer to this problem since the idea of constructive identification would be incompatible with both options.

Second, and more important, there is a distinction to be drawn between questions of *identity* and questions of *identification*, since it is only the latter with which we are concerned here. Identity is basically a matter of sameness. The typical form of an identity question would be, 'Is A the same f as B?' where f stands for the pertinent sortal concept (the same what?) (Wiggins 1980: 15). Generally, though not in all cases, identity concerns spatio-temporal continuity: 'Is A (= the man standing in the corner) the same person as B (= John, my classmate from high school)?' Or, in law: 'Is the legal system A (= in Zimbabwe) the same as B (= (formerly) in Rhodesia)?'

On the other hand, questions of identification are typically of the form: 'Is A an f?' In this case, neither sameness nor continuity are considered, but seeing something, or singling it out, *as* an f. (It is being neither claimed nor denied that we constantly perceive things as such-and-such; our subject is a type of question, not the nature of perception.[2])

This distinction would be rather trivial and hardly worth mention, were it not assumed by some philosophers that the latter depends upon the former. It is sometimes maintained that one

---

[1] See e.g. Anscombe (1956); Davidson (1980: introd.); Hacker (1988).
[2] Cf. Strawson (1979).

cannot specify the criteria for identifying an X as an f, unless one can specify the criteria for the identity of f.[3] The concession that people are often able to identify things, under covering concepts for which it is very unlikely that they could specify criteria of identity (think of modes of behaviour, musical timbres, etc.), sometimes leads such philosophers to far-reaching conclusions. For instance, that in this latter case, the identifiables are not real entities.[4]

Fortunately we can avoid such philosophical complexities, and for two reasons. First, nothing in the following discussion will depend on either admitting or denying any possible conceptual connections between identity and identification. Second, we could not be accused of taking an unwarranted position in such a dispute. The intentionalist identification thesis explored below does not amount to, nor is it meant to be, a specification of *the* criteria of identification for anything at all. One can discuss certain conceptual constraints on the identification of things under a certain kind of covering concept, without attempting to pursue the further task of providing a full account of the criteria of identification (a task which, in many cases, would be rather futile anyway).

There is another reason why the distinction between identity and identification is worth mentioning here. Below, I shall try to argue against the plausibility of constructive identification in art. Yet I readily admit that, in some cases, identity in art can be value dependent, along the lines of the constructive model. Many works of art are tokens of a type, and it is sometimes of interest to ask whether two tokens are actually tokens of the same type or not (see Wollheim 1978; 1980). In some of these cases, it is plausible to hold that the answer may depend in part on evaluative or aesthetic considerations, but this cannot be taken to establish that the identification of works of art as such is possibly constructive.

2. CONSTRUCTIVE IDENTIFICATION AND THE OBJECTS OF ART

I shall now try to point out certain considerations which support the implausibility of constructive identification in art. Recall, my

[3] If I understand him correctly, Wiggins (1980) seems to hold such a view. This view seems also to have been presumed by Wollheim in *Art and its Objects* (1980), but it is not clear in Wollheim (1978). See also Williams (1973 : 15–16).

[4] This view is elaborated and powerfully criticized by Strawson (1976).

claim is that the artist's intention to create an object as a work of art (or as, for instance, a novel) constitutes an essential element of our conception of what it is for something to be identified as a work of art. Thus, to begin with, for something to be a work of art it must be an artifact. We do not identify trees, or landscapes, or even marvellous sunsets on bright summer evenings, as works of art (except of course, in a figurative form of speech, or when attributing the object's creation to a supernatural entity). In short, art has to be created.

But of course, not all created objects, that is, artifacts, are works of art; we only single out certain kinds of artifact as works of art. Now the crucial point here is this: those subscribing to the possibility of constructive identification in art must maintain that works of art are identified as such on the basis of certain aesthetic features they happen to possess. But this is a serious distortion, since we normally discriminate between the concept of an *aesthetic artifact* and the concept of a *work of art*. Nor is this distinction groundless.

To begin with, it is difficult to imagine why these aesthetic features could not apply to other artifacts.[5] More importantly, we sometimes speak of a work of art having no aesthetic merits whatsoever, often because it is simply bad or unsuccessful, sometimes because it was meant to be so. Consider the ideology of certain twentieth-century genres which explicitly deny any such aesthetic purposes or merits.[6] It is true that these revolutionary genres often create new standards of aesthetic appraisal, new tastes as it were. But it would be a serious distortion to describe their identification as art as wholly dependent on their success in implementing such new standards of aesthetic appraisal. We often identify them as works of art long before we know whether such a development is possible. In short, any attempt to base the criteria for art's identification on aesthetic features alone is bound to fail. (For similar reasons, it seems unhelpful to employ aesthetic functions, as is sometimes suggested.)

---

[5] Note that there are certain aesthetic values which incorporate a reference to the artistic intentions in the requisite sense, like e.g. 'creativity'. Thus, when I speak about 'aesthetic features' I mean those which do not comprise any reference to the intentions to create a work of art, not even implicitly.

[6] The examples I have in mind are early Dada, and conceptual art. See Lynton (1980: chs. 4 and 10).

And yet, does it not make sense to say, 'This was not meant to be a work of art, but it is'? It seems to; we understand what has been said. But compare this, for example, with instances of insincere speech-acts. The fact that in normal circumstances we presume a speech-act to be sincere (cf. Searle 1969 : 60) does not entail that we cannot make sense of deviations from this condition, deviations which are parasitic on what it standardly means to perform a speech-act of a certain kind. Or, to take a similar example, consider the practice of voting. One could hardly be described as voting for such-and-such without forming the relevant intention. Yet we can easily imagine deviations from this. Suppose someone who is absolutely unfamiliar with the practice of voting is persuaded to perform the acts considered as a vote for something without even knowing what he is doing. Such a person might be said to have voted without the requisite intention. But again, the possibility of such an unusual case is parasitic on our standard understanding of what it means to vote. Similarly, one need not deny that in exceptional or unusual circumstances, art could also be created unintentionally, as it were. Still this seems to have little bearing on what it standardly means to identify something as a work of art. In other words, the intention to create a work of art is a *criterion* for its identification as such, but not a logically necessary condition. Criteria are, by their nature, defeasible; one can always imagine circumstances in which a given criterion does not hold. But this fact, that criteria are defeasible in a way that necessary conditions are not, does not render the former irrelevant or useless.[7]

An objection based on counter-examples may seem in place at this point: from an historical perspective, we seem to have identified as works of art numerous things which were not created as such. To mention a few examples, consider ancient cave paintings, Oceanic art, African art, and perhaps even things as close to our culture as medieval icons. Admittedly, transcultural comparisons pose difficult problems in the context of almost any discussion about the concept of art and its limits. In the present context, however, only one particular claim would amount to a real counter-example to the thesis suggested here. Suppose one wanted to claim that African warrior-masks were works of art. Nothing in this contention would amount to an objection to the

[7] For a more detailed account of the defeasibility of criteria, see Ch. 7, sect. 4.

intentionalist identification thesis advocated here, provided it was presumed that the pertinent African culture had a concept of art sufficiently similar to ours. It is only when we presume (as I believe it would be right to do) that the pertinent African culture had no concept of art whatsoever (or that if it did, it was one too remote from ours to be translated to 'art' in our language), hence precluding the creation of the warrior-mask as a work of art, that its identification as such becomes a relevant counter-example. But in this case, the contention that the warrior-mask was a work of art would be utterly perplexing. It would require an explanation of what justifies the mask's classification as a work of art on the basis of its appearance alone. One could justifiably claim that it *resembled* a work of art in various respects, or that it could have been one had it been created as such, but not that it in fact was one.[8] In classifying an artifact, then, either it is presumed that the purposes in play in its creation are close enough to those we consider artistic, in which case it can be said to have been created as a work of art, or the purposes in play are not taken to be artistic, and hence classifying it as a work of art would amount to a distortion.

Now consider the opposite case: can we say 'This was meant to be a work of art, but in fact it is not'? Again, it seems to make sense. But could it mean anything other than, 'It was meant to be a work of art, but is really a very bad one'? On the account suggested here the two amount to the same, in normal circumstances. In general, to be able to say that something is bad art, it must be intended as art in the first place. A shopping list is not bad poetry, it is none at all. Of course, a kind of shopping list can be intended by its author as poetry, and might then be said to be a piece of poetry, though perhaps a poor one.[9]

To sum up so far, the thesis that intentions play a conceptual role in the identification of works of art is required for the following two purposes: it allows for discrimination between works

---

[8] The fact that these beautiful artifacts, once discovered by European artists, have had an enormous impact on various modern genres, particularly on primitivism, does not prove the contrary; similar inspiring impact can be attributed to beautiful Tahitian women as well.

[9] Indeed it was characteristic of Dada, at some point, to employ this strategy of turning such banal objects into works of art, as it were, simply by presenting them as such. Marcel Duchamp's *Fountain*, an ordinary urinal, exhibited at a New York gallery in 1917, is a famous example.

of art and other aesthetic artifacts, and for discrimination between bad art and non-art.

This much might well be conceded by Dworkin. But, he would argue, identification in art, as in other interpretative enterprises, is basically a matter of agreement, of the consensus which happens to prevail at the pre-interpretative stage. One can easily envisage a very different conventional setting, in which the criteria would be quite different. As he puts it in the case of law, it 'cannot flourish as an interpretive enterprise in any community unless there is enough initial *agreement* about what practices are legal practices. . . . We all enter the history of an interpretive practice at a particular point; the necessary preinterpretive agreement is in that way *contingent and local*' (1986 : 91, my emphasis). There is a fairly obvious sense in which it is true that the identification of art is— within certain limits—a matter of consensus. Undoubtedly, in different cultures different things are identified as works of art. This means, for example, that we will probably be unable to specify universal criteria for the identification of works of art; that the criteria are at least partly contingent and culture dependent in a rather strong sense. But this is beside the point. Nothing in the argument so far presumes it possible to provide a *definition* of art (or law for that matter). Nor am I claiming that the conceptual relation between intentions and the identification of works of art is one of *entailment*. To begin with, it is not the case that anything one intends to create as a work of art is, *ipso facto*, a work of art. Surely people can intend to create a work of art without actually succeeding in doing so; intention is a criterion for the identification of art, but by no means the only one. Other criteria, such as public acceptability, institutional recognition and support, local and temporary conventions, etc., play equally important roles. Second, as I have already indicated, it is in the nature of criteria— as opposed to necessary conditions—to be defeasible. One can always imagine some unusual set of circumstances under which the pertinent criterion does not hold.

Furthermore, it is arguable that the concept of art, as opposed, perhaps, to the concept of aesthetics, is a cultural product *par excellence*. This means that the reference or extension of 'art' consists in what people in a given culture think it to be. But again, there is no presumption to the contrary here; the argument advocated so far does not present 'art' as an *indexical* word, referring to a 'real entity' whose existence and nature are independent of our knowledge. In other words, there is no need to be a realist with respect to the concept of art in order to deny the possibility of constructive identification; the latter is undermined by *conceptual* considerations.

Thus imagine, for example, a newly discovered culture in which the concept A stands for the following practice: shiny green stones, of which there is a scarcity, are collected by some of the people in this culture and exhibited in a way very similar to that in which portraits are exhibited in galleries. (One could push the similarity further: the culture includes distinguished stone collectors, private collections of shiny green stones, A experts, and so on.) Now, even if we could see the point in all this, there seems to be very little here which would warrant the conclusion that A amounts to a peculiar concept of art, or involves a peculiar artistic genre. Shiny green stones are not works of art, we would say. The concept A is simply too remote from our concept of art to be translated into 'art' in our language. Is this only a matter of agreement, of our shared convictions about the practices we identify as art? Yes, it is, but neither more nor less so than *language* is, in general.

Dworkin rightly distinguishes between conventions, properly so called, and shared convictions (1986:136). It is typical of the latter, but not of the former, that they can turn out to be wrong or false. The belief in the existence of witches was false, and the practice of burning them an iniquity. Rules of grammar, however, are neither true nor false (and neither right nor wrong). Furthermore, people cannot agree or disagree on something that makes no sense. It should be relatively easy to envisage the negation of anything that is purely a matter of shared convictions. For instance, it is a widely shared conviction that it is wrong to torture people just for fun. Yet we can make perfect sense of a denial of this view, that is, within our own language, our own conceptual scheme. This does not seem to be the case, however, with the contention that shiny green stones are not works of art. In short, it is the concept of art which rules out the possibility of constructive identification of works of art, not a contingent and local agreement.

Before we turn to the issue of constructive identification in law, another possible reply should be mentioned. It might be claimed that we got the question wrong from the outset. Instead of asking

'How do we identify something as a work of art?' we should have concentrated on the interpretative nature of art criticism, and asked about the identification of whatever is subject to interpretation in it. Surely, so the argument would continue, objects of art are not interpreted in isolation. Art criticism would be utterly incomplete if critics ignored the background on which works of art are created and understood, in particular, the pertinent genres to which given works are taken to belong. In other words, one cannot interpret a work of art without having formed a vision of the genre to which the work is taken to belong. Now, genres can be identified constructively: one need not presume that genres must be created as such. It is possible to account for the emergence of genres in terms of something like an 'invisible-hand explanation'; genres seem to manifest an overall pattern or design which could only have evolved through the successful attempts of a group of artists to realize the pattern or design. But in fact this semblance is often false. The overall pattern may not have been in anyone's mind, so to speak, at any particular point.

All this should be conceded. But the interpretative perspective should not obscure the fact that we can normally, and with no particular problems, distinguish very clearly between works of art and the genres of which they are instances. The fact that the interpretation of the former typically involves a certain vision of the latter is not evidence to the contrary. One never confuses genres with works of art, simply because genres are not the *kind of things* which can be works of art. The distinction here is quite instructive. It can shed light on the parallel distinction, in the case of law, between legal norms and institutions, and the (political) morality (or ideology, if one prefers) of which a given legal institution is taken to be a realization.

3. RAZIAN AUTHORITY AND CONSTRUCTIVE IDENTIFICATION IN LAW

I have tried to argue, thus far, that the identification of something as a work of art must typically rest on, *inter alia*, the presumption that it was intended to be a work of art; the object has to have been created as such. This rules out the possibility of constructive identification of works of art. But law, of course, may be quite different. The example of art is instructive, nevertheless, at least in one limited respect: it has shown that the value dependence of the interpretation of works of art does not entail the possibility of constructive identification. The latter is undermined by a conceptual constraint. A similar line of reasoning will be suggested here with respect to law. But it is similar only in a very abstract way. There are particular conceptual reasons due to which constructive identification in law is rendered impossible. These reasons, I shall argue, can be derived from Professor Raz's analysis of the concept of authority and its bearing on the concept of law. It is to these that I now turn.

Raz's doctrine of authority is well known, and a brief presentation of its essentials should suffice here.[10] It is presumed by this doctrine that all (efficacious) legal systems have *de facto* authority. This entails that the law either *claims* that it has legitimate authority over its subjects, is held to possess it, or both. (This feature of law, that it claims to be a legitimate authority, involves only the presumption that we discriminate between the kind of claims laid down by law, and those which would be laid down by a gang of robbers.) Raz's main argument then, is as follows: for something to be able to claim the possession of legitimate authority, it must typically be of *the kind of thing which is capable of possessing it*. Only certain kinds of thing can be considered as possessing authority, and only that which can be authoritative can either possess or fail to possess legitimate authority. Hence, since law claims to possess legitimate authority, although it can fail to possess it, it must have the requisite features of what might be called authority-capacity. Raz identifies two such features:

First, a directive can be authoritatively binding only if it is, or is at least presented as, someone's view of how its subjects ought to behave. Second, it must be possible to identify the directive as being issued by the alleged authority without relying on reasons or considerations on which the directive purports to adjudicate. (1985 : 303)

[10] The following discussion is based on 'Authority, Law and Morality' (Raz: 1985). Admittedly, the discussion will do little justice to the complexity of Raz's analysis of authority, nor will it attempt to capture all the possible aspects and implications of this analysis. In particular, Raz's argument that the authoritative nature of law undermines not only the coherence thesis but also what is often called 'soft positivism' cannot be explored here. The discussion will be guided by our interest in the possibility of constructive identification in law, and will thus be confined to a rather limited perspective. For further details and other implications of his analysis, see *The Morality of Freedom* (1986b) chs. 1–4; see also the Symposium on the works of Joseph Raz, 62 *Southern California Law Review*, 3 and 4 (1989), and Raz (1989).

Patently, both features of authority-capacity undermine the possibility of constructive identification. The first reflects the idea that only an agent capable of communication with others can have authority over them. As we have seen, nothing can be more straightforwardly opposed to the constructive identification thesis than the idea that law must be a product of communication, or at least presented as such.

Seeing how the second feature of authority-capacity is derived requires a closer look at Raz's analysis of practical authority. He takes the case of arbitration to represent a paradigmatic example of authority. The arbitrator's decision is meant to reflect certain reasons, to sum them up, and present their right balance. (Raz calls these 'dependent reasons'.) Since the arbitrator is there to settle a dispute, his decision must itself be taken as a reason for action on the part of the disputants. Thus, it must be distinguishable from those reasons which would have applied to the disputants directly, had there been no arbitration in the first place. (Raz also calls the latter reasons dependent reasons.) Thus, Raz's main insight is that 'the only proper way to acknowledge the arbitrator's authority is to take it to be a reason for action which replaces the reasons on the basis of which he was meant to decide' (1985 : 298). The outcome is the second feature of authority-capacity. If the authority's directives are meant to replace some of the reasons on the basis of which he was meant to decide, it must be possible for the disputants to *identify* his directive *independently* of those reasons. Again, this runs counter to the constructive identification thesis. According to the latter, the identification of law depends, partly, on considerations about what the law ought to be, namely, on considerations which the law is there to settle.

Hence, to maintain the constructive identification thesis one must either show what is wrong with Raz's analysis of authority, or show why legal norms need not be authoritative directives.[11] First, however, it will be useful to see how Raz summarizes his concept of authority, in the following three theses (1985 : 299):

---

[11] Notably, the requisite features of authority-capacity fit the standard sources of law, that is, not only legislation and judicial decisions, but custom as well. The latter, as lawyers know very well, is not only a matter of a regularity of behaviour but one which is guided by certain norms which are taken to be binding by the pertinent community. Thus, custom reflects the judgement of the bulk of a given community about how people ought to behave in the circumstances. See Raz (1985 : 306).

The Dependence Thesis:
All authoritative directives should be based, among other factors, on reasons which apply to the subjects of those directives . . . Such reasons I shall call dependent reasons.

The Normal Justification Thesis:
The normal and primary way to establish that a person should be acknowledged to have authority over another person involves showing that the alleged subject is likely better to comply with reasons which apply to him . . . if he accepts the directives of the authority as authoritatively binding and tries to follow them, than if he tries to follow the reasons which apply to him directly.

The Preemption Thesis:
The fact that an authority requires performance of an action is a reason for its performance which is not to be added to all other relevant reasons when assessing what to do, but should replace some of them.

The dependence thesis is unlikely to be disputed. In particular, it is difficult to see how someone can claim legitimate authority unless he claims to decide (at least partly) on reasons which apply to the alleged subjects. Of course, authorities can deceive, or fail to act on such reasons, but this is beside the point. Furthermore, suppose it is conceded that an authority might act on reasons aimed to benefit, say, X, when X is not an alleged subject of the authority. Even in this case, in claiming legitimacy, the authority would have to claim that the alleged subjects have a reason to benefit X, a reason which applies to them directly.

The normal justification thesis is also less controversial than might meet the eye. Some may tend to resist the claim that justifying one's compliance with an authority involves holding that the authority knows better what ought to be done, as it were. This might be conceded in certain cases. The alleged authority of parents over their young children, for instance, is typically justified by the assumption that parents are more likely to know what is best for their children. Yet one would be inclined to deny that this holds in other cases, particularly in that of political authorities. However, nothing that strong is entailed by the normal justification thesis. What has to be shown is that the authority is somehow better situated to decide what its subjects ought to do, which is not always a matter of 'knowing what is best', so to speak. Legitimacy in issuing authoritative directives may be due to the special circumstances of the given situation, rather than to any personal merits or expertise. This is typically the case when the authoritative directives are meant to solve co-ordination problems, or in prisoner's dilemma situations (Raz 1986b : 56).[12]

Furthermore, even those who might wish to claim that the justification of political authorities can only be derived from certain doctrines about the special tasks they are meant to perform, must nevertheless appeal to the normal justification thesis. Suppose it is held that the main task of political authorities is to maintain the peace and to monopolize the use of force in society. (These are dependent reasons.) The justification of political authority would then depend on its degree of success in maintaining peace, and on the relative merit of this objective as compared to other, potentially competing values. In any case, the justification of authority would be incomplete and the question begged, in the absence of an explanation as to why public peace (or anything else) could not be maintained just as well were people to fail to comply with the authority's directives. Thus again, what is appealed to is the normal justification thesis.

Finally, it should be emphasized that the normal justification thesis provides a necessary, but not a sufficient, condition for the legitimacy of authorities (Raz 1986b : 56). For a given authority to be legitimate, further conditions must be satisfied. In general, it must be shown that there are no reasons against complying with the authority which override the reasons for complying with it (ibid.). In particular, Raz emphasizes the need to satisfy 'the condition of autonomy', that 'the matter (over which someone is said to have authority) is not one which it is more important that people should decide for themselves than that they should decide correctly' (Raz 1989 : 1180).

The pre-emption thesis is the one most likely to prove controversial.[13] Fortunately, however, for the purposes of our discussion it is unnecessary to defend this thesis. As Raz himself

---

[12] I do not intend to claim that the solutions of all co-ordination problems require authoritative resolutions. On the contrary, most that we encounter are resolved without the help of authorities.

[13] The pre-emption thesis entails that an authority's directives yield a kind of exclusionary reason for its alleged subjects, i.e. those who have reasons to comply with the authority's directives in the first place. Assessing what to do, the subject has to exclude reliance on the dependent reasons. The concept of exclusionary reasons was presented in Raz (1975 : 35–48). For a critical review of Raz's account of exclusionary reasons see e.g. Moore (1989b).

clarifies (1985 : 305), the pertinent features of authority-capacity do not necessarily depend on the pre-emption thesis (though they are entailed by it). Suppose the pre-emption thesis is denied, that is, authorities' directives are held to yield reasons for action which are not meant to replace any of those on whose basis the authority was to decide, but only meant to be *added* to the balance of reasons the subjects must assess. This seems to be the view advocated by Dworkin (1986 : 429) in his reply to Raz's analysis:

[Raz] is right that any successful interpretation of our legal practice must recognize and justify the common assumption that law can compete with morality and wisdom and, for those who accept law's authority, override these other virtues in their final decision about what they should do. . . . Raz thinks law cannot be authoritative unless those who accept it *never* use their own convictions to decide what it requires, even in this partial way. But why must law be blind authority rather than authoritative in the more relaxed way other conceptions assume?

Suppose this view is accepted, the pre-emption thesis rejected, and the authority's directives taken to result only in additions to the overall balance of reasons for action. Even in this case, an authority's directive would have to be identified *as such*. It has to be identified as a directive issued by an authority, and the reasons it yields as reasons to be added to, and weighed against, other reasons for action. In other words, the requisite features of authority-capacity as identified by Raz may be defended without subscribing to his view that an authority's directives create reasons for action which exclude the consideration of (or always override) the reasons which would otherwise apply directly to the alleged subjects. It is quite sufficient to admit (as Dworkin seems to in this passage) that they create distinct reasons which *can* override other prudential or moral reasons for action. In any case, the alleged subjects would have to be able to identify authoritative directives independently of, and as distinct from, other reasons. If determining what the law is involves considerations about what the law is there to settle, how can it compete with, even if it does not necessarily override, that which the law is there to settle? To conclude: the argument quoted above hits the wrong mark; repudiating the pre-emption thesis does not save the constructive identification thesis.

The main argument against the Razian analysis, however, is a decidedly different one. Dworkin would argue that Raz's account, irrespective of the details, must have gone wrong somewhere since it does not fit the practice of adjudication. Furthermore, as far as Raz's analysis is a conceptual one, it fails on its own terms: judges and lawyers do not use the term 'law' as this analysis would have it. Norms and principles are often considered legally binding despite the fact that no one in any authoritative capacity has issued them. Admittedly, Raz's analysis makes allowance for the possibility that a norm is considered to be a legal norm because it is *presented* as an expression of an authority's view about how its subjects ought to behave, without this actually being the case. But this only brings us back to the pretence story:[14] a subscriber to the Razian analysis of law must maintain that adjudication often involves a kind of pretence, which occurs whenever judges claim to follow the law, where in fact there is no law to follow since the pertinent norm does not result from any authoritative directive.

Notably, on Dworkin's own account, the force of this objection is somewhat more limited than might seem to be the case. Fit, it should be remembered, is a rather flexible notion; it admits of degrees and it is sensitive to various evaluative considerations. So the question is not 'Does it fit?', but rather, 'Which account fits better? Furthermore, the suggestion that Raz's analysis fails on its own terms is potentially misleading. True, a conceptual analysis must fit ordinary usage. But one cannot ignore the possibility that language itself is so very often conceptually misleading. As Wittgenstein has shown, a great deal of philosophical confusion stems from the tendency to project a conceptual scheme from one language game to another, just because the two are superficially similar. Judges and lawyers should not be presumed to be exempt from such confusions.

It is presumably clear to anyone familiar with the politics of law, that at least sometimes judges have very good reason to claim that they are following the law when they are in fact inventing it. This kind of pretence is far from seeming nonsensical or mysterious. In other words, the question now facing us is not whether the pretence story makes any sense at all. It is, rather, a question of quantity, as it were: what level of pretence (and confusion) can be allowed without the result being an absurd picture of adjudication? Admittedly, it is difficult to say how one would go about trying to answer this question. Instead, let me mention a few

---

[14] See Ch. 1.

possible considerations which might mitigate the mystery of the alleged discrepancy between theory and practice.

First, a more accurate picture of the proportions should be of assistance: how often do judges claim to follow legal norms while in fact relying on extra-legal material? In view of the vast number of legal disputes which never even reach the courts, and the vast number of 'easy' cases settled unproblematically in the humdrum routine of adjudication (especially in the lower courts), a more precise idea may be formed of what people regard as the law of their land. (Paradoxically, both laymen and law students get a rather distorted picture in this respect. The former typically assume that law settles more than it actually does. Law students, on the other hand, typically read about the more problematic questions submitted to the courts of appeal, and are hence prone to the impression that most legal cases are hard ones.)

Furthermore, Dworkin's most convincing examples concern constitutional cases from the American Supreme Court, which of course is not surprising, for two main reasons. First, a legal system based on a written constitution is bound to be concerned with special problems. Predictably, these will emerge from the tensions between the relative importance of the constitutional provisions and their condensed and rather laconic formulation. (Think for instance how much depends on the interpretation of the words 'due process of law' in the Fourteenth Amendment.) Second, in a democratic country where the (appointed) Supreme Court has the power to overturn first-order legislation, the court is bound to be under enormous political pressure. It has more political power than either the public or the judges themselves would like to admit. (Again, one should not distort the picture by ignoring the actual politics. People are not ignorant of the enormous political power vested in their Supreme Court judges. This is manifest in the great concern about the judges' appointment and their political records.[15])

Thus, as one looks at the politics behind the constitutional structure of the American legal system, the cloud of mystery seems to dissipate. Hard cases in American constitutional law, particularly those involving controversial instances of judicial review, are

---

[15] This only serves to show that people are more aware of the judges' power and practice to create new law, even in fundamental issues at the front of American politics, than one might think from the picture as depicted by Dworkin.

typical examples where a kind of pretence in adjudication makes perfect sense. But of course, the need for pretence does not always have to be so straightforwardly political. To mention just one example, consider the possibility of overturning a judicial decision by an act of legislation: its acceptance is likely to be more readily achieved when the judicial decision is presented as a novelty in the first place, rather than as an interpretation of the existing law.[16] Thus, somewhat paradoxically, the more reason judges have to fear the possible overturning of their decision (that is, one which creates new law) by legislation, the more reason they have to present it as if it were an interpretation of the existing law.

Finally, but not of least importance, it should be kept in mind that many hard cases can be found where judges do not pretend at all to apply or interpret the existing law; they explicitly admit to a gap in the law, and to the fact that their decision (if followed as a precedent) will amount to the creation of new law. In short, the examples—when taken at face value—are not conclusive; the apparent discrepancy goes either way.

A somewhat similar objection to the Razian analysis of law's authoritative nature has been raised recently by Moore. Although it does not dwell on the pretence problem, it also maintains that the Razian analysis yields an unacceptably simplistic view about what judges do when they interpret the law:

> The problem of Raz's exclusionary reason account of a statute's authority is that it excludes just the materials a judge needs to make a fully reason based interpretation of any statute. For *plain meaning* and *legislative intention* are inadequate materials for the application of any statute to any case. (Moore 1989*b* : 891, my emphasis.)

The objection is not made explicit here, as it is in Moore's earlier writings, the details of which cannot be explored by the present discussion. Two prevalent sources of confusion should, however, be mentioned; both will be taken up again in the next two chapters.

The first part of Moore's objection may be understood in both a weak and a strong sense. It is arguable that Raz's pre-emption thesis puts too strong a constraint on interpretation of the law. When an authoritative directive is ambiguous or otherwise

---

[16] A pertinent piece of folk psychology: people are happier to find others wrong than to admit their own mistakes.

unclear, reference to the dependent reasons might be required in order to establish the content of the authority's directive more precisely. When judges interpret the law, they often have to rely on considerations about that which the law is there to settle, yet— within certain limits—they can still be said to be following the law, not inventing it.

Be this as it may, the objection that Moore is putting forth is much stronger than this. His contention is that authoritative directives can never be applied without relying on the dependent reasons. As he puts it, 'plain meanings *cannot* guide judicial interpretations of statutes by themselves' (1989*b* : 891).

As far as this view depends on the assumption that all understanding of language and communication involves inter-pretation, it involves a fallacy. As we have seen elsewhere,[17] it ignores the fact that an understanding of the language is required to make interpretation possible in the first place. In short, Moore is right in presuming that Raz's analysis would be rendered implausible and rather vacuous if it were the case that law could never be applied straightforwardly, as it were. But law, like any other form of communication, can simply be understood, and then applied. Interpretation is the exceptional, not the standard mode of understanding language.

The second part of the objection involves another fallacy, one which should be obvious by now. Raz's analysis dwells on the role of intentions in the *identification* of law. It repudiates the constructive identification thesis on the grounds that a directive cannot be identified as a legal directive, unless it is presumed to have been intended as such. But we have already seen that the role of intentions in the identification of things under a covering concept has no direct bearing on the way a text should be interpreted. Raz is not committed to the view that one is confined to an attempt to retrieve the authority's intentions in order to determine the content of an authoritative directive. On the contrary, Raz's analysis can be employed to elucidate some of the conditions under which it would be reasonable to allude to the authority's intentions when assessing how to read its directives. These possibilities will be explored in Chapter 8. The following is merely a schematic outline

[17] Ch. 2.

Generally, the desirability of deferring to a given authority's intentions depends on the kind of authority in question and one's reasons for complying with its directives in the first place. If one's reasons for complying are based on the assumption that the authority *knows* better what should be done in the circumstances, then it would be sensible to take its intentions into account when its directive is not perspicuous. Suppose I have acknowledged someone's authority over me concerning the question of what kind of computer I should buy, as I take him to be an expert on such matters. Now suppose he has advised me to purchase a certain computer, while—as it happens—there are two kinds of computer that fit his description. Given that he intended me to buy one particular kind, to attempt to clarify his intention would be the sensible thing to do.

Arguably, as we have seen, one's reasons for complying with political authorities are mainly of a different nature. One would have to be a hopeless optimist to presume that political authorities were experts in all the realms subject to their jurisdiction. In numerous cases, one's reasons for complying with the directives of political authorities are not based on the assumption that legislators *know* better what ought to be done. Thus, when their directives are open to different interpretations, a judge has no particular reason, that is, a reason based on the authoritative nature of law *ipso facto*, to decide the case according to the legislator's intentions (even if the legislator had such an intention and it is discernible).[18]

To conclude, Moore errs in assuming that the authoritative account of law renders adjudication implausible as it would require constant reliance on legislative intentions. He would seem to be challenging windmills here.

[18] This is not to say that one cannot put forward other reasons, which are not based on the authoritative nature of law, why judges should be concerned with legislators' intentions. But this of course is beside the point.

7

NO EASY CASES?

MOORE'S objection to the Razian analysis of law, mentioned at the end of the previous chapter, is in fact only a particular instance of a more general argument aimed at undermining legal positivism: the latter can be said to be committed to the thesis that a distinction exists between (so-called) easy cases, where the law can be applied straightforwardly, and hard cases, where the issue is not determined by the existing legal standards. The objection I intend to examine here consists in the claim that this is in fact an illusory distinction, there being, in all the relevant respects, no easy cases as the positivist would presume.

This chapter sets out to disprove the above argument. I shall begin by explaining why legal positivism is, indeed, committed to the distinction between easy and hard, and in what sense this is so. I shall then go on to defend the distinction in question against the various arguments offered against it.

I. A SCARECROW CALLED FORMALISM

One of the main tenets of legal positivism is its insistence on the conceptual separation between law as it is and law as it ought to be.[1] As stated in the previous chapter, this separation thesis necessarily involves the assumption that judges can (at least in some standard sense, that is) *identify* the law and *apply* it without reference to considerations about what the law ought to be in the circumstances. In other words, the distinction between the law as it is and the law as it ought to be entails a parallel distinction between the activities of *applying* the law and *creating* it. This also suggests a particular view about the role of interpretation in adjudication. Interpretation is typically meant to designate a (partly) creative activity; it has to do with determining the meaning of that which is in some relevant respect unclear or

---

[1] This formulation is notoriously too crude and conceals various and rather distinct positions, but for our present purposes, these complexities can be ignored.

indeterminate. Put somewhat loosely, one could say that interpretation adds something new, previously unrecognized, to that which is being interpreted. Taken together with the previous point, it entails that legal positivism cannot accept the view that law is always subject to interpretation. To a greater or lesser extent, judges grantedly participate, through their interpretative activities, in the process of creating the law. First, however, there must be a law there to interpret.

The fact that the distinction between easy and hard cases is entailed, or rather required, by the distinction between the law as it is and the law as it ought to be, is of course of little help in the present context. The argument offered by the line of criticism presently under discussion is that the latter should be rejected precisely because the former is indefensible. What we should ask then, is whether the distinction between easy and hard cases has any conceptual basis which is independent of the legal positivist doctrine. The most prominent attempt to propound such a foundation is Professor Hart's distinction between the *core* and *penumbra* of concept-words, which he placed at the root of judicial reasoning. Consider this, by now very famous, passage:

A legal rule forbids you to take a vehicle into the public park. Plainly this forbids an automobile, but what about bicycles, roller skates, toy automobiles? What about aeroplanes? Are these, as we say, to be called 'vehicles' for the purposes of the rule or not? *If we are to communicate* with each other at all . . . [and] *behaviour be regulated by rules*, then the general words we use—like 'vehicle' in the case I consider—must have some standard instance in which no doubts are felt about its application. There must be a *core* of settled meaning, but there will be, as well, a *penumbra* of debatable cases in which words are neither obviously applicable nor obviously ruled out. (1958 : 63, emphasis mine.)

This short passage epitomizes Hart's thinking on our present subject. Simple as it sounds, however, it has been gravely misunderstood. This chapter sets out to defend the view encapsulated in this passage, in two ways. First, I shall try to undermine the various criticisms put forward against it. Second, I hope to demonstrate that Hart's insight here is well entrenched in a highly sophisticated conception of meaning and language, namely, that of Wittgenstein.

The gist of Hart's thesis may be summed up as follows: the formulation of legal rules in a natural language makes their meanings depend, primarily, on the meanings of the concept-words used in these formulations. Since the meaning of a concept-word consists in (*inter alia*) its *use*, there must always be standard instances in which the application of the concept-word is unproblematic. This is what Hart calls the core of meaning. However, since most of the concept-words in our language are somewhat vague and without a totally determinate meaning, their application to the facts will always involve some borderline cases. These are what he calls the penumbra, consisting in the absence of agreement as to the word's applicability. In these cases, the fit between facts and concept-word is an issue which must be determined according to various non-linguistic considerations, such as the presumed purpose of the rule. But, and this is the controversial point, when the facts do fit the core of the pertinent concept-words of the rule in question, the application of the rule is obvious and unproblematic, and this is what is meant, in (the rather unfortunate) jurisprudential jargon, by the term 'easy' case.

It is important to bear in mind, however, that the view presented here is very schematic; adjudication is of course much more complex a practice than Hart's simple example might be understood to suggest. The following are only a few examples: first, most of the rules confronting a judge are already directly or indirectly 'loaded' with previous interpretations. Second, in instances requiring the extraction of rules from precedents, their formulation would typically be much more difficult to determine. Third, the individuation of legal rules often depends upon other legal rules or fragments of them (for instance, a rule determining the amount of income tax for a certain level of earnings must be supplemented by the rules defining 'income', 'tax', etc.).

Notwithstanding these complexities, and many others I have not mentioned, it would be a mistake, or at least premature at this stage, to dismiss Hart's distinction between easy and hard cases as over simplistic. In particular, it would be misguided to pronounce Hart's thesis necessarily inadequate since adjudication is not merely a matter of applying rules. First, it should be realized that Hart is not offering a comprehensive theory of adjudication based on the distinction between easy and hard cases. The distinction is meant to illuminate one important aspect of judicial reasoning which is, however, by no means the only one. Secondly, one can hardly deny that the application of rules is at least the core of judicial reasoning. No reasonable account of the latter could be provided, without an explication of what understanding, following, and applying a rule consist in. It still remains to be seen whether complexities of various kinds cast any doubts on this basic model, as it is suggested by Hart, but this should not prevent anyone from taking the basic model seriously, despite its apparent simplicity.

Before embarking on our main project, that is, examining Hart's thesis in detail, several somewhat crude misconstruals should be set aside. First, one cannot overemphasize the warning that the terms 'easy' and 'hard' cases are potentially misleading. The distinction has nothing at all to do with the amount of intellectual effort required in order to decide a legal case. As Raz once pointed out, deciding an easy case in, for example, tax law (that is, a case which is wholly determined by the legal standards) might be much more difficult than deciding many another hard case (Raz 1977 : 182). Nor is there any intended implication here that application of the law in easy cases is in some way 'mechanical' or 'automatic', as is sometimes suggested. There is nothing mechanical about the application of a rule to a particular case, nor is there necessarily anything complex or difficult about solving most of the hard cases. If any distinction were to be drawn between more and less 'mechanical' applications of rules, it would pertain to the complexity of the operations required by the rule, and not to the distinction between easy and hard cases, in the sense being used here.[2]

More significantly, the distinction between easy and hard cases (whether in legal positivism in general, or in Hart's particular version of it) is sometimes associated with a philosophical scarecrow called judicial formalism (see Moore 1981 : 155–63). The latter is taken to suggest that judicial reasoning, that is, the application of rules to given facts, is a matter of *logical inference* expressible in terms of analytical truths, while the positivist doctrine that there are easy cases is taken to be some type of endorsement of formalism. Needless to say, formalism is then easily undermined and the entire move considered a serious critique of legal positivism. The truth is that formalism is so

---

[2] e.g. think of the difference between carrying out an order to continue an arithmetical series, say $n + 2$, and attempting a more complicated one, $13 + n^2 \times 0.5$, both of which would be 'easy' cases.

obviously false as to require an explanation of why it should be associated with Hart's doctrine in the first place. It is easily discernible that whatever it is that connects a rule to its application cannot consist of logic or analyticity.[3] The move is even more perplexing when we recall that it was Hart himself who repeatedly exposed such a view as a fallacy (1958 : 67; 1967 : 100–6).

To pinpoint what seems to lie at the source of this confusion, consider Hart's example once again. A legal rule forbids the entrance of vehicles into the public park; Hart's contention that 'plainly this forbids an automobile' is understood to be a statement made true by its very meaning, hence an analytical truth. Given this construal, the view that in easy cases the legal conclusion is logically deduced from certain premises, that is, rule formulations and statements expressing the classification of the pertinent particulars, would seem easily attributable to Hart. But in fact the picture here is utterly confused. The concepts of logical inference and analyticity apply only to interrelations between rules or expressions, not to their application to the world. As Hart puts it, 'logic is silent on how to classify particulars' (1958 : 67), but it is precisely this classification to which his distinction between core and penumbra pertains. In other words, we must keep separate what might be called 'rule-rule' and 'rule-world', relations; logic and analyticity pertain only to the former, not to the latter kind of relation. The fact that in both cases the criteria for correctness are semantic should not obscure this crucial difference. Suppose someone is pointing at a red object in front of him, saying, 'This is red.' When asked to justify this assertion, one can only appeal to the *meaning* of 'red'; one would say that this is what 'red' means, thus appealing to a *rule* about how a word is used in English. Surely, though, it makes no sense at all to say that we have a logical inference here, or that the ostension expresses an analytical statement. (This is unlike the statement 'Bachelor = unmarried man' which does not concern the application of rules, or expressions, but the semantic relation between them.)

In short, formalism is a scarecrow; neither Hart nor any other legal positivist must subscribe to the view that the application of legal rules is a matter of logical inference. This is not to say that

---

[3] This should not be confused with a different thesis, namely, that the law of universal instantiation ($(X)Fx$ infer Fa) ultimately mediates between the rule and its application. For a rejection of this idea see Baker and Hacker (1985 : 92–3).

Hart's distinction between easy and hard cases is unproblematic, but only that one should concentrate on the serious problems, of which formalism is not one.

2. THE HART — FULLER DEBATE

Professor Fuller's objections to the Hartian distinction between easy and hard cases may still constitute the most elaborate criticism of this thesis, one deserving a close examination. Fuller (1958:661 ff.) understands Hart's thesis to be based on three assumptions, of which he accepts none. The first of these would construe interpretation of a legal rule as a matter of interpreting the concept-words it deploys. The second would hold that the interpretation of concept-words in legal rules is (or ought to be) determined by the ordinary use of these terms in natural language. The third alleged assumption of Hart's, possibly taken to be entailed by the previous two points, is that the meaning of concept-words is insensitive to the particular legal context in which these words are meant to function.

Fuller's main criticism then, is aimed against these three assumptions. However, he also attributes to Hart the view that unless these assumptions are maintained, 'we must surrender all hope of giving an effective meaning to the ideal of fidelity to law' (Fuller 1958:664). Fuller accordingly attempts to add another level of criticism in showing that the ideal of fidelity to law is not jeopardized if one rejects the allegedly Hartian position.

Let us take a closer look at the details of Fuller's account. Hart's first alleged assumption, that the interpretation of a legal rule is purely a matter of determining the concept-words it deploys, forms the target of Fuller's most vigorous attack:

The most obvious defect of his theory lies in its assumption that problems of interpretation typically turn on the meaning of individual words.

If the rule excluding vehicles from parks seems easy to apply in some cases, I submit this is because we can see clearly enough what the rule 'is aiming at in general' so that we know there is no need to worry about the difference between Fords and Cadillacs. (1958:662–3)

By way of demonstrating, Fuller asks us to consider whether the rule excluding vehicles from the park would apply to a group of local patriots who want, as a memorial, to mount on a pedestal in the park a truck used in World War II. 'Does this truck, in perfect working order, fall within the core or the penumbra?' he then asks (1958:663). His point here is actually twofold: first, that understanding a rule is always a matter of determining its purpose, and that it is only in the light of this purposive interpretation that one can judge whether the rule's application to the facts of a given case is to be relatively easy or difficult. Second, since the purpose of a rule can only be determined in the light of considerations as to what the rule is there to settle, 'it is in the light of this "ought" that we must decide what the rule "is" ' (1958:666).

The basis for the criticism of Hart's second alleged assumption is somewhat more obscure, partly because it is not fully stated. Instead, we are left with a vague disavowal of 'common usage' as the basis for the analysis of meaning, as it is said to ignore or underestimate the 'speaker's purpose and the structure of language' (1958:669). In all, this is meant to imply that Hart's concept of interpretation is based on an inadequate theory of meaning. Fuller, though, does not discuss the kind of theory of meaning Hart supposedly has in mind, nor does he elaborate on the grounds for its inadequacy. The reader is more or less left in the lurch. In any case, the question of whether Hart's thesis is based on a particular conception of meaning, and to what extent, is an interesting one in its own right, and I shall discuss it in the sequel.

Hart's third alleged assumption as Fuller outlines it, and accordingly Fuller's objection, in fact amount to a misunderstanding. The idea that concept-words used in the formulation of legal rules ought to be interpreted so as to assign them the same meaning in each and every occurrence, irrespective of the particular context in which the rule functions, is one which quite obviously ought to be dismissed outright. There is no reason to contend that the word 'vehicle,' for instance, should be assigned the same meaning in the rule forbidding vehicles in the park, and a rule concerning the insurance of vehicles. But the real question is whether or not Hart is committed to maintain the contrary. The answer to this, I think, is 'No'. To begin with, Hart can only be taken to be committed to the view that the *core* of concept-words, as opposed to their penumbra, remains constant across different rules. Thus, he would say that an ordinary automobile should be taken as a standard example of 'vehicle' if anything is, so that any rule concerning 'vehicles' must be taken to apply to *inter alia*, ordinary automobiles. Conversely, it is quite clear that he would not hold this true with respect to the question of whether or not bicycles are also 'vehicles' for the purposes of different rules. But even this point (which Fuller seems to ignore) should not be overstated. Hart was very much aware of the fact that numerous concepts form family-resemblance concepts, in which even the core, that is, standard examples, might vary from case to case. (This point will be explained in greater detail below.)

Furthermore, there is no need to deny that in some unusual circumstances a judge might face the possibility that the application of a rule to a given case in keeping with the core of the pertinent concept-word would lead to unacceptable results, and hence decide that even an ordinary automobile was not a 'vehicle' for the purposes of the rule at hand. The question is whether or not in this case the judge properly can be said to have *applied* the rule, and this clearly depends on the soundness of the point raised by Fuller's first objection (and perhaps the second as well). We are thus left with Fuller's first two objections, and I shall begin by considering the second.

Recall that what we are faced with is the question of whether Hart's distinction between core and penumbra commits him to any particular theory of meaning, and, if so, to what extent. It is a biographical fact, based on Hart's own account (cf. 1983: introduction), that he has been greatly influenced by various philosophers of language, particularly Wittgenstein and Austin. But I would suggest that as someone who has learnt from (the later) Wittgenstein, Hart would have avoided any attempt to construct what is usually called a *theory* of meaning for a natural language. One of the main insights of Wittgenstein's later work consists in pointing out the futility of such a project and the misconceptions it would involve (cf. Hacker 1986: ch. 6; McGinn 1984: 29), and there is no evidence to suggest that Hart has ever dissented from this point. On the contrary, Hart seems to share Wittgenstein's view that an adequate account of meaning and language must not obscure the fact that the meaning of the words we use is completely overt and manifest in their use. In other words, as long as the idea of a theory of meaning is understood in its contemporary sense (for example, Davidson's), namely, as a quasi-scientific explanation of meaning, it should not be assumed that Hart had any such theory in mind.

Wittgenstein's impact is, however, the most evident in Hart's treatment of the indeterminacy of sense, which underlines his distinction between core and penumbra. He is usually understood to have adopted Wittgenstein's views here, and it might be instructive to trace some of these ideas back to their source. The requirement that sense be determinate has been propounded by Frege (and the early Wittgenstein) and preoccupied him for various theoretical reasons. In general, he thought an ideally scientific language would have to be one in which all expressions had a determinant sense. He defined the latter as follows: A word/ sentence has a determinate sense if and only if, for every possible object, there is a definite answer to the question of whether it is within the extension (or reference) of the word/sentence or not. It is worth mentioning that Frege did not consider this requirement to be satisfied in our natural languages. On the contrary, he saw natural language as hopelessly contaminated by vagueness. (See Dummett 1981 : 31–5, 48, 316, 440.)

The later Wittgenstein not only discarded this Fregeian version of the requirement for the determinacy of sense, but also was anxious to show that it made no sense whatsoever. It is only if one presumes that there is more to the meaning of an expression than what is perspicuous in the practices of using it and explaining its meaning, that it would make sense to impose this requirement on any language, be it natural or scientific (see Baker and Hacker 1980b : 225). However, as this presumption is utterly mistaken—as Wittgenstein strove to demonstrate throughout the *Philosophical Investigations*—Frege's notion of the determinacy of sense emerges, in turn, as intrinsically incoherent.

Does this mean that all the words in our language are vague? That of course depends upon what we mean by 'vague'. If we understand vagueness to mean that in the practice of applying a word there are irresolvable disagreements in judgement over certain areas of its application, then it is obviously true that most concept-words are vague. Yet, in order to be more accurate, vagueness should be distinguished from 'open texture' and family resemblance. The former term (coined by Waismann[4]) is meant to designate the *possibility* of vagueness. Even terms which are not vague are potentially so, since one can always imagine circum-

---

[4] This is not to imply that Wittgenstein would subscribe to Waismann's analysis of 'open texture'. See Baker and Hacker (1980a : 170).

stances where there would be irresolvable disagreements in judgements as to the word's applicability. That Wittgenstein would subscribe to the view that most of the words in our language are at least possibly vague is quite undisputable (cf. PI, sect. 187) yet one would be on safe ground in presuming that he would not have attached great significance to this fact; 'The sign-post is in order—if, under normal circumstances, it fulfils its purpose' (PI sect. 87).

More importantly, vagueness should also be distinguished from family resemblance. The latter designates a concept-word which is applied to various phenomena where 'these phenomena have no one thing in common which makes us use the same word for all' (PI sect. 65). Instead, these phenomena are linked to each other by numerous and complex *similarities*, which Wittgenstein illustrates by the famous metaphor of 'family resemblance' (PI sect. 67), and it is only due to these similarities that distinct phenomena are called by the same concept-word. The idea that our language comprises family-resemblance concepts is perhaps one of Wittgenstein's least controversial contributions to philosophy of language, and there is no need to expand on it here. What we do have to address, however, is the question of whether or not the distinction between vagueness and family resemblance has any bearing upon Hart's thesis.

On the one hand the following difference is obvious: in the case of vagueness, the standard examples would share something which makes us use the same word for them all, whereas in the case of family resemblance we would face multifarious standard instances which do not share any single defining feature. This of course, makes the distinction between core and penumbra more intricate in the latter case.[5] On the other hand, Hart's thesis remains basically untouched by this difference: any concept-word, whether vague or one of family resemblance, must have standard examples which manifest agreement in judgements of its applicability. Although no single defining feature shared by all the standard examples can be specified in the latter case, this does not mean that they are not standard examples. Suppose we cannot find any one feature due to which chess, football, and patience are all

---

[5] The difference might also have a bearing on analogical reasoning in adjudication, but this point cannot be explored here.

called 'games'; does this mean that any of them is not a standard example of 'game'? Clearly not. On the contrary, this only shows the crucial importance of the idea that a great deal of agreement must exist as to what the standard examples of our concept-words are. In the absence of such agreement, the successful employment of family-resemblance concepts would have remained a total mystery.

Thus we can see that vagueness, open texture, and family resemblance all support the thesis that the concept-words we employ must have a core of meaning, that is, standard examples which manifest agreement in judgements about the word's applicability. These standard examples are used in our everyday explanations of what words mean, and we often have no better explanation of a word's meaning than to point to its standard examples. Furthermore, standard examples provide the *criteria* for correct understanding of expressions. Under normal circumstances, someone who does not recognize the applicability of a word to its standard examples manifests that he has not mastered its use. And vice versa, since understanding the meaning of an expression consists in the ability to use (and explain) it correctly, the ability to specify the standard instances of its applicability can usually be taken to show that one has understood the meaning of a given expression.

Notably, at some point Fuller seems to be challenging the picture of meaning depicted here. As an example, he takes the word 'improvement' in the rule, 'All improvements ought to be promptly reported', which he claims 'is almost as devoid of meaning as the symbol "X"' (1958:665). He then goes on to demonstrate the disambiguation of 'improvement' in this sentence according to various assumptions about communication intentions and context, with a particular emphasis on the purpose of the pertinent rule. All this is taken to demonstrate something like the profound context dependence of meaning in general (1958: 667–8).

However, Fuller's discussion here is rather confused. If a word is 'almost as devoid of meaning as the symbol "X"', then it cannot be disambiguated. Disambiguation can only take place when an expression has several possible meanings, not when it is devoid of meaning. In other words, either a word has meaning, in which case it can be used, and hence it must also have standard examples, or it is devoid of meaning, in which case it simply cannot be used. Words can be more or less vague, but not without meaning at all. Therefore, what Fuller's example would seem to demonstrate, is that the word 'improvement' is (perhaps) a family-resemblance concept and hence has multifarious standard examples. This in itself, as we have seen, does not undermine Hart's thesis.

3. THE ARGUMENT FROM DEFEASIBILITY

Let us return to Fuller's first and most important objection to Hart's thesis. As we have seen, he claims that Hart's thesis is intelligible only against the assumption that the interpretation of a legal rule is a matter of determining the concept-words it employs, an assumption to which he objects forcefully. Fuller's objection comprises two main theses: first, that understanding a rule must always involve an understanding of its particular purposes; second, and as a consequence of the fact that determining the purpose of a rule typically involves considerations about what the rule is there to settle, 'it is in the light of this ought that we must decide what the rule is' (1958 : 666).

I shall now concentrate on Fuller's first thesis, while assuming that the second is relatively sound. I shall attempt to show that understanding a rule does not necessarily require a grasp of its purpose, and if this is accomplished, Fuller's second thesis will in turn be rendered harmless.

One of the prominent arguments thought to support Fuller's thesis is what might be called 'the argument from defeasibility':[6] since it is the case that any legal rule—if construed literally— might, under certain circumstances, have utterly immoral or otherwise absurd results, a judge must always ask himself whether the case before him is one in which the results would be unacceptable if the rule were thus applied. The fact that the answer is often obvious, so the argument continues, does not mean that the question need not always be asked and answered. Thus the application of a legal rule to any set of facts necessitates that

---

[6] The term should not be thought to imply that the argument explored here dwells upon Hart's ideas as expressed in his inaugural lecture (see 1983 : 21–48). There he suggested the existence of a kind of defeasibility endemic in legal language which renders it *sui generis*, a view which he seems to have abandoned shortly afterwards. See Baker (1977). As opposed to Baker, though, I do not find that this thesis is being restated in *The Concept of Law*.

the judge consider the purpose of the rule and ask himself whether the purposes at play would not in fact be defeated were the rule to be construed literally. This, in turn, is taken to entail that it never makes sense to speak of a straightforward, or literal, application of a rule, as Hart's thesis maintains (see Moore 1981 : 277–9).

There are several strands of confusion here which ought to be unravelled. Immediate reflection should find the argument rather puzzling: it seems to hold that since any rule, if construed literally, *can* result in absurd consequences, it follows that no rule can be construed literally, which is an obvious fallacy. Thus, if the argument from defeasibility is to make any sense at all, its conclusion must be revised. The argument should be taken to lead to a prescriptive conclusion as to what judges ought to do. This, in fact, is just how Moore understands (and subscribes to) Fuller's argument; Fuller's best argument, he says, 'is a normative one urging judges to *disregard* that meaning when it does not fit into their notion of the rule's purpose' (1981 : 277). Understood in view of such a prescriptive conclusion, the argument would be stated as follows: Any rule, if construed literally, can lead to absurd consequences, and accordingly judges should always ask themselves whether this danger is present and, when it is, decide according to standards which would avert the iniquity.

But if the argument is understood in this way, it cuts no ice in the dispute with Hart (or with any other legal positivist for that matter). Moore's version of the argument confuses the question of what *following a rule consists in* (which interested Hart), with that of *whether a rule should be applied in the circumstances*. Even if we concede that judges should always ask themselves the latter question (which is far from clear), it does not follow that rules cannot be understood, and then applied, without reference to their alleged purposes or any other considerations about what the rule is there to settle.

Let me expound this point, since it is of crucial importance. It should be kept in mind that our discussion commenced with the positivist doctrine about the separation between law as it is and law as it ought to be. We have seen that for this thesis (in either the Hartian or Razian version) to be acceptable, it must be accompanied by the assumption that judges can *identify* the law and apply it, without reference to considerations about what the law ought to be in the circumstances. Clearly, whether this latter assumption is warranted or not, depends on considerations about what under-standing and following a rule consist in. In particular, it turns upon the question of whether there is a sense in which following or applying a rule does not consist in, or is not mediated by, an interpretation of this rule.

The argument from defeasibility, construed as Moore under-stands it, tackles a different question altogether, namely, whether the rule *should* be applied (or not) in the circumstances. Needless to say, the answer to this normative question is bound to be affected by the moral contents of the particular law and legal system in question. This, however, is something which neither Hart nor Raz have any reason to deny.

Perhaps Moore would reply that I have missed an important point in his argument, namely, that his objection to the Hartian thesis is based from the outset on moral, rather than conceptual, considerations. This, though, would put him on safer ground only on the basis of the assumption that Hart's thesis makes a moral difference in the first place, which is simply a mistake. Moore's assumption that it does seems to be drawn from the view which he attributes to Hart, that legal cases *should* be decided 'on the basis of linguistic intuition alone' (1981 : 277). Yet this is just another confusion. Hart's commitment to what follows from linguistic or conceptual analysis alone carries him only so far as to ground a conceptual distinction between easy and hard cases. It does not extend beyond that, to the question of how judges ought to decide various cases, that is, from a moral point of view. In other words, an easy case is not one in which *ipso facto* a judge should, as a matter of moral duty, apply the rule in question.

Perhaps Moore was misled here by the argument which Fuller attributes to Hart, namely, that his thesis is supported by considerations about the 'ideal of fidelity to law' (Fuller 1968 : 664). But this is a rather puzzling point. To begin with, it should be noted that Hart himself does not propound any such argument explicitly, either in the article (Hart 1958) to which Fuller's review is addressed or, to the best of my knowledge, in any other place. Nor does such a position fit his general line of thought: Hart has never described fidelity to law as an *ideal*. Is it at all reasonable to suppose that one so clearly concerned with the conceptual separation between law as it is and law as it ought to be would ground his descriptive conception of law on considerations about 'the ideal of fidelity to law'? Would that not be too obvious a fallacy?[7]

In short, the argument from defeasibility—construed as a *moral* objection to Hart's thesis—does not seem to hit the right target. Moore, however, offers another version of this argument, based upon semantic rather than moral considerations. A scrutiny of this argument, which will distance us temporarily from Fuller, is offered by the next section.

4. INDEXICAL PREDICATES AND EMPIRICAL DEFEASIBILITY

Hart's thesis, it might be argued, suffers from the following flaw: it is confined, at best, to those concept-words whose meaning determines their reference. However, as we have seen in Chapter 5, on Putnam's analysis of indexical words such as natural-kind predicates, meaning does not determine reference, but vice versa; it is the 'real nature' of the entities designated by indexical words that determines their meaning. To capture the relevance of this objection, let us substitute our worn-out example of the 'No vehicles in the park' rule with a legal rule that comprises an indexical concept-word. Thus, consider a rule attaching certain legal consequences to a person's 'death' (for example, that a physician is entitled to remove his organs for body-transplants).[8] Now surely, on Hart's account, the appropriate application of this rule would depend on, *inter alia*, the construal of the extension (or reference) of 'death'. Hence easy applications of this rule would be possible only if it is true of 'death', as it is of 'vehicles', that there are some standard instances in which no doubts arise as to the word's applicability. If, however, we presume the indexicality of 'death', so the argument would run, there is an important sense in which no such standard examples exist.

To be sure, none (at least in this context) offer the absurd claim that it is impossible to be completely sure of a person's death. The point, of course, is more subtle, namely, that whatever might be

---

[7] At one point Fuller seems aware of these difficulties when he suggests the following, rather diagnostic observation: 'I believe we can say that the dominant tone of positivism is set by a fear of a purposive interpretation of law and legal institutions, or at least by a fear that such an interpretation may be pushed too far' (1958:669). As nothing of the sort has been suggested by Hart, however, one is bewildered about the source of this diagnosis, let alone its accuracy.

[8] The example is Moore's, and so is the gist, though perhaps not all the details, of the objection presented here. See Moore (1985:293–7).

conceived to be the relevant standard instances of indexical predicates, such examples are *defeasible* in a sense that other, non-indexical instances are not. This defeasibility consists in the fact that the standard examples employed to explicate the meaning of indexicals are, at best, only approximations of the real reference of the concept-word, and not—as I have argued in the previous section—criteria for its correct use. Hence, in principle, it is always possible *to discover* that a certain instance formerly thought of as a standard example of 'death', or any other indexical word, in fact constitutes a mistake as it does not fall within the reference of the word after all. For example, whereas several decades ago we might have thought that a person suffering from total cardio-vascular and respiratory failure for thirty minutes to be indisputably dead, we now know that this is not necessarily the case. Nor would we say that the meaning of 'death' has changed since. When people use an indexical predicate, they intend to designate its reference 'rigidly', that is, whatever its real nature turns out to be (Moore 1985 : 297).

Let us take a closer look at the kind of defeasibility described as characteristic of indexical words. Its most interesting feature is the fact that it is contrasted with the notion of criterion. On a Wittgensteinian account, standard examples of a concept-word typically function as criteria for its correct use; they are constitutive elements of the word's meaning (though not, as some commentators have thought, identical to it). Thus the fact that ordinary automobiles are standard examples of 'vehicle' is a fact about the *meaning* of 'vehicle', not a fact about the world. On the view examined here, however, this is not true of indexical words. The fact that a piece of metal is held to be a piece of gold, is allegedly a fact about the world, and not about the meaning of 'gold'.

Thus, the defeasibility in question is empirical;[9] it derives from the fact that no statement about the real reference of indexical concept-words is maintainable without doubt. Or, to use a

---

[9] As Moore's argument is not confined to natural-kind predicates, the term 'empirical defeasibility' would not capture the full scope of his thesis. On Moore's account, many other types of concept-word are indexicals as well, notably moral concepts, and even legal terms of art, like 'malice' for example. I allowed myself to ignore this complexity since it does not affect my arguments here; if at all, it renders Moore's view even more controversial and less plausible than my presentation here would indicate.

Dummettian phrase, the indexicality of a predicate entails a 'verification-transcendent' truth about its real reference. Any piece of evidence which might support an item's inclusion in (or exclusion from) the extension of a given indexical predicate, can only render the conclusion more or less probable, but never certain.

Now consider the judicial application of a rule which contains an indexical predicate, like (allegedly) 'death'. The judge must unquestionably engage in reasoning which requires him to classify certain particulars, that is, to decide whether they fall within the extension of 'death'. Thus, assuming the indexicality of 'death', any such classification would amount to an empirical statement (or presumption) about the world, that is, about the real reference of 'death'. As such, it must be supported by evidence, evidence which can only render the conclusion, at best, very probable, but not certain. Moreover, the type of evidence required cannot pertain to the rules or conventions of language. It must be scientific evidence, and hence, in principle, empirically defeasible.

Upon reflection, an easy reply to this argument seems to present itself immediately. Suppose we concede the argument so far. Still, one might argue, in most legal contexts, the kind of defeasibility claimed to be characteristic of indexical predicates does not undermine Hart's thesis. Generally, our certainty about the extension of an indexical predicate is no less than our certainty on the most basic scientific theories and world-views. The now recognized fact that such theories, no matter how strongly adhered to, may turn out to be false, rarely affects our humdrum activities despite the fact that we often rely on these theories. Most people who buy and sell gold, for instance, are not terribly worried by the prospect of scientific revolutions or the defeasibility of the evidence presently taken to support the identification of gold. There seems to be no reason, then, to consider adjudication any different. True, every classification of a particular under an indexical covering-concept might turn out to be false, but this seems to have little *practical* bearing upon the possibility of there being easy cases in law. The level of certainty required in law is no different from the level of certainty required in a great number of other activities where we rely on scientific, and hence defeasible, evidence.

Although this answer is basically correct, it underestimates the alleged force of the argument from defeasibility. Proponents of this argument, and particularly Moore, have a more ambitious plan in mind than merely casting doubts on the reliability of judicial classification of particulars. Moore is sceptical of the Wittgensteinian analysis of meaning as relied upon by Hart, not of judges' ability to classify particulars.

Moore divides contemporary theories of semantics into two basic conceptions of meaning, realism and conventionalism. Conventionalism, in turn, comprises two basic, closely related conceptions of meaning. Both rely on the idea that meanings are conventionally determined by certain criteria, but one takes the notion of criterion to be analysable in terms of necessary and sufficient conditions, while the other, notably Wittgenstein's, maintains 'some loose assemblage of the conditions [which] will be sufficient for the correct application of the word' (Moore 1985: 292 n.).

According to Moore, however, both conventionalist accounts of meaning fail for the same reason, namely, their inability to account for the indexicality of predicates like 'gold' or 'death', etc. In particular, they both entail that whenever a change occurs in our view of the real nature of the reference of an indexical predicate, and hence in the criteria for its correct use, a change must also occur in its meaning. But this, as Moore has learnt from Putnam, is unacceptable. So Wittgenstein must be wrong, at least with respect to indexical predicates (Moore 1985 : 297–8).

Unfortunately, this view of Wittgenstein's conventionalism is far too simplistic. It rests upon a misconstrual of his analysis of the complex relations between the notions of meaning, reference, and criteria. Admittedly, the concept of criteria is not one of the clearest in Wittgenstein's writings, and he seems to have changed his mind about it during the years. Some points are clear enough, however, and their elucidation suffices to render the argument from empirical defeasibility quite harmless.

To begin with, it must be noted that Wittgenstein did not identify criteria with meaning. Although he did speak about 'defining criteria', he did not envisage a particular set of definitive criteria which would determine the correct use of a given expression in terms of necessary and sufficient conditions. (Moore, indeed, seems to concede as much.) On the contrary, on a Wittgensteinian account one should typically expect a multiplicity of criteria for the correct application of a given concept. The criteria for understanding, for instance, are multifarious: one can manifest understanding by performing an appropriate action, by explaining that which he has understood, through the manner in which he or she responds to something, or by whatever other means.

Secondly, it is important to realize that *all* criteria are defeasible, not only those which determine the use of indexical predicates. This is so as all criteria for the correct applicability of a concept-word are *circumstance dependent*. The manifestation of pain-behaviour, for instance, is—under normal circumstances—a criterion for the assertion that one is in pain. But of course, one might pretend to be in pain, or intend to deceive, etc. Yet, as Wittgenstein readily admitted, there is no hope of enumerating all the variant circumstances which alter the criteria. Nor does this fact undermine the role of criteria in determining meaning: 'if a circumstance makes the use doubtful, I can say so, and also *how* the situation is deviant from the usual ones' (1967 : sect. 144).

Hence it should be clear that Wittgenstein did not conceive the relation designated by '*p* is the criterion for *q*' as one of *entailment*. Thus, to revert to one of our examples, the fact that a half hour of cardiac-respiratory failure is, under normal circumstances, a criterion for calling a person 'dead', does not entail that a given person is in fact dead. Just as pain-behaviour does not entail that one is in fact in pain.

To capture the full significance of this point, another distinction should be mentioned here, that between criteria and evidence. From the academic year 1933/4 onwards, Wittgenstein uses the concept of criterion with an emphasis on its contrast with what he called *symptoms*. The latter, as opposed to criterion, signify empirical evidence which is learnt from experience. Thus, for example, a certain chemical reaction might be a symptom of the identification of 'gold', something which can be learnt from experience, whereas the fact that 'gold' is a kind of metal (and not, for example, the name of an animal) is a criterion for its use (see Hacker 1986 : 308).

The distinction is of crucial importance. As Hacker rightly observed, 'evidential relationship presupposes the independent identification of the relata. A criterion, however, defines, or partially defines that for which it is a criterion' (ibid.).

It follows that the relation between meaning and a theory about reference is more complicated than Moore seems to have presumed. If a given phenomenon is considered a symptom of a concept's applicability, the fact that this evidential relation eventually turns out to be false has no bearing on the meaning of the concept. Similar changes in criteria, on the other hand, do typically involve appropriate variations in meaning. Interestingly, Wittgenstein had anticipated the kind of objection raised by Moore. Consider the following section:

The fluctuation in grammar between criteria and symptoms makes it look as if there were nothing at all but symptoms. We say, for example: 'Experience teaches that there is rain when the barometer falls, but also teaches that there is rain when we have certain sensations of wet and cold . . . In defence of this, one says that these sense impressions can deceive us. But here one fails to reflect that the fact that the false appearance is precisely one of rain is founded on definition. (PI sect. 354)

The connection between the barometer and the occurrence of rain is surely an evidential, symptomatic one; the fact that it can turn out to be false has no bearing on the meaning of 'rain'. But our sensations of wet and cold, and whatever else constitutes our perception of rain, are—in normal circumstances—criteria for the correct applicability of the word 'rain'; not because they cannot turn out to be false, but because they define, as a matter of linguistic convention, what we mean by 'rain'. If, for some bizarre reason, a change occurs in those criteria, it would indeed be the case that the meaning of 'rain' has changed as well. Likewise, cardiac-respiratory failure is not a criterion for the correct use of 'death', but a symptom, or a piece of evidence, which is associated with this unfortunate state of affairs on the basis of experience. On the other hand, the fact that we associate death with the absence of any vitality is a criterion for its use. If one day we discover that dead people are capable of reading philosophy, no doubt our concept, and hence the meaning, of 'death' will require a dramatic revision.

Two conclusions emerge so far. First, that the most plausible examples of indexical predicates the theory of whose reference can change without causing any changes in meaning, do not constitute counter-examples to Wittgenstein's analysis at all, as they involve a revision of symptoms rather than criteria. Second, that according to Wittgenstein, a change in criteria does carry with it a respective change of meaning.

The matter, however, cannot be settled so easily. One of the most interesting points emphasized by Wittgenstein in this context is that criteria and symptoms fluctuate, particularly in science.[10] Scientists often define a concept without really deciding whether an item in their definition is a symptom or a criterion. Thus, for instance, the presence of a certain kind of bacteria in a person's throat might either be a symptom of the occurrence of a certain disease, or a criterion for the use of the concept-word signifying that disease. The point of this observation is not to complain of the deplorable laxity of scientific terminology; from a scientific point of view the distinction is usually not too important. Yet this fluctuation emphasizes how difficult it is decide whether changes in scientific theories yield consequent changes in meaning or not, thus stressing that the answer to this question often depends on the way scientists themselves view the relation between a phenomenon and that which it is a phenomenon of. Hence, typically, the actual history of the pertinent scientific development must be consulted. To see whether meanings have changed or not, one must look carefully into the ways in which people have understood and used the given concept.

To my mind, this Wittgensteinian analysis is much more reasonable and accurate than the aspect of Putnam's theory relied upon by Moore. On Putnam's account, at least as Moore would have him subscribe to it,[11] no change in the acceptable theory of the reference of any indexical predicate yields a change in its meaning. I find this thesis unconvincing for two reasons: first, contrary to the impression arising from Putnam (1975 : 197, 236), the alternative is not necessarily the opposite, Feyerabendian conception, according to which *every* change in a theory about the reference of an indexical predicate entails a change in its meaning. Putnam worries rightly that unless Feyerabend's view can be repudiated, scepticism is inevitable; if the meaning of our theoretical terms varies with each successive explanation of their reference, then the separate explanations are not explanations of the *same* thing, and accordingly the newer ones are no better than

---

[10] See Hacker (1986 : 309), and refs. there.

[11] See Moore (1981 : 202 ff; 1985 : 300). It should be noted that Putnam can hardly be said to have criticized Wittgenstein's conception of meaning. The picture of meaning Putnam strove to undermine, as he explicitly made clear, is the one which conceives of meaning as a *state of mind*, something which Wittgenstein strove to undermine himself, as Putnam of course knows.

their predecessors. Yet Wittgenstein's distinction between symptoms and criteria should alleviate this worry considerably. Most scientific theories affect the symptoms of, rather than the criteria for, the use of indexical predicates.

Secondly, Putnam's view, when construed in an unqualified manner, seems exaggerated in the opposite sense as well. All too often the meaning of words does change, sometimes radically, as a consequence of surprising discoveries about their reference. It seems quite extraordinary to insist that accumulation of knowledge about the world does not bring with it a change in the meaning of the words we use. Suppose we discover, for instance, that the animals we now call 'tigers' are in fact sophisticated machines composed of silicon chips, perhaps implanted here many centuries ago by aliens. Would anyone want to insist that the meaning of 'tiger' remains the same? I suspect that apart from devout Putnamians (which I am not sure that Putnam himself still is) no one would make such a claim. We would say, instead, that we have discovered that there are no tigers; those things formerly thought to be tigers have in fact emerged as something else (cf. Putnam 1975:243). However, if we continue to use the word 'tiger' to name these things, 'tiger' would surely have acquired a very different meaning, not only a different reference. Being a kind of animal is not a symptom, a piece of evidence which renders the classification of certain particulars as 'tigers' more or less probable; it is a criterion for the use of this word.

Consider a less dramatic, and hence perhaps more plausible, example. Take the differences between our conception of the reference of 'atom' and, say, that of the Greek atomists. Let us also presume that some of the differences consist not only of variations in the accepted symptoms, but also of the criteria for the meaning of 'atom'. Are we forced to say, on a Wittgensteinian account, that we no longer refer to the *same* substance? And hence that we cannot make sense of the contention that we now have a better theory about 'atoms' than the Greeks did? Surely not. The fact that the meaning of 'atom' in our idiolects is different from the meaning of 'atom' in those of the Greeks does not entail that we are not referring, *roughly*, to the same substance. Rough approximations are all one needs here. As with the circumstance dependence of criteria, one normally understands the difference or deviation, and has the ability to explain how it is different.

We are now in a position to conclude that not much is left of the argument from defeasibility. Construed as a moral objection to Hart's thesis, it is irrelevant. Construed as a general objection to Wittgenstein's conventionalism it turns out to be idle.

To return to Fuller's arguments, it is not completely clear whether Fuller meant them to be understood along the lines suggested by Moore. I would suggest that Fuller's most interesting objection to the Hartian thesis is meant as a conceptual one, based on considerations about what understanding a legal rule consists in. Basically, Fuller seems to maintain that understanding a rule always consists in (*inter alia*) a grasp of its purpose. Notably, if this view is correct, it would amount to a serious objection to the Hartian thesis, one which would refute it on its own terms. Furthermore, if we add to this the assumption that typically, determining the purpose of a rule involves interpretative hypothesis about what the rule is there to settle, not only Hart's distinction between easy and hard cases, but also the separation thesis distinguishing the law as it is from the law as it ought to be, would be refuted. Thus, a careful examination of Fuller's suggestion is of great importance.

5. WITTGENSTEIN ON FOLLOWING A RULE

The question to be addressed at this point is whether or not it makes sense to claim that one can understand a rule only in view of the purposes it is taken to advance. Note that this is not the same question as whether all interpretation is or should be purposive, as it were. The reason is quite straightforward. A negative answer to the former question might be based precisely on the point that understanding and following a rule do not consist in, and are not mediated by, imposing an interpretation upon it.

It has already been argued, in Chapter 2, that the notions of understanding an expression (or explaining its meaning), and interpreting it, should not be used interchangeably. There is no need to repeat this argument here. However, it might be thought that even if this is generally conceded, it still remains an open question as to whether one can be said to be acting in accord with a rule, without the rule being thus interpreted. The idea that interpretation is always required in order to determine which acts are in accord with a rule (and which go against it), seems supported by the idea that rules as such are indeterminate. In other words, there seems to be a gap between a rule—which constitutes a sign, and its application—which constitutes an action, a gap which can only be bridged by interpretation.

Repudiating this idea (along with the various misconceptions involved in it) was one of Wittgenstein's main concerns in his rather extensive discussion of following rules in the *Philosophical Investigations* (sects. 143–242). Needless to say, a full account of this discussion of Wittgenstein's would go far beyond the scope of this work (or of my competence, for that matter). Instead, I shall try to summarize those of his arguments which have a direct bearing on our present concerns.

Wittgenstein's concern with what following a rule consists in derives from his conception of meaning. Knowing the meaning of an expression is not an inner state of mind, but rather an ability (or an array of abilities) to use the expression in accordance with the rules of the language. Hence, the relation of the meaning of an expression to its use(s) is a particular instance of the relation of a rule to its application.

Let us begin with the clarification of two general points. First, as has already been mentioned, one of Wittgenstein's most important observations about language is that the meaning of expressions in language are perspicuous throughout. Using language is a rule-governed activity, like a game, hence the rules in question are normative, and like all normative rules, they explicitly guide actions, serve as standards of evaluation, play explanatory roles in making actions intelligible, play a crucial role in instructing learners how to engage in the pertinent activity, etc. The moral to be drawn from this is that rules must be perspicuous, that is, that it does not make sense to speak of 'hidden rules', or rules that can be discovered only through scientific or quasi-scientific exploration (Hacker 1988 : 162–5; McGinn 1984 : 119).

Furthermore, the rules constituting a language-game should be clearly distinguished from the background state of affairs in which there is a point in having such rules and against which they are intelligible.[12] Every rule-guided activity presupposes a particular background which is not part of the activity itself but makes it possible and relevant. The game of tennis, for instance, is possible only against the background of the laws of gravitation, the fact that

[12] Baker and Hacker (1985 : ch. 5); Pears (1988 : 425). See also Ch. 2, sect. 2.

we are normally capable of telling whether a ball has fallen inside or outside the marked lines, the fact that the desire to win a game fits the human predicament, etc. All this is part of the background against which there is a point to having the game. Yet in normal circumstances, none of these points would be cited as being part of the rules constituting the game. Furthermore, as Wittgenstein observed, although we can envisage things being otherwise, 'the more abnormal the case, the more doubtful it becomes what we are to say. And if things were quite different from what they actually are . . . this would make our normal language-games lose their point' (PI sect. 142).

The distinction is relevant here for the following reason: had Fuller's thesis been confined to the contention that rules in general, or legal rules in particular, are made intelligible only against the background of (*inter alia*) certain purposes which they can be taken to advance—that is, in the sense of background outlined above—it would have been a sound observation. But in the present context, it would have been quite innocuous as well. The distinction between easy and hard cases as maintained by legal positivism concerns the question of what following a rule consists in, not the question of what makes it possible to follow the rules of this, rather than another, game.[13]

The second point and perhaps the key to the whole discussion, is that Wittgenstein conceived of the relation between a rule and its application as a grammatical one, that is, one which is internal to language. To understand a rule is to be able to specify which actions are in accord with it (and which would go against it), just as to understand a proposition is to be able to specify its truth conditions. In other words, it does not make sense to say that one has understood a rule if one cannot identify the actions which are in accord with it. (See Baker and Hacker 1985:91; Pears 1988: 468.) This should be clarified in some detail.[14]

---

[13] It is possible that many of the arguments presented by Fuller's book (1969) on the 'inner morality of law', as he calls it, can be accounted for along the lines suggested here. If so, this would also suggest that, contrary to appearances, many of his theses are in fact reconcilable with legal positivism. But of course, this is a wide topic which exceeds the interests of this chapter.

[14] The following discussion will not dwell on Wittgenstein's alleged 'rule scepticism' as it struck Kripke (1982). The latter has been repeatedly—and cogently—criticized by numerous writers. See Baker and Hacker (1984b); McGinn (1984); Pears (1988).

Wittgenstein begins his discussion of following a rule with the idea of the indeterminacy of rules. He asks us to consider the following example: a pupil is ordered to continue an arithmetical series, say from 1,000 on, according to the rule $n + 2$; he then writes '1,000, 1,002, 1,004, 1,008 . . .' Two main questions are exemplified here. First, any rule, it seems, can be misinterpreted, and it is not clear what this misinterpretation consists in.[15]

Second, the actions in accord with a rule seem to be under-determined by the rule's formulation: whatever one does can be brought into accord with the rule on some interpretation of it. Both contentions, however, manifest profound misunderstandings. Thus, consider sect. 198:

'But how can a rule shew me what I have to do at this point? Whatever I do is, on some interpretation, in accord with the rule.' This is not what we ought to say, but rather: any interpretation still hangs in the air along with what it interprets, and cannot give it any support. Interpretations by themselves do not determine meaning.

And the same point in sect. 201:

It can be seen that there is a misunderstanding here from the mere fact that in the course of our argument we give one interpretation after another; as if each one contented us for a moment, until we thought of yet another standing behind it. What this shows is that there is a way of grasping a rule which is *not* an *interpretation*, but which is exhibited in what we call 'obeying a rule' and 'going against it' in actual cases.

This is the crucial point: if a rule could not determine which actions were in accord with it, then no interpretation could do this either. Interpretation is just another formulation of the rule, substituting one rule for another, as it were. Hence it cannot bridge the gap between rule and action. A rule, in other words, is a sign and its meaning cannot be determined by another sign; the meanings of rules, like those of all symbols, must be determined by the actions themselves, that is, by the way the rules are *used*.

---

[15] Wittgenstein here considers, and undermines, a whole array of possibilities. For instance, can we say that the pupil's misinterpretation of the rule consists in the fact that he had not captured the intention of the one who gave him the order? Would the latter say, 'Well, this is not what I had in mind'? The suggestion is perplexing: does it make sense to say that all the steps were in his mind before they had actually been taken? (PI sect. 188) For a survey and exegesis of Wittgenstein's arguments, see Baker and Hacker (1985: 81–227).

Hence also, understanding a rule consists in the ability to specify what actions are in accord with the rule, which is not an interpretation of the rule, but is exhibited by 'obeying the rule' or 'going against it', that is, in practice. Consider this subsequent part of sect. 198:

'Then can whatever I do be brought into accord with the rule?'—Let me ask this: what has the expression of the rule—say a sign-post—got to do with my actions? What sort of connexion is there here?—Well, perhaps this one: I have been trained to react to this sign in a particular way, and now I do so react to it.

But that is only to give a causal connexion; to tell how it has come about that we now go by the sign-post; not what this going-by-the-sign really consists in. On the contrary; I have further indicated that a person goes by a sign-post only in so far as there exists a regular use of sign-posts, a custom.

This completes the previous point. If the meaning of rules and signs is determined by their use, one might surmise that any action can be made to be in accord with the rule. In other words, one still remains puzzled as to how rules can determine the actions in accord with them, if it is the actions which determine the meaning of the rule. But of course, there is a normative connection between rules and actions,[16] consisting in the existence of a custom of using the sign or rule thus and so, and not otherwise. Which is to say that learning how to follow a rule is learning to master a technique (PI sect. 199). Yet Wittgenstein is careful to warn us against a potential misunderstanding: it might be thought that instead of explaining what following a rule consists in, he has provided a kind of causal or psychological explanation of how, for example, one learns to follow a rule. This of course, is not the point. Something *is* a signpost only in so far as there exists a regular use of that sign for particular purposes, and it is this regularity of use which provides the meaning of the sign.

Wittgenstein's contention that the use of rules consists in there being a custom is potentially misleading; one is inclined to think that 'custom' is meant to indicate the necessity of a community of

---

[16] *Contra* Kripke, Wittgenstein does not take a sceptical standpoint here: 'if everything can be made out to accord with a rule, then it can also be made out to conflict with it. And so there would be neither accord nor conflict here' (PI sect. 201)—which is obviously absurd—not a sceptical standpoint to be taken seriously. See n. 14, above.

users, a social practice. But, as Baker and Hacker (1984b : 20) made clear, this conclusion is wrong: Wittgenstein's emphasis here is on the multiplicity of the occasions of use, not on the multiplicity of users. As they put it, 'The contrast here is not between an aria and a chorus, but between looking at a score and singing' (ibid.; see also Pears 1988 : 500).

A further misunderstanding might arise from the idea that the meaning of rules is determined by their use: 'Hence there is an inclination to say: every action according to the rule is an interpretation. But we ought to restrict the term "interpretation" to the substitution of one expression of the rule for another' (PI sect. 201). Suppose one concedes Wittgenstein's analysis so far, but still wishes to insist that every action according to a rule involves interpretation. Now, one cannot say that the action is *mediated* by interpretation, since, as we have seen, the gap between a rule and its application cannot be bridged by another formulation of the rule. One could say, however, that although interpretation does not mediate between rules and actions, still acting according to the rule is an interpretation of the rule. But this would be misleading since in one sense it is vacuous, and in another wrong. It is vacuous if by 'interpreting' we simply mean 'this is how he understood the rule' and can thus also say that he has misunderstood it. However, if 'interpreting' is taken to mean something which amounts to yet another formulation of the rule, then obviously the suggestion above would be wrong: acting according to the rule does not constitute another formulation of it, but rather exhibits that one has understood the rule correctly.

Wittgenstein might be presented with counter-examples. Does not a performance of a symphony, for instance, amount to an interpretation of it? On the face of it, Wittgenstein's proposal of limiting the term 'interpretation' to the substitution of one expression of the rule for another is too restrictive. This would be a misunderstanding, however, since Wittgenstein need not deny that there are occasions in which actions manifest a certain interpretation of a rule. It would, however, be wrong to suggest that *every* instance of following a rule is an interpretation of it, which would be irreconcilable with the normative aspect of rules and rule-following. To interpret a symphony, whether by its being performed in one way or in another, one must first have a pretty good idea of what the scores mean.

The idea that all rules must be subject to interpretation might still be thought to be essential, if we connect Wittgenstein's discussion of vagueness with his own conception of what understanding a rule consists in. The idea here would run as follows: rules formulated in our language, such as legal rules,[17] are bound to employ general concept-words with various degrees of vagueness. However, if we concede Wittgenstein's point that understanding a rule consists in the ability to specify which actions are in accord with the rule, we are led to the conclusion that we can never have a complete grasp of a rule; our understanding of rules will always be deficient, as there will always be instances where one cannot tell whether or not the rule applies. Hence, if we want to allow for a complete understanding of rules, so the argument continues, we must also admit that every rule is bound to be interpreted.

The answer to this is that the quest for completeness is misguided here. One of Wittgenstein's most important observations in discussing the concept of explanation is that the quest for completeness—if understood as a demand for the removal of every possible doubt—is incoherent: 'an explanation serves to remove or to avert a misunderstanding—one, that is, that would occur but for the explanation; not every one that I can imagine' (PI sect. 87). The same holds true of a complete understanding of rules. The assumption that there must be more to understand there derives, in both cases, from the same source of confusion. It follows from the presumption that a complete account of the meaning of an expression is a Merkmal-definition, that is, providable in terms of necessary and sufficient conditions (Baker and Hacker 1980b: 29–45). Thus, just as it is misguided to presume that unless one can specify necessary and sufficient conditions for the applicability of a concept-word, one's grasp of its sense is in some way incomplete, it is equally misguided to assume that the complete understanding of a rule must remove all possible doubts about its applicability.

This should not be taken to mean that the distinction between complete and incomplete understanding or explanation is out of place. It is only that we should jettison the association of completeness with necessary and sufficient conditions. An ex-

---

[17] To be sure, there is nothing unique to legal rules here; all rules can be formulated in language, including the rules of language itself.

planation would be complete, if it fulfils its particular purpose, that is, if it removes the misunderstanding that otherwise would have existed. Equally, 'the sign-post is in order—if, under normal circumstances, it fulfils its purpose' (PI sect. 87). And one has a complete grasp of a rule, if under normal circumstances, one is able to specify which acts are in accord with the rule, and hence, which would go against it.

It should be emphasized that all this is not meant to imply that in all cases of disagreement on the applicability of a given rule (due to vagueness, for example), Wittgenstein would maintain that 'anything goes', as it were. It very well might be the case that interpretation is required to determine the applicability of a rule in certain circumstances, and interpretation can, of course, be based on *reasons*. But interpretation here should not be confused with understanding the meaning of the rule. If the formulation of a particular rule is inadequate for purposes of determining a particular result in certain circumstances, then there is nothing more to explain or understand about its meaning; what is required is a new formulation of the rule—one which would remove the doubt—and this is what the term 'interpretation' properly designates.

We can return to Fuller's thesis at this point, as its inadequacies should be clear by now. His assumption that one can understand a rule only in view of the purposes it is taken to advance, violates the distinction between following a rule and interpreting it. To follow a rule, one needs to understand and act according to it, with the intention of doing so. As we have seen, the relation between a rule and its application is a grammatical one, that is, internal to language. Understanding a rule consists in the ability to specify which actions are in accord with the rule (and hence which would go against it). Thus, it does not make sense to say that one has understood a rule yet does not know which actions would be in accord with it. On the other hand, assumptions about the purposes a rule is meant to advance are interpretative assumptions which do not mediate between a rule and its application but rather between one formulation of the rule and another. Hence, the thesis that one always needs to determine the purpose of the rule in order to be able to specify which actions are in accord with it, amounts to contending that the application of a rule always requires its translation into another rule, which is an obvious absurdity.

Thus, unless it can be shown that there is something unique to adjudication which requires this constant translation procedure, as it were, we have no reason to doubt that legal rules *can* often be simply understood, and then applied, without the mediation of interpretative hypotheses about the rules' purposes. Interpretation is required only when the formulation of the rule leaves doubts as to its applicability in a given set of circumstances. In such cases, assumptions about the purposes the rule is meant to advance would take a prominent—perhaps even pre-eminent—role in solving the particular difficulties encountered.

8

LEGISLATIVE INTENT AND THE AUTHORITY OF LAW

So far, the role of intentions in interpretation has been discussed from different perspectives and in various contexts. At the more abstract level, I have argued for a distinction between the role they play in determining the content, as opposed to the identification, of that which is a possible object of interpretation. Applying this distinction to the law, I have argued that the authoritative nature of law accounts for the conceptual role intentions play in identifying legal norms as such, which still leaves open the issue of whether the legislator's intentions have any particular role in the interpretation of statutes. It is this question which I shall try to answer here.

   Although the topic is familiar, a few introductory remarks are in order; these will form the chapter's first section. The following two sections will then concentrate on the attempt to clarify the intentionalist's thesis irrespective of its validity. The fourth and last section is devoted to the question of justification. In other words, I shall attempt to elucidate the conditions under which it would be reasonable for judges to defer to the legislators' intentions in statutory interpretation.

I. WHAT IS THE ISSUE?

Should legislative intent play a role in statutory interpretation, or indeed can it play any such role? This is one of the age-old questions of common law jurisprudence. Yet as is often the case with such philosophical stalking-horses, some of the issues involved are muddled by a lack of clarity in the definitions of the pertinent questions. It is the task of clarifying the issue which I intend to address first. The most immediate difficulty encountered stems from the plurality of doctrines under consideration. Roughly speaking, we can, of course, identify two main camps: those who favour deference to legislative intent, under certain circumstances, referred to below as intentionalists, and those who oppose such deference. Yet each standpoint actually comprises a very wide range of positions. In fact there is hardly any position which has not been argued for by one scholar or another, from outright sceptics, who claim that 'there is no such thing as a "legislative intent"', to those who claim that legislative intent is the only legitimate source for statutory interpretation.

I shall not attempt a survey of all these positions. Instead, I shall begin my discussion with a general and rough definition of the thesis I wish to assess here. In outlining a position that favours deference to legislative intent, one which is at least initially plausible, I shall also be pointing out the kinds of obstacle such a thesis would have to overcome, thus providing an effective framework for the subsequent discussion.

The kind of plausible doctrine I have in mind here would comprise the following general theses: first, that laws, at least in certain cases, are enacted with specific intentions, and that this is a matter of fact which is discernible through an ordinary fact-finding procedure. Second, that in certain cases the presence of such a fact, namely, that the law was enacted with a specific intention, provides the judge with reason to decide a legal dispute in accordance with the legislative intent.

The characterization of a plausible version of intentionalism in terms of these two theses aims at clarifying that the intentionalist faces a dual task which is both explanatory and justificatory. On the one hand, he must face the sceptics who argue that—as a matter of fact—there is no such thing as legislative intent, at least not in any helpful sense. On the other, he must answer those who claim that even if legislative intent were a discernible fact, it should not constitute a reason for judicial interpretations of statutes.

Each of these tasks comprises various subquestions. At the descriptive level, the intentionalist must show it possible to identify both the 'legislator' whose intentions are meant to count, and the kind of intentions which are potentially relevant to statutory interpretation. (These two questions will be addressed in the next two sections, respectively.) At the level of justification, two questions arise, apart from the general one of why it is ever a good reason to defer to legislative intent; one regarding the scope of the doctrine, and the other, its alleged force. The first is the question of whether the doctrine's applicability is confined to certain kinds of case, or applies whenever a legislative intent bearing upon the issue at hand can be discovered. The second, the question of the doctrine's force, is as follows: granted that legislative intent constitutes a reason for decision in a given case, what kind of reason is it? Should it replace all other, potentially conflicting, reasons for decision, only some of them, or none? How should it be weighed against such other, potentially conflicting, reasons for the decision—is it a very weak reason, binding upon judges only in the absence of other good reasons for decision, or is it a very strong one, not easily overridden by other types of reason?

Thus, to reiterate, we can say that the question of justification comprises three main issues: why should legislative intent be a reason for decision, in which cases, and what is the relative weight to be attached to this type of reason when it is applicable? Needless to say, although these are conceptually separate questions, their answers are likely to be intermixed in various ways, depending on the particular doctrine espoused.

Finally, to complicate matters a bit further, it should be noted that the very nature of the justificatory question is itself subject to controversy. This is an issue I would like to address before going on to examine the other questions in detail. Both proponents and foes of intentionalism sometimes conduct their arguments as if the issue is to be determined on the basis of considerations pertaining to the concept of law. Others, denying this, contend that the issue can be resolved satisfactorily, only if it is first recognized as thoroughly dependent on moral and political arguments. Both positions are confusing, however, as both are partly right and partly wrong. This is so as there are at least two ways in which intentionalism can be claimed to be a matter of law, and at least two ways in which it can be claimed to be a matter of morality.

Intentionalism can be a matter which falls within the realm of law if, and to the extent that, some of the questions mentioned above are determinable, and determined, by legal practice. In certain legal systems, for instance, the question of whose intentions count as the intentions of the legislator might be determined by legal practice, in which case it is trivially a matter of law. Yet intentionalism can be claimed to belong to the concept of law in a much stronger sense. It may be construed as a doctrine which claims that deference to legislative intent is always a matter of law, as deference to legislative intent forms part of what it is to follow the law. I hope it is evident from my arguments in the previous chapter that this is not a plausible view; I have argued there that the existence of easy cases is made possible not by the fact that the legislator's intentions are clear and decisive, but by the fact that rules can often be simply understood, and then applied, without the mediation of interpretation. Hence, it will be presumed here that intentionalism, like any other interpretative strategy, pertains to the kind of reasons judges should rely upon when deciding *hard cases*; that is, when the issue is not settled by the existing legal standards, and interpretation is required to determine the appropriate solution of the case.

This assumption about the role of intentionalism also clarifies why there are two possible ways in which it can be a matter of moral and political argument. Granted that judicial decisions of hard cases often make a moral difference, proposing deference to legislative intent as a source of decision-making in such cases is, *ipso facto*, morally significant. Yet it does not follow that the considerations capable of supporting intentionalism are necessarily moral ones. As they pertain to the reasons that judges should rely on when confronted with hard cases, such considerations are bound to be based on evaluative judgements of various kinds, moral and political ones possibly included. But they are not thus included because the judicial decision makes a moral difference. We have already seen that considerations supporting interpretative strategies are bound to be sensitive to the purposes and values one finds embodied in the relevant enterprise. However, it would be a mistake to identify these evaluative judgements with the particular effects of a given interpretation as compared with an alternative one of the same object. Such an identification would constitute the double confusion of identifying evaluative considerations with moral (or aesthetic) ones, and identifying reasons purporting to support a given interpretative strategy with its likely effects. In both cases the latter form part, but not all, of the former. Hence, I will presume that the debate over the desirability of intentionalism in law is bound to be affected by various evaluative considerations. Whether these are primarily moral and political is something which remains to be seen.

2. WHOSE INTENTIONS?

The argument over the role of authors' intentions in interpretation is not, of course, unique to law. Art critics, to take one familiar example, often debate a very similar point. Yet there is one general problem which is unique to law, and which art critics are usually spared. I refer to the problem of identifying 'the author'. Works of art, like most other objects of interpretation, are typically created by a single 'author'. Even if the historical identity of the author is in doubt, it is usually the case that there is such an author, and that it is a person to whom one can attribute intentions. On the other hand, statutory interpretation in a modern legal system presents a special problem in this respect, as 'the legislator' is often not a single person, but a whole legislative body composed of numerous members. Hence the question, 'Can we attribute an intention to a group of people, sometimes even numbering several hundreds?'[1]

Lawyers, in particular, would not find it difficult to answer this question, as they would point to the fact that we often do attribute such intentions in similar situations. For instance, we attribute intentions to corporate bodies, such as commercial corporations, trade unions, cities, etc., on the basis of what can be called, the concept of *representative intentions*. That is, by means of identifying certain individuals whose intentions would *count as* the intentions of the corporate body itself. This does not involve a kind of fiction, as is sometimes suggested by lawyers, but rather a set of established rules or conventions which determine these matters. We are vindicated in attributing intentions to the corporate body because rules or conventions determine that the intentions of certain individuals are *considered*—within certain established limits—*the intentions of the corporate body itself.* Hence also, when these people act in their official capacity, they normally know and take into account that they act on behalf of the corporate body.

It should be noted that rules or conventions have a twofold function here: both of establishing the practice and of allowing for the identification of the particular instances falling under it. That

---

[1] I am ignoring an additional complication here: even with respect to a single legislator, it is not always clear whether he has formed a certain intention in his official capacity or not. A legislator might hold certain intentions, or rather hopes, unofficially, as it were. Can we say that in this case he has the intention that his intention not be taken into account by the courts?

is, rules help us explain how actions and intentions may be attributed to a corporate body at all, while serving to identify its actions and intentions in particular cases. Needless to say, the latter is parasitic upon the former. Unless we have some idea what it would be like for a corporate body to perform actions and form intentions, satisfactory identification remains impossible. The point is, however, that we often do have a fairly good idea of what it would mean for a corporate body to perform actions and exhibit intentions, and we know how to identify these. That is, when an existing set of rules or conventions determines whose actions and intentions represent, or count as, the actions and intentions of the corporate body itself.

In other words, it is characteristic of the concept of representative intentions that the rules which vindicate the attribution of intentions are constitutive of the practice. The situation here is not unlike other, more familiar instances, where certain actions gain their social meaning, as it were, only on the basis of certain rules or conventions. To give one closely related example: numerous speech-acts—like issuing a command, or uttering the words 'I do' in the appropriate circumstances of a marriage ceremony, etc.— would not have the social effects they do outside the rule- or convention-governed practices of which they are parts. Hence, each and every performance of such a speech-act involves an implicit invocation of the appropriate conventional procedures which are taken to determine the social meaning of the speech-act in question (that is, of course, apart from the conventions determining the literal meaning of the words used by the speaker).[2] In a familiar sense, this is true of legislation as well. The performance of certain actions counts as an act of legislation if and only if these actions are carried out in accordance with (and as an instance of following) certain rules or conventions. Hence, these rules or conventions must also determine whose actions are appropriate for the successful performance of an act of legislation and in what circumstances.

---

[2] See Austin (1955). Notably, Austin seems to have maintained that all the speech-acts for which he coined the phrase 'illocutionary acts' are essentially conventional in this way. But Strawson's (1964) illuminating account of the issue makes it clear that only certain types of illocutionary act are essentially conventional, while the performance of others involves no reliance on convention- or rule-governed practices of any kind.

Unfortunately, however, at least in the Anglo-American legal systems, conventions do not extend so far as to determine whose *intentions*—amongst the various members of the legislative body—and in what combination, count as the intentions of the legislative body itself.[3] In this, legislative bodies are quite unlike most other corporate bodies, where rules determine not only whose actions, but also whose intentions count as the intentions of the corporate body itself.[4]

Notably, most jurists seem to concede this fact.[5] Some, however, tend to reach sceptical conclusions at this point. The sceptic concludes that since there are no rule- or convention-governed practices of identifying the intentions of certain individuals taken to represent the intentions of the legislative body, then attributing intentions to the latter is in fact a fiction, a myth. There are actually two prevalent versions of this sceptical argument. As the more extreme one has it, legislative intent is a fiction due to conceptual considerations. The more moderate version of scepticism holds that even if we had an idea of what it meant for a legislative body to have an intention, its actual existence and discoverability would, at best, be a rare occasion.

Let us begin by taking a closer look at the more radical version. The following argument may be taken to be representative:

1. Intention is a mental predicate. It is only those possessing certain mental capacities who can be said to form intentions.
2. A group of people, as opposed to its individual members, does not possess a mind; only individual people have the requisite mental capacities to form intentions.
3. Unless there are determinate ways of identifying certain individuals whose intentions represent the intentions of the group, no intention can be attributed to a group of people, as such.

[3] There is, of course, an underlying assumption that the actions of the legislators have been carried out intentionally. But this is not the relevant sense of 'intention' here, as it only says that something was not done by chance, or under the influence of drugs, etc. Needless to say, this is not the kind of intention which might have any bearing on statutory interpretation.

[4] Perhaps this is due to the fact that such rules would have to determine a hierarchical structure within the legislative body, something which is utterly opposed to our conception of representative democracy.

[5] See MacCallum (1968); Brest (1980 : 212), though, seems to suggest that those rules which determine whose actions, and in what circumstances, count as an act of legislation, also determine whose intentions count for the purposes of intentionalism. But I could not find any arguments in the text which could be taken to support this claim. On his recommendation to follow the majority view, see text below.

4. On the assumption that the conditions of (3) do not obtain in the case of legislative bodies, these cannot be said to have any intentions whatsoever.

The argument is, of course, quite familiar, and so are the metaphysical controversies it raises over the concept of a group-mind. I cannot hope to resolve this metaphysical dispute here. Fortunately, however, this is unnecessary, since the sceptic's argument fails irrespective of such metaphysical controversy. To see this, we must distinguish between the idea of a *group*-intention, which the sceptic rejects, and that of *shared* intentions, which he seems to ignore. The former is purportedly the intention of a group, organization, etc., as such, which is somehow distinct from the intentions of any of its individual members. Presumably, the sceptic is opposed to the ontological perplexities raised by the potential references of this concept. But the idea of shared intentions involves no such ontological perplexities. Even the sceptic would probably agree that many people can have the same (or very similar) intentions. Arguably, this is often what we mean when we attribute intentions to a group in a non-representative manner. In saying, 'the Nation aspires to independence', for instance, we mean that the relevant intention is shared by all or most individual members of the group in question. Similarly, we often attribute intentions to political parties, minority groups, artistic genres, sports clubs, and the like.[6]

It should be emphasized that attributing shared intentions to a group is not a purely quantitative matter of counting, as it were, how many members of a given group share a certain intention. An additional element must obtain, establishing a non-accidental connection between the identification of the group and the pertinent intention. It is natural, for example, to speak of a nation aspiring to independence, as those who share the pertinent intention (and, perhaps, those who oppose it) also share the expectation that this intention be held by their group, as such. The said intention is significant for them precisely (though not only) because they expect it to be shared by other members of the

---

[6] It should be emphasized that the distinction between group-intention and shared intention does not concern differences between the *objects* of intention. In other words, both types of intention pertain to the question of what is the intention of a collective body or organization, and not to the intentions which concern a *collective good*. The latter kind of intentions are, I think, what Rousseau had in mind in distinguishing between the 'general' and the 'particular' will.

group, while even expecting membership in the group to be identified, in part, in terms of this and similar intentions.[7] Had we discovered, for instance, that the very same people also happen to share an extraordinary fondness for strawberries, we still would not say anything like, 'It is the nation's intention to eat great quantities of strawberries.' The affection for strawberries, even if it is shared by all the members of a certain nation, has nothing to do with the identification of the group as a nation.

Now, let us return to law. Considerations mentioned so far seem to support what is usually called the *majority model* of legislative intent (cf. MacCallum 1968; Brest 1980). On the assumption that there is no particular reason why legislators cannot share certain intentions, it would be natural to maintain that legislative intent is present when most of the legislators share a particular intention *vis-à-vis* a law they have enacted. This leaves no place for doubt that perhaps the intention is only accidental to the identification of the legislative body as such. After all, it is the business of legislators to enact laws. Furthermore, at least within the present framework of our constitutional practices, the majority model seems particularly suitable. It is in accord with the rules which determine whose actions, and in what combination, count as an act of legislation. Ordinarily, this has to do with a majority vote. Thus, if it is normally the case that the actions of the majority are sufficient for the successful enactment of a law, it seems equally sufficient that the requisite intention be held by the majority of legislators (MacCallum 1968 : 263).

Hence, the majority model seems to offer a very plausible construct allowing for the attribution of intentions to the legislator, being an instance of one of the most common modes of attributing intentions to groups; that is, employing the concept of shared intentions. It is not surprising, however, that several difficulties arise with respect to the applicability of this model. To begin with, as has often been pointed out,[8] at times there is no majority view—at least not in any compelling sense—of the particular issue bearing upon the case before the court. Just as legislators can share intentions, they can also have conflicting and incompatible ones *vis-à-vis* a law they have enacted, each perhaps

---

[7] Cf. Raz (1986b : 208).
[8] See e.g. Dworkin (1985 : 47).

hoping (though often with no illusions) that his or her intention will eventually be realized in practice.

More problematically, the majority model is ambiguous. It is unclear whether the majority it is based on comprises those who voted for or against the bill, or those who share an intention with respect to the particular issue at hand. This ambiguity is not easily resolved. Consider the following example: suppose the issue before the court is whether or not a certain statute, R, applies to the case in question, say x. Let us assume that there are one hundred members of parliament, sixty of whom voted in favour of R, and forty of whom opposed it. Let us further assume that the following facts are known: of the sixty members of parliament who supported the bill, thirty did so (partly or mainly?!) because they were convinced that R would apply to x, while thirty-five of those who opposed the bill did so because they thought the same, namely, that R would apply to x. Thus, we have a majority of members of parliament who thought that R would be taken to apply to x. But we also know that this is not the majority who would support the bill thus understood. Suffice it to say that in such cases there is a strong inclination to admit that either construal of the majority model would be utterly inadequate. Moreover, I do not believe that any single criterion is capable of removing all cases of the ambiguity.

Nevertheless, the conclusion which emerges so far should not be overstated. True, it is sometimes embarrassingly difficult to answer the question of just whose intentions count. In such cases—and in so many others as we shall see shortly—the appropriate conclusion should be that the 'legislator' had no particular intention with respect to the issues bearing on the case before the judge. But it would be a great distortion to maintain that this is always the case, even with respect to large legislative bodies, such as parliaments. Admittedly, it is a question of fact whether the existence and discoverability of legislative intent, understood in terms of shared intentions, is or is not a rare occasion, one which is not easily determinable. But it seems quite unlikely that this occasion is so rare as to be ignored altogether. Nor do I think that the opponents of intentionalism place too much weight on an attempt to deny this. Suggesting that there are never cases where the majority of legislators share a certain intention *vis-à-vis* a law they have enacted would render the phenomenon of legislation a rather mysterious achievement. After all, legislation is often a result of a well-recognized desire on the part of a political party to bring about a particular change in the political, social, economic, etc., situation of the country. So let us turn to other questions requiring an answer of the intentionalist, particularly those concerning the appropriate notion of 'intention' on which he wishes to rely.

3. WHAT KIND OF INTENTIONS?

A person who performs an action—especially one as complex as legislation—typically has a variety of intentions. Hence, the intentionalist, even if he were to concentrate on a single legislator, must face a whole array of difficult questions: Which intentions are potentially relevant and why? Are some of these legally relevant intentions more important than others? How does one cope with the cases where various intentions are in conflict or otherwise incoherent?[9]

Before I venture to suggest some answers to these questions, let me emphasize that any classification of the various intentions with which a given act is being performed is necessarily limited and partial, as the possibilities of placing the dividing lines are almost endless. The distinctions must thus be guided by certain assumptions about theoretical relevance. In our case, they must be sensitive to the reasons one would have for assigning legal significance to the various types of intention.[10]

Bearing this qualification in mind, let me suggest the following distinction. At the most abstract level, it is useful to distinguish between what the legislator *aims* to achieve (or avoid) by enacting the law, and his thoughts (or assumptions, expectations, etc.) about its *proper application*.[11] I shall consider each of these broad categories separately.

[9] Dworkin (1985 : 52–4) rightly contends that one cannot answer these questions by relying on the intentions of the legislators themselves. Even if the legislators have an 'interpretive intention' (as Dworkin calls it) which consists in their intention with respect to the kind of intentions they intend to be relevant or dominant, this cannot be taken to solve any problem. An attempt to rely upon the interpretative intentions would only beg the question, 'Why are these interpretative intentions relevant?'

[10] For this reason, it would also be a mistake in the present context to attach too much weight to the analysis of the concept of intention, and its related notions, like motive, desire, hope, expectation, purpose, etc.

[11] This distinction, though in various forms, has been long recognized. See MacCallum (1968 : 237).

Aims and Further Intentions

When we ask ourselves what it is that the legislator sought to achieve by enacting the law, we will always find that certain purposes are manifest in the language of the law itself, as a matter of logic, while others, though they exist, are not. Consider, once again, the 'No vehicles in the park' rule. Surely it must have been one of the intentions of the legislator that if anything is a vehicle it should not enter the park. The legislator cannot deny as much without breaching the rules of language or logic, or what speech-act theorists call the condition of sincerity.[12] Admittedly, this is a rather trivial point, but trivialities sometimes tend to be forgotten, or muddled.[13]

Apart from the aims which are manifest in the language of the law itself, the legislators are likely to have had a variety of, what I shall call *further intentions*,[14] in enacting the law. Thus, to revert to our example, the legislator might have enacted the law in order to enhance the safety of people who use the park; to reduce the level of pollution in the vicinity; to protect the safety of squirrels in the park; and, let us also presume, to enhance his chances of winning the forthcoming elections.

There are three points that I wish to emphasize about further intentions. First, it should be realized that hardly any act of legislation is performed without any such further intentions whatsoever.[15] Of course it is possible to enact a law without having any idea why such a law is required, but we may hope that this does not happen too often.

[12] See Austin (1955 : 15); Searle (1969 : 60).

[13] Dworkin's distinction between abstract and concrete intentions is a good example of how this triviality can be muddled. His notion of the abstract intention stands for the intention which is manifest in the law itself, and his notion of the concrete intention draws upon the legislator's thoughts about the proper application of the words used in the statute, which I shall dwell on in some detail below. The terminology would have been innocuous, had Dworkin not further maintained that the difference consists in different 'levels of abstraction' (1985 : 48). This was bound to yield unnecessary questions e.g. 'Are there intermediary cases between the two?' 'Is the distinction a matter of fact or a question of theoretical convenience?' and the like. I believe that the following discussion will show this to be a superfluous complication.

[14] The terminology is borrowed from Moore (1985 : 344). On the notion of further intentions in speech-acts in general, see Strawson (1964 : 161–3).

[15] There is one general exception to this: when the intention which is manifest in the language of the law itself is held by the legislator to stand for an *ultimate* purpose, in which case the further intention is identical, as it were, with the intention which is manifest in the language of the law itself. Such laws are, however, quite rare.

Second, it is often difficult to distinguish the further intentions with which an act has been performed from the agent's motive in performing it. Admittedly, motive is an extremely problematic concept,[16] and I cannot explore its various meanings here. Suffice it to say that there is often a substantial overlap between motives and further intentions. An agent may, for instance, be motivated by desire for revenge, while at the same time it may be the case that revenge was what this agent strove to achieve by his action. Likewise, certain moral convictions the legislator holds may explain both his motive in enacting a given law, and what it was that he strove to achieve by it. But this is not always the case; there are motives which do not figure in any proper description of what the legislator sought to achieve by enacting the law (that is, in terms of further intentions). These are typically motives that the legislator is not (fully) aware of. The Marxist notion of 'class-consciousness' is often given as an example in this context.[17] An analysis of such hidden motives and their potential role in legislation is an interesting topic in its own right, but it has little bearing on our present concerns. It would be quite extraordinary if intentionalism were taken to extend to such hidden motives as well. In any case, I shall not dwell on this possibility.

The third, and perhaps most problematic point, stems from the distinction that lawyers would wish to draw between the merit or worthiness of the further intentions, and their legal relevance, or legitimacy. It might be a good idea, for example, to enhance the safety of people who use the park, while protecting the squirrels may not be such a good idea. However, to the extent that one espouses intentionalism, one must support deference to both intentions, as both seem equally relevant. On the other hand, the legislator's intention of making himself more popular by enacting this law, is a kind of intention which, I take it, even enthusiastic supporters of intentionalism would be reluctant to take into account. (Suppose the legislator had discovered that there were more pedestrians than drivers among his potential voters and that this knowledge formed part of his reason for enacting the law shortly before elections. One does not bring such facts to the

---

[16] Cf. Anscombe (1956).

[17] For a discussion of this point in the context of intentionalism in historical studies in general, see e.g. K. Graham, 'How Do Illocutionary Descriptions Explain?', in Tully (1988: 153 ff.).

court's attention, except perhaps for the purpose of discrediting such intentions.)

It is not always as easy to recognize the difference between relevant and irrelevant intentions as this example might be taken to suggest. It is even more difficult to specify any general guidelines according to which such a distinction could be substantiated. In particular, the main question is whether we can come up with a criterion which is independent of the content of the particular intentions in question, or will the line eventually be drawn only on the basis of moral and political considerations delineating a sphere of legitimate intentions with which laws should be enacted? There is perhaps at least a partial content-independent criterion, pertaining to the kind of speech-act performed. Certain types of speech-act, such as insinuating, deceiving, showing off, etc., have the rather unique feature that the speaker's further intention is *essentially non-avowable*; rendering it explicit would be self-defeating. The whole point of insinuating, for instance, is that the hearer suspects, but only suspects, the intention to induce, for example, a certain belief. Once this intention is rendered explicit, the speech-act cannot remain one of insinuating (Strawson 1964 : 163). Similarly, when it is one of the intentions of the speaker to use a speech-act for purposes of manipulation, it is his intent that the former intention remain unrecognized by the hearer.

With due caution, this can be applied to our problem as well. It may serve as a sufficient condition for the identification of further intentions which one would initially be reluctant to take into account, that the legislator himself is most likely to disavow them. More precisely, in such cases it is not part of the legislator's intention to secure the effect he strives to achieve through others' recognition of his intention to secure it. On the contrary, there is a strong element of self-defeat in rendering such intentions explicit. But of course, this is only a partial criterion, which will often require supplementation by other, primarily moral, considerations.

Application Intentions

Apart from their various aims in enacting a given law, legislators often have certain intentions or expectations as to the proper application of the law they have enacted. Let us term these the legislators' *application intentions*. Thus, to take a typical example, consider the question of whether or not the 'No vehicles in the park' rule also applies to bicycles. The following possibilities exist:

1. It is possible that the legislator has not given the question any thought at all; it simply did not occur to his mind.
2. The legislator may have thought about the question, but either failed to make up his mind or intended to delegate the decision to the courts, which practically amounts to the same thing.
3. Finally, there is the possibility that the legislator had a determinate intention that the rule should—or should not— apply to bicycles as well.[18]

Needless to say, the plausibility of intentionalism with respect to application intentions derives from the existence of the kind of intentions designated by option (3), whereby the legislator has had a determinate intention with respect to the issue bearing on the case before the court. Yet as the situations described in the former two options are not all that rare, advocates of intentionalism have often attempted to define their doctrine in such a way as to encompass situations of these types as well. There are two common stances which aim to overcome the lack of a determinate legislative intent, as described in (1) and (2). The first is based on what might be called the idea of counter-factual intention. In situations such as these, it is argued, the judge must ask himself what it is that the legislator would have decided had he been directly confronted with the issue and a decision required of him. But how would one go about answering such a question? After all, it would even prove extremely difficult to answer such a counter-factual question with respect to one's own intentions. Furthermore, it is far from clear what kind of facts should be taken into account: should judges take into account only the explicitly stated aims of the legislator, or various presumed aims as well? Should the judge go to the trouble of finding out the legislator's personal inclinations too? Imagine, for instance, the judge saying something like this: 'I know this legislator, and I know that he loves cyling. In fact, he takes a ride every morning in the park.' Is this the kind of fact judges should be allowed to consider? And if not, how is one to tell what the *legislator* would have intended? In

---

[18] Note that the phrase 'not intending that x' is ambiguous between having no intention about x, and intending that not x. The former is an instance of either (1) or (2) above, and the latter is an instance of (3).

short, the idea of a counter-factual intention is quite unhelpful, to say the least.

The second alternative sometimes suggested in this context is a prescription to judges to ask themselves what it is that they would have intended had they been in the legislator's place. This, however, is ambiguous: either it is tantamount to the counter-factual thesis, in which case we are back with the same perplexities, or it is just an awkward way of saying that the judge should decide the case according to those policy considerations which are expected of legislators. This, admittedly, is not a vacuous suggestion. It can be contrasted with other, potentially conflicting grounds for judicial reasoning, which are guided by the presumption that judges, ex officio, should adopt a point of view which differs from that of the legislator. But for our present purposes, this thesis is irrelevant, as the kind of reasoning suggested to judges on this option is indifferent to the actual intentions of the legislator. If I have to decide what it is that I would have done were I in place of A, there is nothing I need to know about the actual intentions of A. Hence also, according to the suggestion under consideration here, the correct decision can easily be at odds with the actual intentions of the legislator. It is thus advisable not to discuss this suggestion under the title of 'intentionalism' at all. In any case, I shall presume that application intentions are potentially relevant only when, as a matter of fact, the legislator has had a determinate intention bearing on the issue before the court, and my discussion will be confined to this option.

There are two further points to be noticed about the application intentions. First, they should not be confused with communication intentions.[19] An act of legislation, like any other speech-act, must be performed on the basis of an understanding that certain conventions and other states of affairs obtain. These necessarily include linguistic conventions which determine the meaning of the utterance in the given situation. And, of course, they also include a great deal of background knowledge—referring to conventions and other states of affairs—allowing for the successful performance of an act of communication. Thus, when a speaker expects to be understood, he must expect the hearer to share the pertinent knowledge of these conventions and states of affairs and be aware of the speaker's intention to rely on them. But such expectations

[19] On the definition of communication intentions, see Ch. 2, sect. 2.

can, of course, be frustrated, and this is another sense in which we can speak of the potential frustration of the legislators' intentions. It should be realized, however, that in this case the frustration of the legislative intent is a standard instance of *misunderstanding*, and as such, has nothing to do with the question under consideration, that is of the appropriate interpretative strategy judges should adopt in the resolution of hard cases. As I have repeatedly argued in the previous chapters, understanding an act of communication, and interpreting it, are two separate things which ought not to be confused.

The second, and more important point, is this: between the legislators' application and further intentions (or the aims which are manifest in the law), means–ends relationship of sorts would typically have to obtain. Suppose a statute, *R*, was meant to achieve a certain purpose, say *P*. The application intention of the legislator that *R* should be taken to apply to *x*, for instance, would typically be based on his assumption that *R* thus applied is more likely to enhance *P*. Of course the legislator can be mistaken (or insincere), and as a matter of fact, applying *R* to *x* might be inconsistent with the intention of achieving *P*. But in this case, either the legislator would have to admit that his application intentions were inadequate, being likely to defeat his own purposes in enacting the law, and hence better ignored; or else he would have to admit that *P* was not an adequate formulation of his further intentions. In either case, however, the application intentions ought to be taken into account—from the legislator's own point of view—only if, and to the extent that, their realization is likely to enhance his further intentions.

It should be emphasized that this is not a matter of the intensity with which the legislator holds his various intentions, as it were, but a matter of logic. It very well might be the case that the legislator has a clearer or stronger sense that *R* should be interpreted to apply to *x* than any of his further intentions in enacting *R*. But in any case, his application intention must be indicative of his further intentions. The legislator cannot maintain, without being utterly incoherent, that his application intentions ought to be assigned precedence to his further intentions. That would amount to the absurdity that when the means are inappropriate for achieving the ends, one should nevertheless stick to the means. On the other hand, when the further intentions are assigned precedence over the application intentions with which they are inconsistent, no logical incoherence is attributed to the legislator, but only a factual mistake, as it were.[20]

To sum up so far I have distinguished between three main types of intention that are potentially relevant from the legal point of view. Apart from the intentions that are manifest in the language of the law itself, legislators typically have further intentions in enacting a given law, sometimes including certain intentions bearing on its proper application. I have also suggested that some of these further intentions may be essentially non-avowable, in which case they are rendered legally irrelevant. Finally, I have pointed out that considerations of consistency require that the legislator's application intentions be taken into account only if, and to the extent that, they are in accord with his further intentions.

4. WHY SHOULD INTENTIONS COUNT?

The two previous sections attempted to substantiate the first general thesis espoused by intentionalism, namely, that laws are enacted, at least in certain cases, with specific intentions which are potentially relevant for statutory interpretation, and that this is a matter of fact which can be discerned by ordinary fact-finding procedures. We must now address the question of whether the presence of such a fact should ever constitute a reason for judges to decide an interpretative question in accordance with these intentions. That is, we must now turn to the question of justification. However, before taking up this task, two clarifications are called for.

Firstly, I must emphasize that I shall not be concerned here with constitutional interpretation, nor do I intend my arguments to have any straightforward application to the latter. There are two main differences between constitutional and statutory interpretation which, I believe, justify this caution.

---

[20] To be sure, legislative intent may turn out to be incoherent in many other ways than the one described here, e.g. when the legislator's further intentions or application intentions are internally inconsistent. However, as Dworkin rightly argues (1985:50–1) in such cases it would be impractical or even impossible to decide which intentions ought to be regarded as the dominant ones. Hence in such cases, the practical result is that the legislator had no intention with respect to the pertinent issue, as if she had not made up her mind.

First, and most important, is the difference residing in the possibility of judicial review in American constitutional law. In non-constitutional cases, the courts' decisions are subject to alteration and overruling by ordinary statutes. If the legislator does not approve of a judicial decision, the situation is easily amendable through an ordinary law-making process. The case is quite different in constitutional law: overruling a Supreme Court decision when it has invalidated an act of the political branches on constitutional grounds is an extremely difficult, almost impractical process. Hence, within the present framework of the American democratic system, judicial review creates a special problem, put nicely by Ely: 'a body that is not elected or otherwise politically responsible in any significant way is telling the people's elected representatives that they cannot govern as they'd like' (1980 : 4–5). There is of course nothing equally dramatic in the ordinary interpretation of statutes. Presumably, a substantive difference in the power-relations between the judiciary and legislative bodies, such as the one manifest in the two cases, is bound to yield different questions, and different doctrines, also bearing on the justification of intentionalism.

The second difference, related to the previous one, stems from the fact that as far as the Constitution can be taken to express the views of certain people, they are the views of people who have been dead for centuries. This engenders an obvious worry, pertaining to the question of whether, and how far, people can control the conduct of future generations. There are, of course, not only old constitutions but also ancient laws. But again, the difference is striking: given the relative importance of the Constitution in the functioning of the legal system and the difficulties involved in the amendment process, the inter-generation problem emerges as one of the main worries of constitutional jurisprudence. On the other hand, as far as it is a problem for statutory interpretation, it is one which can be isolated as a particular problem pertaining to a particular class of laws.

The second clarification is this: considering the various justifications of intentionalism, I shall be assuming that there are no conventions, followed by the community at large, which comprise a general practice of reliance on legislative intent[21] for purposes of

---

[21] For obvious reasons, I shall not be concerned with those intentions which are manifest in the language of the law itself. Generally, the frustration of such

interpreting statutes. This assumption ought to be emphasized for the following reason: had there been such a conventional practice, judges would have had a reason to respect it on grounds of the ideal of protected expectations. If the parties to a legal dispute can show that they had a justified expectation that the relevant statute be interpreted according to the legislators' intentions (assuming the legislator had had such an intention bearing on the case), judges would normally be obliged—other things being equal—to respect these expectations. I shall assume, however, that at least in the Anglo-American legal systems there are no such conventional practices, that is, people do not normally expect statutes to be interpreted by the courts primarily according to the legislators' intentions.

How can intentionalism be justified, then, if it is not supported by legal practice? The most popular line of thought, one which, I suspect, many lawyers, and perhaps even more laymen, find appealing, is the argument based on democratic principles. It is often stressed in this context that since judges are not democratically elected or politically responsible for their decisions, they ought to respect the choices of the elected representatives of the people.

But the details of this argument are far from clear. To begin with, this argument—which seems to rest on the appropriate respect judges should pay to democratic *procedures*—should be distinguished from a different line of thought, associated with the principle of majority rule. The latter is neither an attractive ideal, nor grounds for the conclusion the intentionalist seeks to establish. Majority rule, conceived independently of the checks and balances built into any reasonable structure of a democratic government, amounts to nothing more than an espousal of populism. That populism is not an attractive ideal is, I take it, a generally conceded point. There are certain situations, of course, in which a given choice is morally correct only because it is the choice of the majority. But these are exceptional cases which cannot be taken to constitute the only, or even the primary, grounds for the preference of democracy over other types of government. Furthermore, when a judge is confronted with such a case, he would have

intentions would result in the breach of the rule in question. And in any case, the intentions which are manifest in the law itself are of little help to judges faced with hard cases.

a moral reason to decide according to the wishes of the majority, which has nothing to do with deference to legislative intent.

Be this as it may, the principle of majority rule, stripped of its procedural elements, would not support intentionalism as it would require that judges be guided by the intentions of the majority of legislators, only if, and to the extent that, these intentions reflect the wishes of the majority in the pertinent population. But this, of course, is not always the case, as it often happens that the intentions of the majority of legislators are in conflict with the wishes of the majority of voters. Hence, to the extent that one wishes to abide by the majority rule, one had better advise judges to consult opinion polls rather than the intentions of the legislators. Thus, the argument under consideration should not be construed as an espousal of populism; not only because the latter is not a very attractive ideal, but also because it would not support intentionalism anyway.

Bearing this in mind, it is clear that the premise of the argument from democracy, construed as a procedural matter, does not entail the conclusion that the intentionalist seeks to establish. One can readily concede that judges ought to respect the political choices of people's elected representatives. But this only begs the question: what is it that the representatives have *democratically* chosen? Opponents of intentionalism may argue that it is not accidental to democratic procedures that they result in authoritative texts, that is, in statutes. One of the main objectives motivating parliamentary debates to culminate in a vote on a particular text, is to establish, as precisely as possible, what it is that, agreed upon, is sufficient to gain majority support (Ely 1980 : 17). Hence, at most, respect for democratic procedures entails that judges should apply the law whenever this is possible. Perhaps it also entails that the *final say* on legal matters should rest in the hands of the legislative bodies. This, however, falls far short of admitting to the intentionalist's conclusions.

Finally, even if one could make sense of the argument from democracy, its applicability to any but contemporary laws would be utterly problematic, as the contemporary constellation of the legislators' intentions might be different from the intentions of those who enacted the law. Suppose that when a statute, R, was enacted, say ten years ago, the majority's intention was that R should apply to x. Suppose further, that the constellation of the legislators' intention has changed since, and the majority now holds the opposite, namely, that R should not apply to x. Which constellation of the legislators' intention should the judge follow according to the democratic principle, the past or the present one? Attaching a decisive weight to the principle of democracy would force one to choose the contemporary constellation of the legislators' intentions as the one which should be followed. After all, what is the point in respecting the majority view if it is no longer the majority view? But this is a perplexing result. It entails that intentionalism is not limited to the legislators' intentions in enacting the law, but extends to intentions which have not been expressed in any institutionalized way. Needless to say, considerations belonging to the concept of law render this option unacceptable. The legislators' thoughts about how their subjects ought to behave are legally irrelevant, unless they have been expressed, that is, communicated, in one of the established ways recognized by the legal practice. Thus, if intentionalism is to make any sense at all, it must be confined to the original intentions of those who enacted the law. But, as we have seen, whenever the latter is not in accord with the contemporary constellation of the legislators' intentions, the argument from democracy renders intentionalism quite unattractive on its own terms.[22]

Let me turn now to a different line of thought which I find much more promising. Generally, I will suggest that the primary way of justifying reasons for complying with the intentions of the legislator involves the very same considerations which are taken to vindicate compliance with an authority's directives in the first place. In other words, I will argue that the justification of deference to legislative intent must be derived from the conditions which can be taken to establish that one person should be acknowledged to have authority over another. These conditions have been discussed in Chapter 6, and I will not repeat them here. The present argument is confined to showing that the same analysis, based on Raz's conception of the concept of authority, can be employed to elucidate the conditions under which it would be reasonable to defer to the authority's intentions when assessing how to interpret his directives. In particular, I will argue that the justification of intentionalism hangs on the distinction between two types of reason for acknowledging an authority's legitimacy. I

[22] Cf. Gans (1988 : 105).

have mentioned the distinction in Chapter 6, but will now expand on it in some detail.

Generally, as we have seen, the legitimacy of a practical authority derives from its mediating role; that is, an authority should be acknowledged as a legitimate one if, and to the extent that, its alleged subjects are likely to comply better with the reasons for action which apply to them when abiding by the authority's directives, than they would were they trying to follow those reasons independently of the authority's resolutions. I have argued in Chapter 6 that this thesis, which Raz calls the 'normal justification thesis', is in fact compound, consisting of two distinct types of justification. In some cases, compliance with the authority's directives can only be justified on the basis of the assumption that the authority is likely to have better access to the right reasons bearing on the issue than its alleged subjects; the authority 'knows better' what ought to be done, as it were. In cases of this type the justification of authority involves assumptions about the relative expertise of the authority as compared to its alleged subjects.

As we have seen, however, this is not the only way of understanding the 'normal justification thesis'. Often it is enough to show that the authority is *better situated* than its alleged subjects to make the pertinent decision; that is, without thus being committed to the presumption that there are certain reasons for action, whose identification and ascertainment are more accessible to the persons in authority. By and large, this is the typical kind of justification available when the function of the authoritative resolution is to solve co-ordination problems. It should be noted that the concept of co-ordination is being used here in a rather inclusive and somewhat loose sense. I will presume that a problem of co-ordination arises whenever the fact of having an established and salient decision is more important (morally or otherwise) than the particulars of the actual decision taken (that is, within a certain, reasonable, range of options).[23] In situations such as these, the legitimacy of the authority in question derives from its ability to solve the co-ordination problem, an ability which does

---

[23] Similar considerations apply when the function of the authority is to solve 'prisoner's dilemma' situations. These differ from co-ordination in various, familiar respects, but these differences do not affect my discussion here. I should also reiterate that I do not presume that all co-ordination problems, as such, require an authoritative resolution; most humdrum co-ordination problems are settled by other means.

not involve expertise of any kind. This latter point is of crucial importance as it shows that the legitimacy of authorities to issue directives may be acknowledged even with respect to issues, or fields of conduct, where no possibility of expertise is recognized.

This distinction, between what I shall call the expertise and the co-ordination theses, bears upon the plausibility of intentionalism as follows: the case for deferring to the authority's intentions— when its directives require interpretation—is typically much stronger in the case of expertise than in the one of co-ordination. When one's reasons for acknowledging the authority of another are based on the assumption that the authority is more likely to have a better access to the right reasons bearing on the pertinent issue, it would typically be most sensible to take the authority's intentions into account when his directives require interpretation. An example can illustrate this point. Suppose one acknowledges the authority of one's doctor, considering him the best available expert on the relevant medical problems. Now, suppose further that the doctor's medical prescription is ambiguous, as there happen to be two different medicines which fit it. Under normal circumstances, attempting to clarify the doctor's intention would be the most sensible thing to do.

On the other hand, if one's reasons for complying with an authority's directives are based on the co-ordination thesis, there is no need to presume the person in authority to be an expert in the pertinent field. Hence there does not seem to be any particular reason to defer to the authority's intentions in order to solve interpretative questions as *ex hypothesi*, the person in authority was not presumed to have a better access than the subjects themselves to the reasons on which they should act.

Admittedly, in both cases, the task of filling in the gaps left by the need to interpret the authority's directives can be carried out by someone else who would thus have to be acknowledged as yet another authority. But there is this crucial difference: in the case of expertise, there would be reason to confer the discretion on the second authority only if, and to the extent that, the latter is believed to have at least equal expertise in the pertinent issue. On the other hand, an authority that was not presumed initially to possess any particular expertise on the question under consideration can be replaced by anyone else whose position enables him to solve the problem equally well.[24]

Thus, when the expertise justification thesis is available, there is reason to take the authority's intentions into account when assessing how to interpret the latter's directives. But even in this case, the reasons do not carry absolute weight, as it were. When contrasted with other, competing considerations (for instance, the advice of another expert), their relative weight would have to be sensitive to the degree of likelihood that the authority indeed has better access to the right reasons bearing on the particular issue. The more reason one has to believe that the authority knows better what ought to be done in the circumstances, the more weight one would attach to the authority's pertinent intentions. Furthermore, one can see that deference to the authority's intentions should *replace* other reasons for decision only within the bounds of expertise considerations. One's reasons for complying with the judgements of one's physician are confined to those considerations which apply to the questions of the most appropriate medical treatment. They should not include reasons which are not based on expertise, like, for instance, the reasons involved in a decision to commit suicide instead of taking the treatment.

Now, it is being assumed here that the alleged legitimacy of the legal authorities derives from both sources. According to this assumption, legislators exercise both types of authority, depending on various factors, like the particular realm of conduct, the nature of the decisions required, the kind of evidence available to the legislators, etc. Sometimes the legitimacy of their directives derives from the expertise justification thesis, and at other times, it derives from the co-ordination justification thesis.[25]

Thus, the conclusion I am driving at should be apparent by now. The intentionalist's thesis gains its plausibility from the availability of the expertise justification thesis, and its applicability is confined to those cases. When the legitimacy of the legislator's authority—

---

[24] Or else the problem can be solved in other, i.e. non-authoritative ways, such as a throw of dice.

[25] I am ignoring a possible complication here, which is due to the possibility of a *mixed* justification. When considerations of co-ordination are mixed with considerations of expertise, one would have to separate between the reasons based on each type of justification and decide upon the relevance of intentionalism accordingly. I do not wish to insist, however, that this task can always be carried out satisfactorily.

in a certain realm of conduct—derives from the co-ordination justification thesis, judges have no particular reason to defer to the legislators intentions in filling in the gaps arising from the need to interpret their directives. This task can be performed equally well by the judges themselves, exercising their own independent discretion.[26] We have also seen that when there is reason to defer to the legislators intentions, the relative weight assigned to this reason must depend on the degree of expertise that the legislators are presumed to possess. Furthermore, this reason should not replace other reasons if the latter are not within the confines of expertise considerations.

At this point, though, one might raise an objection which runs along the following lines. Consider the role of authorities in the solution of co-ordination problems. Let us presume that potential litigants have a justified interest in avoiding litigation as far as possible, and also that they have a justified interest in the predictability of the judicial decisions in case these are eventually required. Let us further assume that the dispute concerns the interpretation of a statute and that there is a legislative intent bearing on the case. Now, would the parties concerned not be better off relying on the relevant legislative intent when they plan their conduct? And, if the case eventually reaches the court, will the judges not have a strong reason to respect such expectations? In other words, it seems that in cases stemming from co-ordination problems, that is, within the bounds of the co-ordination justifica-tion thesis, intentionalism can be justified through reference to the values of stability and predictability.

The problem with this argument is quite simple: it is based on factual assumptions which do not happen to obtain. Stability and predictability require at least two conditions, neither of which obtains in the case of legislative intent. First, that there be an actual practice, conventionally entrenched, giving effect to a particular way of solving problems. Second, and perhaps more essential, that the relevant sources of decision-making be easily accessible to the parties concerned. As to the first condition, I have already mentioned that people in our society do not generally

---

[26] It should be remembered that judges themselves act in an authoritative capacity, and that in the case of higher courts, this authority often equals that of the legislators.

expect that statutes will be interpreted, at least not primarily, according to the intentionalist doctrine.

The presence of the second condition is even more doubtful: legislative intent is not easily accessible and ascertainable to the public at large or even, in fact, to most lawyers. In order to find out the relevant legislative intent, one typically needs a great deal of material on the legislative history of the statute; not to mention all the obstacles to extracting the legislative intent from the historical material, even if it is available. Hence the suggestion that courts should interpret statutes by deference to legislative intent, because this would enhance the stability and predictability of the law, is one which is not supported by facts.

Let us return to the thesis which I have advocated so far. Its most important implication consists in the conclusion that intentionalism is not a plausible doctrine with respect to those issues or fields of conduct where one cannot recognize the possibility of expertise. The importance of this point becomes apparent once we address the contention, shared by many scholars, that expertise is not available in the realm of morality. Note that such a repudiation of the possibility of expertise in moral issues does not necessarily constitute a sceptical stance. Often, those who insist on the epistemic transparency of moral judgements would tend to deny the possibility of expertise in morality. Others oppose it on moral grounds, claiming that expertise in morality is unacceptable as it is inconsistent with the demands of personal autonomy. The plausibility of these, and similar theses cannot be explored here; suffice it to say that the standpoint one takes on this question has a crucial bearing on the applicability of intentionalism, as legislators' intentions often pertain straightforwardly to moral issues, or arise from moral convictions. Thus, inasmuch as the possibility of expertise in morality is denied, such 'moral intentions' are rendered unacceptable as reasons for statutory interpretation. The grounds for this would be either conceptual or moral, depending on one's particular reasons for the repudiation of expertise in morality.[27]

Care should be taken, however, not to make the mistake of overstatement. Even those who deny the possibility of expertise in

---

[27] The implications of this point to the plausibility of intentionalism in constitutional cases which are morally controversial is quite obvious, but I shall not stress it here.

morality can acknowledge the legitimacy of an authority in issuing directives on matters of moral significance. But according to this view, the legitimacy derives from the co-ordination, and not the expertise, justification thesis. For those who deny the possibility of expertise in morality, an authority's legitimacy in issuing directives which have moral significance is based on the assumption that having an authoritative resolution on the matter is important, even though the authority is not presumed to have better access to the right reasons bearing on the issue in question. Hence it should be realized that there is no contradiction in acknowledging the legitimacy of an authority in issuing directives on certain matters of moral significance, while at the same time denying the applicability of intentionalism with respect to these matters. That is, there is no contradiction to the extent that authoritative resolutions on certain issues of moral significance can be justified on the basis of the co-ordination thesis.

I would like to mention some further implications of the thesis advocated here, even if only briefly. To begin with, once intentionalism is advocated on the grounds of the expertise justification thesis, we can see why judges should sometimes take account of preparatory material on the basis of which the law has been enacted, and not merely of the legislators' intentions. By the former I mean, for example, the opinions expressed in various commissions, the intentions of officials and experts who participated in the drafting process, and the like. Within the bounds of the expertise justification thesis, the opinions of these people, and the evidence they have relied upon, can shed light on the considerations bearing on the case before the court, and serve as valuable sources of decision-making. That is, both independently, manifesting expertise, and also as an indication as to the degree of expertise the legislators are presumed to have. Such material enables judges to substantiate their assumptions on the legislators' expertise, and accordingly, to attach greater or lesser weight to their pertinent intentions.

Similar considerations pertain to the dimension of time: the more ancient the law is, the less attractive intentionalism becomes. The reasons for this are obvious: expertise changes over time, due to the accumulation of experience and the available evidence, to progress in various sciences, and the like. Thus the natural conclusion, that the more ancient a law is the more suspicious one has to be of the relevance of the legislators' intentions.

Finally, the expertise justification thesis makes allowance for a certain discrimination between the legislators' further and application intentions: typically, the latter would have to be more suspect. The reason for this is as follows: recall that application intentions manifest one's thoughts on the appropriate *means* to achieve certain ends. Now, compared with judgements on the appropriate ends to be achieved (that is, further intentions), the former possess a greater degree of ascertainment; they are often verifiable in ways which are not equally available with respect to judgements about ends. Furthermore, as means tend to vary a great deal with the circumstances, legislators, or anybody else for that matter, should not be expected to be able to decide in advance on all the appropriate means for achieving a given end. Hence the legislators' alleged expertise, with respect to judgements about the appropriate means to achieve certain ends, can be more readily contested on the grounds of competing evidence. This entails, again, the rather natural conclusion that judges should be more cautious about the legislators' application intentions than about their further intentions; such intentions should be scrutinized meticulously, since independent reasons and evidence are typically more available in these cases.

The chapter cannot be concluded without mentioning the following objection to the thesis it advocates. It might be argued that the considerations mentioned so far actually prove the implausibility of intentionalism altogether, since, at least in the context of law, the expertise justification thesis is never available. Admittedly, if one's reasons for acknowledging the legitimacy of legal authorities are only supported by the co-ordination justification thesis, intentionalism in law is indeed rendered vacuous; there would be no occasions for its application.

The objection is more cogent than might appear at first glance. The interlocutor need not maintain that no issues at all admit of expertise in law. Nor is he obliged to contend that the legislators— as such—are never experts in any of the realms subject to their jurisdiction. The grounds for denying the availability of the expertise justification thesis would be quite different. The interlocutor could rest his case on moral considerations, that is, the undesirability of deferring to this kind of justification in the context of political obligations. A full account of these considerations would carry us too far from the interests of this study.[28]

[28] See e.g. Raz (1986*b* : chs. 2–4).

Suffice it to say that the interlocutor faces a difficult task here. If his moral arguments rule out the availability of the co-ordination justification thesis as well, and hence result in an anarchist position, the objection to intentionalism would be quite uninteresting. Denial of even a prima-facie obligation to obey the law makes a rejection of intentionalism totally unsurprising.

Furthermore, it should be kept in mind that whether or not to defer to the legislators' intentions is the business of judges in their official capacity. Hence it is their normative point of view which ought to be considered in discussing intentionalism. This is a crucial point, since judges have compelling reasons to acknowledge the legitimacy of political authorities, reasons which do not necessarily apply to their alleged subjects. In other words, one should make allowance for the possibility that certain objections to the legitimacy of political authorities are not normatively available to judges in their official capacity, even if they are based on reasons which are binding ones for ordinary citizens. This, presumably, renders the interlocutor's task even less attainable.

Be the final verdict on this controversy as it may, I hope that the various considerations mentioned so far at least elucidate the kinds of argument available to the intentionalist and his opponents. I hope that I have also succeeded in showing that intentionalism in law is not altogether implausible, although its applicability is quite limited.

REFERENCES

ALEXANDER, L. (1987), 'Striking Back at the Empire: A Brief Survey of Problems in Dworkin's Theory of Law', 6 *Law and Philosophy*, 419–38.

ANSCOMBE, G. E. M. (1956), 'Intention', in A. R. White (ed.), *The Philosophy of Action* (1968), 144–52. OUP, Oxford.

AUSTIN, J. (1832), *The Province of Jurisprudence Determined*. Weidenfeld and Nicolson, London.

AUSTIN, J. L. (1955), *How to Do Things with Words*, (ed.) J. O. Urmson, 2nd edn. Clarendon Press, Oxford.

BAKER, G. (1977), 'Defeasibility and Meaning', in Hacker and Raz (eds.), *Law, Morality, and Society: Essays in Honour of H. L. A. Hart*, 26–57. Clarendon Press, Oxford.

BAKER, G., and HACKER, P. (1980*a*) *An Analytical Commentary on Wittgenstein's Philosophical Investigations*, i. Blackwell, Oxford.

——(1980*b*) *Wittgenstein Meaning and Understanding: Essays on the Philosophical Investigations*, i. Blackwell, Oxford.

——(1984*a*), *Language, Sense and Nonsense*. Blackwell, Oxford.

——(1984*b*), *Scepticism, Rules and Language*. Blackwell, Oxford.

——(1985), *Wittgenstein, Rules, Grammar and Necessity*, ii. Blackwell, Oxford.

BARNES, A. (1988), *On Interpretation*. Blackwell, Oxford.

BREST, P. (1980), 'The Misconceived Quest for the Original Understanding', 60 *Boston University Law Review*, 204–38.

COLEMAN, J. L. (1982), 'Negative and Positive Positivism', in M. Cohen (ed.) (1984), *Ronald Dworkin and Contemporary Jurisprudence*. Duckworth, London.

COOPER, D. (1971), *The Cubist Epoch*. Phaidon, London.

DAVIDSON, D. (1980), *Essays on Actions and Events*. Clarendon Press, Oxford.

——(1984), *Inquiries into Truth and Interpretation*. Clarendon Press, Oxford.

——(1986*a*), 'A Coherence Theory of Truth and Knowledge', in LePore (1986 : 307–19).

——(1986*b*), 'A Nice Derangement of Epitaphs', in LePore (1986 : 433–46).

——(1990), 'The Structure and Content of Truth', 87 *Journal of Philosophy*, 279–328.

DREYFUS, H. (1980), 'Holism and Hermeneutics', 34 *Review of Metaphysics*, 3–24.

DUMMETT, M. (1978), *Truth and Other Enigmas*. Duckworth, London.

—— *The Interpretation of Frege's Philosophy*. Duckworth London.

——(1986), 'A Nice Derangement of Epitaphs: Some Comments on Davidson and Hacking', in LePore (1986 : 459–76).

DWORKIN, R. (1975), 'The Original Position', in N. Daniels (ed.), *Reading Rawls*, 16–53. Blackwell, Oxford.

——(1977), *Taking Rights Seriously*. Duckworth, London.

——(1983), 'My Reply to Stanley Fish: Please Don't Talk About Objectivity Any More', in W. J. T. Mitchell (ed.), *The Politics of Interpretation*, 287–313. University of Chicago Press, Chicago.

——(1985), *A Matter of Principle*. Harvard University Press, Cambridge, Mass.

——(1986), *Law's Empire*. Fontana Press, London.

ELY, J. H. (1980), *Democracy and Distrust*. Harvard University Press, Cambridge, Mass.

FEYERABEND, P. (1972), 'How to be a Good Empiricist', in H. Morick (ed.), *Challenges to Empiricism*, 169. Wadsworth Publishing, Belmont, Ca.

FINNIS, J. (1987), 'On Reason and Authority in Law's Empire', 6 *Law and Philosophy*, 357–80.

FISH, S. (1980), *Is There a Text in this Class?* Harvard University Press, Cambridge, Mass.

——(1983a), 'Working on the Chain Gang: Interpretation in the Law and in Literary Criticism', in W. J. T. Mitchell (ed.), *The Politics of Interpretation*, 271–86. University of Chicago Press, Chicago.

——(1983b), 'Wrong Again', 62 *Texas Law Review*, 299–316.

——(1987), 'Still Wrong After All These Years', 6 *Law and Philosophy*, 401–18.

FULLER, L. (1958), 'Positivism and Fidelity to Law: A Reply to Professor Hart', 71 *Harvard Law Review*, 630–72.

——(1969), *The Morality of Law* (rev. edn.). Yale University Press, New Haven, Conn.

GANS, C. (1988), 'Justice Conditioned and Democracy Based Obedience', 8 *Oxford Journal of Legal Studies*, 92–110.

GRANDY, R., and WARNER, R. (1986), 'Paul Grice: A View of His Work', in Grandy and Warner (eds.), *Philosophical Grounds of Rationality*, 1–44. Clarendon Press, Oxford.

GRICE, H. P. (1957), 'Meaning', 67 *Philosophical Review*, 377–88.

HACKER, P. M. S. (1986), *Insight And Illusion: Themes in the Philosophy of Wittgenstein*, (rev. edn.). Clarendon Press, Oxford.

——(1988), 'Language, Rules and Pseudo-Rules', 8 *Language and Communication*, 159–72.

HARE, R. M. (1964), *The Language of Morals*. OUP, Oxford.

HART, H. L. A. (1958), 'Positivism and the Separation of Law and

Morals', in Hart (1983:49–87). First pub. in 71 *Harvard Law Review* (1958).

——(1961), *The Concept of Law*. Clarendon Press, Oxford.

——(1963), *Law, Liberty, and Morality*. OUP, Oxford.

——(1967), 'Problems of the Philosophy of Law', repr. in Hart (1983:88–119). First pub. in P. Edwards (ed.), *Encyclopedia of Philosophy*, vi. 264–76.

——(1982), *Essays on Bentham*. Clarendon Press, Oxford.

——(1983), *Essays in Jurisprudence and Philosophy*. Clarendon Press, Oxford.

HURD, M. H. (1990), 'Sovereignty in Silence', 99 *Yale Law Journal*, 945–1027.

KELSEN, H. (1960, 1967), *Pure Theory Of Law*, trans. Knight. University of California Press, Los Angeles.

KRESS, K. (1987), 'The Interpretive Turn', 97 *Ethics*, 834–60.

KRIPKE, S. (1972), *Naming and Necessity*. Blackwell, Oxford.

——(1982), *Wittgenstein on Rules and Private Language: An Elementary Exposition*. Blackwell, Oxford.

KUHN, T. S. (1962, 1970), *The Structure of Scientific Revolution*. University of Chicago Press, Chicago.

LEPORE, E. (ed.) (1986), *Truth and Interpretation: Perspectives on the Philosophy of Donald Davidson*. Blackwell, Oxford.

LEVINSON, S. C. (1983), *Pragmatics*. CUP, Cambridge.

LYNTON, N. (1980), *The Story of Modern Art*. Phaidon, Oxford.

MACCALLUM, JNR., G. C. (1968), 'Legislative Intent', in R. S. Summers (ed.), *Essays in Legal Philosophy*, 237–73. Blackwell, Oxford. First pub. in 75 *Yale LJ* (1966), 745.

MACCORMICK, N. (1984), 'Coherence in Legal Justification', in A. Peczenik *et al.* (eds.), *Theory of Legal Science*, 231–51. D. Reidel Publishing, Dordrecht.

McGINN, C. (1984), *Wittgenstein on Meaning*. Blackwell, Oxford.

——(1986), 'Radical Interpretation and Epistemology', in LePore (1986:356–68).

MACINTYRE, A. (1973), 'The Idea of a Social Science', in A. Ryan (ed.), *The Philosophy of Social Explanation*, 15–32. OUP, Oxford.

MACKIE, J. L. (1977), *Ethics, Inventing Right and Wrong*. Penguin Books, New York.

MOORE, M. (1981), 'The Semantics of Judging', 54 *Southern California Law Review*, 151–294.

——(1982), 'Moral Reality', *Wisconsin Law Review*, 1061–156.

——(1985), 'A Natural Law Theory of Interpretation', 58 *Southern California Law Review*, 277–398.

——(1989a), 'The Interpretive Turn in Modern Theory: A Turn for the Worse?', 41 *Stanford Law Review*, 871–957.

MOORE, M. (1989b), 'Authority, Law, and Razian Reasons', 62 *Southern California Law Review*, 827–96.

NAGEL, T. (1979), 'The Fragmentation of Value', in *Mortal Questions*, 128–41. CUP, Cambridge.

PEARS, D. (1988), *The False Prison; A Study of the Development of Wittgenstein's Philosophy*, ii. Clarendon Press, Oxford.

PUTNAM, H. (1975), *Mind Language and Reality*. CUP, Cambridge.

——(1983), *Realism And Reason*. CUP, Cambridge.

QUINE, W. V. O. (1953), 'Two Dogmas of Empiricism', in *From a Logical Point of View* 2nd edn., 20–46. Harvard University Press, Cambridge, Mass.

——(1960), *Word and Object*. MIT Press, Cambridge, Mass.

RAWLS, J. (1971), *A Theory of Justice*. OUP, Oxford.

——(1980), 'Kantian Constructivism in Moral Theory', 77 *Journal of Philosophy*, 515–72.

——(1985), 'Justice as Fairness: Political not Metaphysical', 14 *Philosophy and Public Affairs*, 223–51.

RAZ, J. (1975), *Practical Reason and Norms*. Hutchinson, London.

——(1979), *The Authority of Law*. Clarendon Press, Oxford.

——(1985), 'Authority, Law and Morality', 68 *Monist*, 295–324.

——(1986a), 'Dworkin: A New Link in the Chain', 74 *California Law Review*, 1103–19.

——(1986b), *The Morality of Freedom*. Clarendon Press, Oxford.

——(1989), 'Symposium: The Works of Joseph Raz, Facing Up: A Reply', 62 *Southern California Law Review*, 1153–235.

——(1990), 'Facing Diversity: The Case of Epistemic Abstinence', 19 *Philosophy and Public Affairs*, 3–46.

ROOT, M. (1986), 'Davidson and Social Science', in LePore (1986 : 272–304).

RORTY, R. (1982), *Consequences of Pragmatism*. University of Minnesota Press, Minneapolis.

RUSSELL, B. (1959), *The Problems of Philosophy*. OUP, New York.

SEARLE, J. (1969), *Speech Acts*. CUP, Cambridge.

——(1978), 'Literal Meaning', 13 *Erkenntnis*, 207–24.

——(1986), 'Meaning, Communication and Representation', in Grandy and Warner (1986 : 209–26).

——*et al.* (eds.) (1980), *Speech Act Theory and Pragmatics*. Synthese Language Library (vol. x), London.

SIMMONDS, N. E. (1987), 'Imperial Visions and Mundane Practices', 46 *Cambridge Law Journal*, 465–88.

SOPER, P. (1987), 'Dworkin's Domain', 100 *Harvard Law Review*, 1166–86.

SPERBER, D., and WILSON, D. (1986), *Relevance, Communication and Cognition*. Blackwell, Oxford.

STRAWSON, P. F. (1964), 'Intention and Convention in Speech Acts', in *Logico-Linguistic Papers* (1971), 149–69. Methuen, London.

——(1969), 'Meaning and Truth', in *Logico-Linguistic Papers* (1971), 170–89. Methuen, London.

——(1971), 'On Referring', in *Logico-Linguistic Papers* (1971), 1–28. Methuen, Londdon.

——(1976), 'Entity and Identity', in H. D. Lewis (ed.), 6 *British Contemporary Philosophy*, 193–219.

——(1979), 'Perception and Its Objects', in MacDonald (ed.), *Perception and Identity*, 41–60. Cornell University Press, Ithaca, NY.

TAYLOR, C. (1971), 'Interpretation and the Sciences of Man' 25 *Review of Metaphysics*, 3–51.

——(1985), 'Self Interpreting Animals', in *Human Agency and Language*, 45–76. CUP, Cambridge.

TULLY, J. (ed.), (1988), *Meaning and Context, Quentin Skinner and his Critics*. Princeton University Press, Princeton, NJ.

ULMAN-MARGALIT, E. (1983), 'On Presumption', 80 *Journal of Philosophy*, 143–63.

WEINRIB, E. J. (1988), 'Legal Formalism: On the Immanent Rationality of Law', 97 *Yale Law Journal*, 949–1016.

WIGGINS, D. (1980), *Sameness and Substance*. Blackwell, Oxford.

WILLIAMS, B. (1973), 'Personal Identity and Individuation', in *Problems of the Self*, 1–18. CUP, Cambridge.

——(1981), *Moral Luck*. CUP, Cambridge.

WINCH, P. (1958), *The Idea of a Social Science and its Relation to Philosophy*. Routledge and Kegan Paul, London.

WITTGENSTEIN L., *Philosophical Investigations*, Eng. trans. by G. E. M. Anscombe (1958), 2nd edn. Blackwell, Oxford.

——(1967), *Zettle*, ed. E. Anscombe and G. H. von Wright. Blackwell, Oxford.

WOLLHEIM, R. (1978), 'Are the Criteria of Identity that Hold for a Work of Art in The Different Arts Aesthetically Relevant?', 20 *Ratio*, 29–48.

——(1980), *Art and its Objects*, 2nd edn. CUP, Cambridge.

INDEX

aesthetic hypothesis 36
  see also constructive interpretation
aesthetics 97, 102, 111
Alexander L. 72 n., 108
analytical jurisprudence 2–8, 35
Anscombe G. E. M. 54 n., 106 n.,
  167 n.
argumentative character of law 48–50
Art, interpretation of 42, 107–13
artifacts 108–10
Austin J. 45, 93 n.
Austin J. L. 2, 131, 160 n., 166 n.
authority 114–18, 176–84

background knowledge 26–7, 49, 147–8
Baker G. 135 n.
Baker and Hacker 15 n., 128 n., 132,
  147 n., 148, 149 n., 151, 152
Barnes, A. 22 n.
Bentham, J. 45
bivalence, principle of 86–8, 91
Brest P. 161 n., 163

chain of law 73–7
coherence:
  theory of knowledge 62–6, 69, 79,
    100
  theory of law 61, 69, 103
  theory of truth 63, 79, 99–100
Coleman J. L. 7 n.
communication 21, 26, 28–9,
  see also intention
complexity, criterion of 78–9, 83–4
concept of law 39, 47, 176
  and conception 77
constitutional cases 120, 172–3, 181 n.
constructive identification 104–5
constructive interpretation 36–9, 51–
  60, 69–71, 77
context 77
conventions 26, 112, 160–1
conventionalism 8–10, 141
conversational interpretation 36
Cooper D. 52 n.
co-ordination 91, 177–84
core of meaning 125–6, 128, 130, 133
criteria 109, 141–4

and symptoms 142–4
critical law and morality 97–102

Davidson D. 15–24, 58–60, 63 n.,
  64 n., 106 n.
democracy and legislative intent 174–6
defeasibility 135–8
  see also empirical defeasibility
dependent reasons 115, 117, 122
Dreyfus H. 26
Dummett M. 15, 19, 20 n., 22–3, 79 n.,
  86–9, 93, 132
Dworkin R. M. 2–10, 35–47, 58, 60,
  66–84, 103–6, 111–13, 118–21,
  163 n., 165 n., 166 n., 172 n.

easy cases 124–35, 136–8, 149–54
Ely J. H. 173, 175
empirical defeasibility 138–46
epistemology 7, 62–6
  see also coherence theories of
    knowledge

family-resemblance concepts, 131,
  132–3
Feyerabend P. 75 n., 144
Finnis J. 54, 87
Fish S. 21, 31 n., 73–82
fit 71–3, 78, 82–4, 105
following a rule 146–53
formalism 127–9
foundationalism 62–4, 68, 79
Frege G. 14, 15, 132
Fuller L. 129–31, 134–5, 146, 148, 153

Gans C. 176 n
Grandy R. and Warner R. 24 n.
Grice H. P. 24–5, 27
grounds of law 3 n.

Hacker P. M. S. 19 n., 20 n., 23 n.,
  106 n., 131, 142, 144 n., 147
  see also Baker and Hacker
hard cases 120–1, 158
Hare R. M. 53 n.
Hart H. L. A. 1–2, 6, 8, 41 n., 45,
  46 n., 97, 125–38

hermeneutic thesis 43–60
Hintikka J. 52, 57
history, interpretation in 38 n.
holism 24, 58–9, 79, 81–2, 100

identification:
    of art 107–13
    of law 114–15, 118–23
identity 71–3, 106
idiolect 18
incommensurability 54–5, 59, 70, 82, 87, 101
indeterminacy 132, 149
    see also vagueness
indexical predicates 94–6, 138–46
institutional concepts 48–9
integrity in law 69–70, 83
intention(s):
    application intentions 168–72, 183
    author's intention 30–4, 159
    communication intentions 24–5, 29, 36, 103–4, 170
    counter-factual intentions 31–3, 169
    further intentions 166–8, 171, 183
    representative intentions 159–60
    shared intentions 162–4
internal point of view 44–7
interpretation:
    analysis of 13–14, 30–4, 149–53
    and meaning 18, 21
    stages of 71–3
    see also communication intentions and constructive interpretation
interpretative community 21, 74–6

Kelsen H. 46
Kress K. 85 n., 95 n.
Kripke S. 94 n., 148 n., 150 n.
Kuhn T. 21 n., 56 n., 62, 74 n.

legal positivism 5–6, 39, 43, 76, 90, 93, 96, 124–6, 148
legitimacy of law, see authority
Levinson 27–8
literary criticism 30–4, 37, 38, 44
literal meaning 23, 26–7
Lynton N. 108 n.

MacCallum jnr. J. C. 161 n., 163, 165 n.
MacCormick N. 62 n.
McGinn C. 14 n., 131, 147, 148 n.
MacIntyre A. 48 n.

Mackie J. L. 80 n.
malapropism 18–19, 21
meaning:
    and interpretation 14, 30–31
    of 'law' 3–6
    theories of 14–24; see also semantics
mental state, intention as 33, 161–2
meta-ethics 64–9
Moore M. 85, 87, 91–3, 95, 98, 117 n., 121–3, 124, 127, 136–46, 166 n.

Nagel T. 63 n.
natural kinds 93–6, 138–46
    see also indexical predicates
natural law 90–3, 96
normativity of law 45–7

objectivity 33, 70, 80–2
objects of interpretation 14, 71
open texture 132–3

paradigms 21–71
Pears D. 147 n., 148, 151
penumbra 126, 128, 130, 133
politics of law 119–21
positivism, see legal positivism
pragmatics 24–31
precedent 4–5
predictability 180–1
pretence in adjudication 6, 119–21
principle of charity 17–18, 23–4, 58–60
purposive interpretation 130, 138 n., 146, 152
Putnam H. 93–6, 101, 138, 141, 144–5

Quine W. V. O. 15, 17, 59, 62, 79 n.

radical interpretation 14–24
    see also Davidson
Rawls J. 62, 64–9, 77 n.
Raz J. 37 n., 41 n., 43, 45–7, 50, 56 n., 68 n., 90, 114–23, 127, 163 n., 176–8, 183 n.
realism:
    in law 9, 90–3, 95–102
    in semantics 86–9, 95
reductionism 88–9, 92–3
reflective equilibrium 64–9, 73, 81
Root M. 14 n., 58–60
Rorty R. 63 n.
rule of recognition 8–9, 39
rules and interpretation 21–2, 41–2
    see also following a rule

Russell B. 63 n., 87

scepticism 80–2
  see also objectivity
Searle J. 25–7, 49, 109, 166 n.
semantic sting 5–9, 53
semantics 14–24, 93–6, 141–54
  see also meaning
sense:
  and force 15
  and reference 7, 94–6, 138–9
Simmonds N. E. 81–4
social practices 40–2
social science 48, 58–9
Soper P. 7 n.
soundness 71–3
sources of law 8, 39
speech acts 26, 109, 160, 168
speaker's meaning 19
  see also communication intentions
Sperber D. and Wilson D. 24–5, 28 n.,
  29
Strawson P. F. 25, 28 n., 29 n., 63 n.,
  87, 106 n., 107 n., 160 n., 166 n.,
  168

Taylor C. 48 n.
text, *see* objects of interpretation
theory and practice, relation of 40–60
theoretical disagreements 4–6
truth 15, 62–9
Tully J. 38 n.

Ulman-Margalit E. 37 n.

vagueness 126, 132–4, 152
validity, conditions of 3–6
values, the role of, in interpretation 39,
  40–3, 54–7, 76–7, 83, 104, 158

Weinrib E. J. 99–100
Wiggins D. 106, 107 n.
Williams B. 63 n., 107 n
Winch P. 48 n.
Wittgenstein L. 14, 26, 119, 131–3, 139,
  141–4, 147–53
Wollheim R. 107
works of art 107–13